CARCERAL ARCHITECTURE

jovis

CARCERAL ARCHITECTURE

FROM WITHIN AND BEYOND
THE PRISON WALLS

Basile Baudez /
Victoria Bergbauer (eds.)

jovis

TABLE OF CONTENTS

INTRODUCTION

TABLE OF CONTENTS

I
INDIVIDUAL

TABLE OF CONTENTS

II
SITE

III
TIME

IV
CARE

TABLE OF CONTENTS

ADDENDA

Grégoire Korganow, *Night Patrol in a Carceral Facility*, photograph from the series "Prisons," 2013.

⁂

Basile Baudez and Victoria Bergbauer

RETHINKING CARCERAL ARCHITECTURE

Architecture is never neutral. The way buildings are constructed affects individuals, communities, and societies. It is thus crucial to reflect on the effects of the built environment, which is always the sum of complex choices and negotiations between ex- and in-clusion. Such a reflection is even more important, however, when these design choices are implemented as a means of punishment through confinement and seclusion. Architectural choices profoundly impact lives both during and after incarceration. The following contributions offer an unprecedented account of prison architecture and its effects beyond the walls of the facility, shedding light on the lasting ramifications of carceral architecture. They speak not only to the construction of prisons per se but explore how the strategies that create these structures of confinement extend and dissipate into society at large. As this volume makes clear, carceral architecture is always more than the space bound by the walls of the prison complex, which seems to imply an entirely separate world of incarceration.

Previous considerations of the current correctional system have overlooked this aspect. Questions around how prisons are built and how the logics of carceral spaces affect people continue to be neglected in the present day. This is surprising given that the United States hold the dubious distinction of being the world's leading jailer, investing an estimated $80 billion annually to incarcerate nearly 2.3 million people. This staggering figure represents 22 percent of the global prison population, despite the U.S. comprising only 4 percent of the world's total population. With at least 1,821 state and federal correctional facilities across the country, the return on the massive investment of locking people behind bars has been negligible.[1] The criminal justice system, symbolized by the spatial logic of prisons, has failed to enhance societal safety. Instead of fulfilling its purported goal of preparing individuals to (re)find their place in civic society, the prison system often leaves justice-impacted people in a worse state than before their incarceration.

Carceral Architecture shows how the construction of confinement plays a crucial role in this failure and proposes solutions for a society that remains caught in the reality of mass incarceration. By centering the voices of those impacted by the correctional system, alongside various stakeholders such as activists, architects, artists, designers, scholars, and students, the following chapters provide a comprehensive overview of prison architecture, its functions, and its far-reaching consequences. The common questions that connect the chapters to each other—and underpin each chapter's individual perspective (ranging from politics, law, activism, and religion to history, education, economics, and care)—probe a system that considers itself "correctional" or "rehabilitative." The interdisciplinary exchange between experts from different fields brings out how the materiality of prison construction continues to haunt individuals long after their incarceration has ended.

Our aim to initiate such a wide-ranging reflection began in 2021, when we set out to organize a conference on the architecture of confinement on Princeton's campus. Our hope was to create a space where diverse perspectives could converge and foster a dialogue that is seldom found in traditional academic or professional settings. Through a series of individual sessions and roundtable discussions, speakers illuminated the architecture of confinement from multiple vantage points. In the workshop that followed the cross-disciplinary conference, participants unanimously stressed the importance of translating this experience into a lasting format.

This collective insight laid the groundwork for *Carceral Architecture*. What follows is an idiosyncratic, multi-voiced exploration of the history and contemporary impact of prison design. Architectural strategies extend well beyond the physical borders of correctional facilities. They infiltrate elements of prison interiors and their equipment, as well as individuals and communities outside the prison walls. Architecture is never the outcome of an objective design process. Rather, as we will see, its procedures represent a complex crafting of space and place that both absorbs and exerts the influence of various psychological, behavioral, political, and legal factors.

It would be reductive, therefore, to consider the construction of prisons solely through the lens of their designers. We can only begin to understand the manifestation of the carceral by approaching it from a multitude of viewpoints both within and beyond the United States. Through this dialogue, we catch a glimpse of an element of the judicial and carceral system that is often hidden from public discourse. Prisons, shrouded behind blank walls, render incarcerated individuals invisible to society. Key architectural considerations—such as location, materiality, spatial volumes, soundscapes, and circulation—that are routinely analyzed for other building types remain largely unexamined in this domain. Architects tend to avoid carceral commissions, and those who take them rarely publicize their involvement. Consequently, carceral facilities, especially in the United States, remain absent from both architectural and societal debates, often left to underfunded contractors and profit-driven developers.

For the first time, this volume places the architectural question of confinement at the forefront, bringing together authors who were personally affected by architectural decisions in carceral settings and individuals who have worked with or for incarcerated people, studied the carceral system, or sought to reform or abolish it. No existing publication examines the history and the implications of carceral architecture holistically and comprehensively, while histories of carceral architecture by architectural historians often focus on specific case studies or offer large syntheses.[2] But interdisciplinary thinking matters in this context especially, since both the design and operation of carceral systems result from the interaction of multiple actors.

It is imperative to address an issue that currently affects millions of individuals worldwide and continues to preoccupy policymakers, students, activists, and architects. A review of how and why contemporary societies continue to pursue strategies of confinement is now long overdue. This volume gathers contributions from thirty-six experts, unpacking the connected issues that produce and perpetuate carceral architecture. In enabling a deeper understanding of the challenges and stakes of the architecture of confinement, they encourage us to imagine the possibilities of a future without prisons.

INDIVIDUAL | SITE | TIME | CARE: these four themes act as guiding threads across the volume and are in constant dialogue with one another. Rather than offering reductive definitions, each section, which opens with the voices of justice-impacted individuals, breaks free from traditional boundaries. The spaces, places, archives, languages, and codes of carceral architecture emerge from analyses, interviews, artworks, artists' photographs, as well as testimonials from currently and formerly incarcerated individuals.

The first theme, "Individual," explores the tension between one's personal experience and overarching architectural systems. How does the individual navigate a space of confinement? Does individuality or collectivity take precedence in structures of imprisonment? And what defines "an individual" or "a collective" when the architecture itself enforces the exclusion and exploitation of specific groups? Christopher Talib Charriez offers an account of how imprisonment profoundly shaped his worldview. In a transcript of the Spring 2022 *Architecture of Confinement* conference, justice-impacted authors reflect on how carceral architecture modified their identities and transformed their relationship with the interior and exterior of these facilities. They share struggles of preserving their individuality while adapting to survive in confinement and discuss the challenges of reintegrating their "reshaped" selves into society. Two subsequent essays address marginalized groups for whom carceral facilities were not initially designed: historian Sowande' M. Mustakeem discusses the trajectories of girls and women in nineteenth-century Missouri, while rl Goldberg's analysis examines the experiences of transgender individuals today. Isabelle Bonzom reflects on the transformative power of art within correctional facilities, where mural painting offers not only visual enrichment but also the possibility of a mental escape for those who are confined.

The second theme, "Site," interrogates the spatial dynamics of confinement. Where is carceral architecture situated? How do interactions between "the free" and "the confined" occur? Is the prison a place, a site, or a space? These questions challenge the supposed neutrality of spatial categories. Contributions examine the porous nature of borders. Chris Etienne highlights the trauma that facilities impose on individuals long after their judicially defined incarceration, highlighting that carceral architecture cannot be reduced to the prison site. The section delves into the historical connections between sites of confinement—slavery plantations and internment camps—and modern carceral facilities. Anna Arabindan-Kesson and Jessica Womack, leading the Art Hx project on visual and medical legacies of British colonialism, analyze the plantation as a carceral architecture that maximized profit through controlling the (re)production of life. Katie Chizuko Solien offers an architectural analysis of Japanese American internment barracks during World War II, while Sarah Lopez traces how the design of immigration detention centers in Texas reflects shifts in immigration policy and private prison practices. Regina Chen, an architect with the MASS Design Group, links histories of incarceration and racial discrimination with practices in urban planning and public health. She explores how facilities can "de-carcerate" and how community-based alternatives can disrupt the prison pipeline.

"Time" examines how carceral architecture shapes temporal experience. Contributors demonstrate how confinement alters one's perception of time. The section opens with Een Jabriel's reflections on coping with a distorted sense of time during incarceration, a topic Juan Moreno Haines—currently serving a life sentence at San Quentin—addresses in a poignant testimony. Historian Spencer J. Weinreich traces the history of prisons, from the persecution of early Christians to contemporary mass incarceration, offering a novel interpretation of solitary confinement as an infliction of abnormal and destructive solitude. Another aspect emerges through the Per(Sister) group of incarcerated women artists in Louisiana, who discuss how art and curatorial strategies can forge solace and solidarity. Falk Bretschneider, Isabelle Heullant-Donat, and Élisabeth Lusset's study of Clairvaux in France—a former monastery repurposed as a prison that is now abandoned—reminds us that carceral architecture is never static but evolves over time.

The final section, “Care,” investigates the paradox of care in environments designed to undermine individuality. Breaking with dichotomous frameworks, authors explore how treatment is administered, experienced, and denied within these spaces. How does access to care for some depend on its denial to others? Joel Negron examines how incarcerated individuals turn to self-care in the absence of institutional support. Tracing rural facilities in the nineteenth century, Victoria Bergbauer considers how space was conceived as a tool of care and rehabilitation for incarcerated children. Andrea Armstrong critiques the exploitation and inequities surrounding access to food in U.S. prisons. Tommaso Bardelli and his colleagues from ITHAKA and the Ennead Lab reflect on the role of educational spaces in fostering growth and rehabilitation. Liz Trumbull traces the manifestation of religion within Philadelphia’s Eastern State Penitentiary, one of the world’s oldest and most notorious prisons.

Finally, to aid readers in navigating this complex subject, the volume offers resources for instructors, teachers, and activists, including a community-engaged course on the architecture of confinement, exemplary architectural projects, and a working bibliography on aspects of the history of carceral architecture.

Carceral architecture is more than simply the design of individual prisons, jails, detention camps, penitentiaries. It extends beyond the locations that confine people, leaching into every aspect of contemporary society. Witnessing its dissemination is a reminder of how important it is to reflect, to educate ourselves, and to advocate for transforming a cruel, ineffective, and costly system into one that upholds justice and preserves human dignity.

1
"Writing on the Wall." MASS Design Group, accessed January 9, 2025, https://massdesigngroup.org/work/design/writing-wall.

2
See, for example: *The Palgrave Handbook of Prison Design* (Springer, 2023), which is intended for architecture students and designers, and Leslie Fairweather and Seán McConville's *Prison Architecture: Policy, Design and Experience* (Routledge, 2000), which focuses on traditional scholarly perspectives. There is also Norman Johnston's concise *Forms of Constraint: A History of Prison Architecture* (University of Illinois Press, 2000). Similarly, broader prison literature, like Yvonne Jewkes's *Handbook on Prisons* (Routledge, 2007), devotes minimal attention to architecture and is largely centered on the United Kingdom.
For further reference, see the concise bibliography at the end of this volume.

Centre Pénitentiaire
du Havre

Grégoire Korganow,
photograph from the series “Périphérie,” 2019.

Fresnes prison. Hooded prisoners are led to the courtroom, 1930, photograph.
Courtesy of Henri Manuel / Fonds Manuel / ENAP – CRHCP, M-24-031.

INDIVIDUAL

INDIVIDUAL INDIVIDUAL

INDIVIDUAL I INDIVIDUAL

INDIVIDUAL INDIVIDUAL

INDIVIDUAL

INDIVIDUAL

INDIVIDUAL I INDIVIDUAL

INDIVIDUAL INDIVIDUAL

INDIVIDUAL INDIVIDUAL

INDIVIDUAL I

INDIVIDUAL INDIVIDUAL

⁂

Christopher Talib Charriez

INDIVIDUAL

Carceral architecture—particularly prisons and correctional facilities—profoundly impacts the experiences of individuals both within and outside its walls. These designs are not merely functional; they shape behavior, influence social dynamics, and affect personal identity. For many, the oppressive structures, gloomy environments, and surveillance inherent in carceral spaces create an atmosphere of confinement that extends beyond physical imprisonment, impacting self-perception and interpersonal relationships.

From the moment I entered prison at the age of nineteen to serve a twenty-five-year sentence, the architecture established a disorienting sense of control and surveillance. Long hallways, high, gray-painted walls, and barred prison cells were all intentional design choices meant to convey authority and limit my autonomy. This physical environment led to feelings of insignificance and entrapment, undermining my sense of self. Inside those walls, every interaction with others was marked by guardedness and defensiveness, influenced by the oppressive surroundings. Conversations were accompanied by an awareness of constant surveillance; informal gatherings were rendered stale by the knowledge that any interaction might be scrutinized. Consequently, meaningful relationships became harder to cultivate, fostering a sense of isolation and loneliness that permeated my entire experience of incarceration. I spent decades conversing with my inner self, more than any time I spent in conversation with people.

Moreover, carceral architecture often reflects a dichotomy of power and subjugation. The stark, institutional designs serve to remind individuals of their status, reinforcing feelings of inadequacy and shame. Every space I occupied was dominated by concrete and metal, and I struggled to assert my identity beyond that of an inmate. This lack of personal agency led to internalized stigma, hindering my self-expression and personal growth. In many cases, the harshness of the environment exacerbated my feelings of hopelessness, making me question my worth and future outside the system. Although I fancied myself educated and resilient, I was not prepared for the world beyond the walls.

On the outside, the impact of carceral architecture continues to shape my interactions with the world beyond prison walls. Burdened by the stigma of incarceration, memories of those environments linger in my subconscious. This persistent presence heightens my mistrust of crowded places and the people within them. While the gray paint, towering walls, and watchful eyes of surveillance cameras may have physically remained in the prison I was released from, their influence persists in my daily encounters with the evolving notion of freedom. The legacy of prison architecture extends beyond its physical confines, compelling a re-evaluation of self and the capacity to connect with others. Ultimately, the design of these facilities fosters environments that inhibit personal growth, reinforce stigma, and perpetuate cycles of isolation—highlighting the urgent need for reform in how we conceptualize and construct spaces of confinement.

⁂

Nafeesah Goldsmith, Een Jabriel, Ibrahim Sulaimani, and Jill Stockwell

BEYOND INCARCERATION

Nafeesah Goldsmith, Een Jabriel, Ibrahim Sulaimani, three activists who have been formerly incarcerated, share their lived experiences of incarceration with Jill Stockwell, director of the Princeton Teaching Initiative, and discuss the possibilities of changing the carceral system and of creating community support.[1]

Jill Stockwell

(JS) There have been significant calls among currently and formerly incarcerated journalists and scholars to move toward "a person-centered or humanizing" vocabulary when referring to those with experiences of the carceral system. I wonder if you could describe this vocabulary and the importance of this language in your experience.

Een Jabriel

(EJ) I think the very first thing we try to be conscious and aware of is humanizing language, and part of that humanization is the removal of certain terms that have a stigma attached to them. So, for example: inmate. I deal directly with the Department of Corrections, and when we speak about our students, we call them "our students," or "our incarcerated students," or "our incarcerated learners," when referring to the individuals that our tutors work with. Now, more often than not, the administration refers to them as inmates, whatever their last name may be. I think the primary focus of what we're trying to do is to humanize individuals by calling them incarcerated people, incarcerated learners, incarcerated students, formerly incarcerated people, formerly incarcerated students, formerly incarcerated learners, justice-impacted individuals, and so on and so forth.

Nafeesah Goldsmith

(NG) I will speak to this from being the chair of the New Jersey Prison Justice Watch coalition, where we are hearing language coming through from different avenues, particularly from our legislators. When talking about inmates we also have to talk about the fact that they are incarcerated citizens, formerly incarcerated citizens or persons or individuals. Eventually, one day, it will just be a name, and we will not have to identify where the person came from. Until then, we must come up with language that not only humanizes the individual, but also reaffirms the humanity in the person who is using the word.

Ibrahim Sulaimani

(IS) Often, when you look at an offender, you don't see a person. You just see someone you were told is a criminal, someone who committed an offense, who deserves to be there. However, when you hear the term carceral citizen, you're like, what is that? And you want to know more about them. And when you learn more about what a carceral citizen or a justice-impacted person is, then those definitions allow you to identify with them, and to see them as a whole person. So, you know, when you see me, you want to know more about what happened to me, as opposed to what I did. And that allows you to see me as a whole person, to see me as a child rather than an offender.

(JS) Thank you for those responses. We have our first question about time, about the idea of marking time. I wonder if our speakers could each comment on how they experienced the passage of time within a carceral setup.

(EJ) One thing I learned while serving time is that, for me at least, the best way to do my time was to lose track of it. Hollywood shows us, when they depict someone as currently incarcerated, people marking X's on a calendar. That's probably the worst thing you can do when serving time, because it almost drags the time along. I remember I once tried to monitor my macros. I recall myself trying to be more aware of what I was eating—protein, carb, fat intake. But, in doing so, I noticed, maybe eleven days in, twelve days, and two weeks in, that I was inadvertently counting every day that I had been present. And it seemed to drag. It seemed to drag out my stay there. And I think for me the best thing to do was, again, kind of lose track of the day to day, and just be productive in whatever way that presents itself. And you know, wake up to, oh, wow, it's Christmas. Oh, wow, Thanksgiving is coming up. Um, that was fast. That's how I was able to really avoid the stress associated with time, but I think it's also a psychological defense mechanism for myself that I developed without really consciously intending to.

(NG) I like that. For me, it's a little different. And I would say it was about projection. When I first came into Edna Mahan [Correctional Facility for Women], I was in reception, and they gave us our bag and our setup, and there was a notepad and a little plastic flexi-pen. So I'm writing, and then the first thing I started to do is write out my goals.

I'd never done that before, but it seemed like the right thing to do, and so I wrote out my goals, and the first thing on the list was to get my General Educational Development certificate. I remember I wrote out six goals for that year. I came into reception in January of 2004 and I got out in February. And that March, I started taking GED classes. I hadn't completed seventh grade. I expected to be in coursework for quite some time. We'd been in classes for about a month and I remember my GED teacher said to me, I want you to take the pre-GED test. I looked at her and I'm like, are you crazy? You know, like you're trying to set me up for disappointment and failure here. And she says, no, you can do it. That belief made me do it, and it brought me back to the fact that that was a goal of mine, right? So why not do it? And I took the test, and I passed it. And I said, no, this can't be right? And she says, now you're gonna take the actual exam, and I got the third highest score in the state. I then learned the manifestation power of writing and believing. And as my time went on, I began to tap into other areas of belief and spirituality, and it made me think about our history. It could be DNA memory, but I'm thinking about the Egyptians and the hieroglyphs. Those hieroglyphics were not talking about just day to day. They were projections for the future that had to be written, and they had to play out. And this is something that we've seen throughout history, and some of us do it when we're brainstorming, right? We're just mapping our thoughts, and then we go for it. I learned to get through my time by writing out my goals. And I realized that I would exceed those goals, to the point where—the last two years that I was there—I had no goals to list. I started thinking about, what are you really going to do when you get out? And this is a part of that. For me, it was learning how to project and to believe in the process and to go through it.

(IS) Well in the beginning, for me, being that I started out so young, I had the perception of jail and prison that many of you have: that it's just, you know, wild. I went in as a fifteen-year-old kid, determined that I wasn't going to be anybody's prey. I became a predator, and I just "wild-ed out" my first year in the Youth Detention Center. It wasn't an easy place to be. The Youth Detention Center was probably far worse than New Jersey State Prison. I went in, got into a lot of fights, got into a lot of trouble, ended up in segregation a lot. And the Youth Detention Center isn't like being in county jail where you have an older gentleman pull you to the side and say: calm down a little bit. Do this. Study this or get into this. Go to the Law Library. They don't have any of that in the Youth Detention Center and so I wasn't initiated into doing time educationally. However, after my first year, I learned very quickly that getting into trouble wasn't productive, because, you know, you're in the hole all the time, and all you do is hear people come in. You can't see out the window or the door or anything, so you just hear people moving about outside the cell, taking showers, laughing, coming from the yard, and you're not a part of any of that. So I learned very quickly that being out of trouble was more beneficial for me. So, two years after that, I was sentenced. I went to East Jersey, to the Garden State Youth Correctional Facility. I met an uncle that I had there. He was serving a two-way life sentence, and he saw the potential in me and he sat me down like: look, you need to stop doing this. You need to stop going to the yard all the time, spending your days in the gym, playing basketball. Go to the library, work on your case. So that's how it began. My educational pursuits. I didn't finish my high school diploma. I was in tenth grade when I was incarcerated. So that's where I started going to school. Two years, three years later, I obtained all the credits necessary to get my high school diploma. After that, there wasn't anything to do because the Pell Grants [a subsidy that provides for students who need it to pay for college] were taken away. College was gone, so I started working in shops. I took upholstery and mechanics, cabinetry and so on, until the point that I was sent to East Jersey State Prison. Then maybe three years later, New Jersey STEP [The New Jersey Scholarship and Transformative Education in Prisons initiative] came in. They introduced college courses, I enrolled, and the rest of my bid was just spent obtaining education. I was just fully absorbed in my education, because as I started to become educated and see things clearly, I also came closer to the door—to getting out and to going home. And being incarcerated so young, never having a job or anything, my thoughts were, well, I gotta obtain education. So the remainder of my sentence was spent, you know, educating myself.

(EJ) There's a distinction in how time is served, because in a county jail facility, for the most part, you don't know how much time you're about to do. Whereas once you're sentenced and you go to an actual state facility, you pretty much know how long you're going to be there. So there's a difference in the way you carry yourself, at least in the way I carried my understanding of what time looked like, and how it would affect me psychologically. I spent nearly three years in a county facility, basically trying to figure out how much time I would end up doing, going back and forth to court, trying to fight my case, even going to trial. The psychological effect associated with that county facility was one of being locked down a lot. I was inside a cell more often than not. The first two years, it was maybe twenty-two hours a day, at least. At the state facility, I was in a dormitory with a lot of bunks. It's just a different feel and a different psychological observation you make being in a cell versus being in an open dormitory. So those are distinctions that definitely need to be made.

(JS) Several years ago, before the pandemic, Een and Nafeesah were part of a performance piece at Princeton advocating for the end of solitary confinement in New Jersey. In that context, we talked a lot about the ways in which individuals who survive incarceration do so by adapting to keeping time, to noticing others in the absence of visible cues. I wonder if you could comment on the ways in which your sense of time is permanently altered. What are the long-term bodily or psychological impacts of that new way in which time is inscribed on experiences and on the body?

(IS) I think you're affected in every way, being away for so long. You develop a state of psychosis, and you lose the perception of reality and relationships and of how things should go normally; everything changes. When I started, I looked toward my family for support. You're kind of ignorant with it. But you slowly understand things, the difficulties of coming to see someone incarcerated and accepting their phone calls. So you push back like, you know, man, no, I'm not going to call so much. I'm not going to create this burden for you.

Don't come up. But in doing that, you also lose the ability to maintain relationships, as you become distant from your loved ones and your friends, and you push them away. And that affects you in a way that lasts for a very long while: I met the great Nafeesah, and she understood me. She made me see love again, and her coming from that same space, she saw me from the space that my mother couldn't. You know, my aunts and my mother and my uncles, they've been there my entire life from the cradle till now, but there are things that they couldn't understand. There are days you just don't want to be bothered, days when you just zone out. And I don't get that [from Nafeesah], because, for a lack of a better word, she's my consoler. So, instead of going to cry in a park somewhere, I can go home and get consoled. But those effects last for a very long time. You take those things with you when you leave prison, and they resonate in you. Even though you put them in your back pocket, they're still there until you have someone who can acknowledge the space that you're coming from, and pretty much tamp it down.

(NG) They say time heals all wounds. And I don't really believe that. I think sometimes it takes time to really create a wound. And the time that I spent away, a lot of things were healed within me, because I had an opportunity to release myself from expectations, right? The expectations you're born with, what your family puts on you, your friends put on you, your children put on you, your work, those social settings—you have all of these different expectations that are put on you. For me, when I went away, I didn't have to worry about meeting those needs. I learned what my needs really were. That really helped strengthen me, but it also created a wound. There were traumas in the environment, the architecture of confinement, right? I cannot tolerate noise still. I do not like the sound of metal on metal, that clinking, it's horrible, it bangs with its sudden interruptions. It's the reaction that I have. It's psychological, but it's also physical. And so, you say to yourself, darn, did somebody just see me jump out of my skin? I wonder if they want to know why. Like, why did they respond to something like that? Maybe that's normal, right? But to me it's not normal because of how it has affected me. I think about the way I'm desensitized to many things. I'm a part of a coalition, so we get a lot of information about what's going on inside jails and prisons, and we'd hear something that other coalition members will say is really horrific. And it's like, yeah, that's how it is. I don't like the fact that I can have that kind of response of "that's how it is." Because it means that [the system] stripped away some of my humanity, and we can't have that.

One last point would be when you're doing time, your time is constructed for you, and it's intentional. The time you wake up, the time you have breakfast, your count time, the time you do your movements, all these things. All around the clock, there's something going on for you, something that you *should* be doing. Any opportunity that I had to not be in the unit during count time, I took it. I took a job that allowed me to be out of the unit when everybody else was inside. It gave me a sense of owning myself. So when I came home, I had time to walk out the door, open up the refrigerator when I wanted to, get in the car and take these long drives at two o'clock in the morning just because I can. For me, time was about taking back myself because I could.

(EJ) I realized that my original experience with solitary confinement was my first experience with being incarcerated altogether. Upon entering the county facility, I got into a fight the very first day, so I had to be placed in lockup. Now, I think one of the ways I was able to cope with this isolation was that I'm an introvert, right? So I benefited from being isolated because of that introvertedness. And over the course of time, I developed a lot of social skills while incarcerated. I was the tier barber so I was responsible for cutting everyone's hair on that tier. As a way to protect myself and to figure out who my enemies were, I had to develop a certain way to ask questions about where a person was from. You know, who they are, who their friends are, who they're associated with, and then taking note if they're associated with some of my known enemies. I learned a lot of tactics, conversational tactics, the kinds of things I hadn't known prior to being inside. I was put in a position where I needed to learn that and develop my barber skills. Eventually I was able to get a license after I was released. But during that process, I acquired the social skills that you need to protect yourself, to read body language. There's no course. You just had to learn by trial and error. You learn some of this stuff just from being in that particular environment and lifestyle, but I think I was forced to really hone in on it. When it came to being locked down, how that changed my senses, I think for me, primarily, it was more the hearing, because the tier I was inside of was like an H-shaped tier with cells on each side. I was at the tip of the H, so when I would look out, it would just be a wall. So again, as part of trying to see, worrying about my safety, and trying to figure out what's going on, I found myself listening. I found myself listening at the door, hearing conversations, hearing people talk who didn't know I was listening. And then you are aware when you're talking that people may be listening. All this is developed instinctively. It's not like I mapped out this plan. I just started paying more attention to what was being said. I started learning code language that wasn't even associated with me, but I had to learn just in case it applied to me. I'm talking about gang members who have their specific language. I was able to learn what gang a person was affiliated with based on hearing certain terms, certain slang associated with a particular street organization. Not being in a gang myself, I had to really make sure I knew about that. Just paying attention to what's being said because I can't necessarily see everything. And that also pertains to guards, hearing certain conversations they may have with one another, maybe pretending to not even listen. So I think now, I'm just better at reading body language, and I have been benefiting from it since my release. That's definitely one of the main things I developed. And just to add to that—reading lips, we learn how to read lips really well.

(IS) Listening to both of them reminded me of a situation. When I first came home, I moved to Cherry Hill with my aunt, in this nice, quiet suburban neighborhood, a good place for you to start out in life. After thirty years, I'm riding her bike around the neighborhood just to get to know the area. And people were out for their morning walk. I got out in May, so it's nice out. And people wave at me, but your prison mind says, like, the hell are you waving at me for, you don't know me, and you take offense to it. You, literally, take offense to it and put your guard up. And I told my aunt about it, and she's just like, oh, that's Edward. I mean, I told him about you because his son was incarcerated.

Grégoire Korganow, *Night Patrol in a Carceral Facility*, photograph from the series "Prisons," 2013.

And it's just like, wait a minute, like, what's my problem? And that's the point I realized that I had a problem, and I had to begin to work on myself, to the point where I went and got help. Being a student in psychology, I could identify with the language, but for them to classify it and put it in terms of: you're a survivor, and this is what you suffer from. And I began to realize, okay, I can fix this. I know what it is now. And it helped me work on myself to the point where I'm a happy man. I'm in a happy space in my life. You know, I make my own hours at work. I can be home with my wife and daughter all day if I want, and I'm here with you, and I'm in a very happy space. I acknowledge that I had to dispel the language that I picked up [in jail] and realize that everybody getting up from the table isn't the same as everybody about to move on somebody. Everybody getting up from the table means they're leaving the restaurant, they're all done with their meal and they're leaving. It doesn't mean that they're about to rob the joint, or flip the tables or come at you. You had to dispel some of those languages, but you could only do that through acknowledging that there was or that there is a problem with you.

(JS) I could keep asking you questions all morning, but I do want to open it up to the audience at this point. First though, I do want to thank the speakers for the gift of the shared experiences you've provided this morning.

Question from the audience

Thank you all so much, for such honest and thoughtful comments and for helping educate us about your experiences. I want to ask you about how individual moments of time may be different.

Thinking about birthdays or holidays, I'd be interested in your reflections on moments of time that were unique or special for you.

(NG) Can I jump on that? Well, when I was in Edna [Mahan Correctional Facility for Women], it was only women there and so many of us are mothers. You see that this is the tenth birthday that this woman has been away from her children. And how she makes the most beautiful crafts to send home to her children, the most beautiful cards she gets made for her children. She orders things from magazines to be sent to her children. You see another mother, not as fortunate to be able to do those things, who had to give her child away, who had to sign her children over to the state because she didn't have the family to support them when she was incarcerated, and so when their birthdays come up, she cries. You know we're there, and we have become sisters, and we've become mothers to one another, and we've maybe become a wife to another person. And you know, we have these families that we've created now. So when it's your birthday, oh, we're going to celebrate. And I'm just saying I know you guys are in Princeton, but I'm going to keep it real with you here. If you could have witnessed some of those birthday parties, you would have second guessed where you were. There are officers who understand that incarcerated individuals have already been sentenced. It is not my job to continue to punish them, and if a little bit of fun, a little bit of laughter is what they need to help me have a good shift, then so be it. But the way we mark time is different. You say, some people look forward to New Year's. And they're like, I got three more years. Like they do their countdown by New Year's. But then others who have lost family members while being incarcerated, already plan to be depressed around that time, and they'll say, oh, man, you know, May 10 is coming up, man, I'm not going to be good. You're scheduling depression. Why? Because the architecture of confinement creates those spaces for you to be able to do that. It does not monitor your real mental wellbeing and mental health. If you know that a woman just gave birth while incarcerated and had to sign her child over to the state, you should be talking to that woman on a scheduled basis, to know that she is okay. Because if not, she'll become another one of those women who takes their life while incarcerated. So time for everyone is definitely marked differently.

(IS) I guess for me, I learned how to mark time. It might seem barbaric, but I learned how to mark time from tragedies. And by that, I mean when something bad happened, you didn't celebrate or anything like that. But you realize that this happened six years ago. You're like, damn well 9/11 happened fifteen years ago. I learned how to count time like that. You don't do the sketching on the wall or the day-to-day calendar, you don't know how to mark time. You get your New Year's and Christmas every year, and you call home and they tell you: we miss you, and we made a plate for you, even though you're gone. The end of the year is a happy point for you, but you don't pay it no mind. And it's not until you realize that Tupac was shot fifteen years ago or, you know, your nephew was born, or someone died ten years ago, and you remember how you felt that day, sad or bad or down or low. But you remember that it happened six years ago, and you start to acknowledge the fact that you got over it. You got through it. You're in the healing process. And the body and the mind repair themselves. It wasn't so much about the tragedy as it was about me being that far away from tragedy that it allowed me to mark time and to be proud that I was further away from it. And happier to be closer to the point that I was striving for, which was going home.

(EJ) Man, I wish we would have had parties. We ain't had no parties. There is so much desensitization that happens internally. And part of that is how emotions are perceived in that environment. You gotta pick your smiles, is what I call it, you gotta be very careful whom you're portraying. I'm typically a silly guy. But I can't be that around everyone because it can be perceived a certain way. I have to shift into a different gear, which is a militant gear that I try to refrain from. One thing I noticed when I was going through my trial, at maybe twenty-two years old, stressed beyond my imagination, very terrified. I'm seeing my family, seeing my mother, in a despair that I've never seen before, and I wanted to cry so bad. I needed to cry, but I just couldn't. It was like this ball here, that I could physically feel, but I just couldn't find a way to release it. It could have been that nobody had to see anything. I could have cried in the shower. That wasn't the issue. I knew I needed to do it, at least for a temporary release, but I couldn't. So it was difficult for me to feel a lot of things, I can't recall feeling. The last thing I remember feeling was when something happened to my mom while I was inside, and I just felt hopeless because I couldn't be there. My grandfather passed. I can't even recall how I felt about it. I had an aunt who passed, you know, I can't recall how I felt about it. And I learned it through letters, because I tried to avoid talking on the phone a lot because, of course, the financial burden, but also because those conversations reminded me of how my decisions had affected other people, and how helpless I was in that regard. So I tried to refrain from that as much as I could. Even certain visits, I try to minimize because while you're happy to see someone, you're disappointed in yourself and you're disappointed in the fact that you can't assist them in whatever their struggles are, especially if that was your role prior to incarceration. So it's difficult to say what felt different. Honestly even now, I just turned forty, and I think a little bit of my callousness toward seeing them came from feeling like I should have been more excited. Luckily, my family, they clown and joke about it. But I don't know if I really appreciated that contact the way I should have because of this long, deep-rooted callousness. Today, it's nowhere near where it once was, you know, thanks to my daughter, who is four. I think I cry more now, just for nothing, I just find myself crying. I'm catching up, you know, on tears I should have shed years ago. My daughter has me shedding them now in a different context. So I'm blessed in that regard, for sure.

Question from the audience
I wanted to ask if you could speak to the work that you do now, whether it be community organizing or working on legislation or supporting formerly incarcerated folks.

(NG) When we talk about power organizing, we're talking about getting together with community folks, right? And we are talking about going straight to power. We're talking about the architecture of confinement here. You're saying you're going to build another prison, or you're going to put in another facility. But what about the culture?

The culture goes into the architecture, right? And the people who are there to manage the lives of the incarcerated persons, right? They're a part of that architecture. For me, the reward is being able to—once again—project, put out the vision, and start working toward manifesting it. What my coalition is all about manifesting is prison-free futures.

(IS) My organization is a transformative justice initiative, and the focus is on the word "transformative". A part of what we do is "meet him at the gate." And what Meet Him at the Gate does is it allows us to meet people coming home from prison. It allows similarly situated people to meet in a space where they're returning home after however much time they've done and they're seeing people like them, who automatically identify with where they've been and where they're coming from. And there's a sort of relief in that. And there's a de-escalation too, because prison is a trauma. It's a space of trauma. I'll give you a perfect picture of that, using myself after thirty years of prison. I had never thought of suicide, never. But my last forty days, I began to contemplate suicide because I didn't know what the world I was going into was made of. As I got closer to coming home and I was looking over the wall, I began to contemplate well, am I ready for this? So that's the trauma of prison, you know? And this is why "we meet them at the gate." We don't just give them a bag of goodies and stuff like that. We give them wraparound services. And we're about transforming minds. And it's in transforming minds and lives that I find happiness. I mean, just the other day, I got a phone call from somebody in a halfway house after thirty-two years in prison. And we brought him some clothes. Everybody in his family died. He was incarcerated at sixteen. He's now in his late forties, and he doesn't have anybody, like, literally, he doesn't have anybody but the people he was incarcerated with. So we brought him some clothes and socks and everything. And he was just like, so grateful. You always hear in rehabilitation circles about that person chasing that first high, and that's my first high–being able to relive that experience of leaving prison again. And every time we're there, we're there to meet somebody at the gate, and we share that with them, I get to relive that again. To see the look of "you don't ever want to go back to that," and we're going to help you feel like you don't ever want to go back to that.

1
The excerpted print conversation stems from a panel session, held at *The Architecture of Confinement* conference at Princeton University in April 2022. The text has been edited for clarity and concision.

⁂

Sowande' M. Mustakeem

FROM THE CITY JAIL TO THE PENITENTIARY: WOMEN, GIRLS, AND CRIME IN THE AMERICAN MIDWEST

Every city has a history etched within the cells of its jails and penitentiaries—some eroding with time, others demolished and long-forgotten—that reveals the past of people once formerly confined. From Kansas City to St. Louis, Missouri, women, men, boys, and girls filtered through a pyramid of carceral power in the American Midwest, most notably at the Missouri State Penitentiary (MSP) of Jefferson City; the oldest penitentiary west of the Mississippi River (where investment enabled penal design and building construction) that, once completed, opened its doors in 1836.

Some of the most iconic MSP convicts (Lee "Stagolee" Shelton, "Pretty Boy Floyd," Sonny Liston, and James Earl Ray)—four men among many other prisoners—are routinely invoked as central to the institution's two-century long memory. However, narrating the history of crime and punishment solely through the gaze of masculinity leaves the evolution of female criminality untold, erasing the lived experience of the different types of women and girls who found themselves behind bars. This essay is led by a set of central queries: once arrested and forced to navigate the multiple spaces designed for carceral confinement, what were the crimes and jailed experiences of both girls and women in the nineteenth century? Moreover, where and how does the architectural past factor into America's carceral evolution and memory?

What follows is more entwined than expected. It probes the jailed lives of seven women and girls from the American Midwest who committed crimes. It also recenters the foundational carceral spaces created by three men: each born in different places and of varying architectural generations that had a significant impact on the visibility of symbolic American power through the design of penitentiaries, city/county jails, "insane" asylums, "lunatic" hospitals, universities, churches, schools, hotels, banks, as well as other public buildings. More than merely imagining them, these architects actualized tangible modern carceral designs that shaped the spatial experience of multitudes of people charged with an assortment of crimes. Some convicts were freed while, for others, the prison became a shallow grave for society's unwanted and discarded. In short, this essay brings together the little known carceral testimonies of Sadie Hayes, Maggie Redd, Lulu Thomas, Lizzie Collins, Hattie Watson, Amanda Umble, and Mary Wesley. Going further, it reveals the significance of two generations of architects: one American-born (from New Jersey), Asa Beebe Cross, and two European, John Haviland (Somerset, England) and Thomas Walsh (Kilkenny, Ireland), who literally shaped the emerging American carceral future through notes, sketches, blueprints, contractual opportunities, business deals, and job creation–from within and beyond Missouri.

In 1883–a year after America's most iconic nineteenth century outlaw, Jesse James, was killed in his St. Joseph, Missouri living room owing to gubernatorial orders–the state of Missouri was faced with another side of violence. This incident involved not only a woman, but the interplay of alcohol and a revolver that led to the death of a police officer. In the early afternoon of October 8, Sadie Hayes went out barhopping with a friend until tensions boiled over between Sadie and her friend's brother. She walked up Eighth Street, near Biddle, her voice growing louder as she shouted curses and open threats to cause harm if anyone dared interfere with the ongoing feud. The police were alerted and Third District Police Sergeant Peletiah Jenks, a father of five, followed up on the station call. As Sadie circled the downtown area openly brandishing a weapon, a crowd began to converge when, within what seemed like seconds, Sergeant Jenks appeared and motioned toward her. Before he could reach Sadie, she allegedly fired her revolver. Moments later, Peletiah's partner found him bleeding on the sidewalk and called for help with transporting Sergeant Jenks to his home nearby where, hours later, at approximately 10:45 pm, Peletiah died from a fatal wound to the forehead. Sadie was arrested, forced into the calaboose and later moved to the St. Louis city jail, located within an infamous state symbol and massive icon of city power that stood for many decades, known globally as the Four Courts.[1]

The first St. Louis jail, made of stone and brick and located at Sixth and Chestnut Street, was designed in 1816 by Theodore Hunt. It was equipped with four cells on a single floor. Measuring 20 by 40 feet, the cost of erecting the building came to an estimated $1,200. Two and a half decades later, at the same location, architect Henry Singleton built the second jail, which was completed in 1842 for a cost of $40,000. Singleton's version, however, extended over four levels. The jail itself, measuring 40 by 60 feet, featured a stone exterior that allowed nine times the previous jailing capacity. While the St. Louis County Court moved toward plans for yet another jail during the American Civil War, they rejected a plan from another architect. The court decided instead for a more integrated criminal justice center that bundled the police department, the four court system, city jail and morgue into a single location. Purchasing an open lot (380 by 280 feet) in 1868 for $125,000—the former site of a previous well-known mansion—catapulted the envisioned carceral future of state power owing to sizeable capacity that "occupied the area between Eleventh and Twelfth Streets from Spruce to Clark Street."[2]

Emil Boehl and Koenig, *Old St. Louis Jail,* 1870, photograph. Missouri Historical Society, N33476. Public domain.

In his ambition to extend the county's interest in a robust carceral presence, Thomas Walsh—the Irish-born St. Louis County architect—voluntarily drew up and submitted plans to the court for immediate consideration. Within a year's time, Walsh's expansive architectural vision for the growing city of St. Louis came true in a powerful and tangible way postwar through the building and opening of the Four Courts between 1870 and 1871. Growing calls from local judges and politicians for greater jailing capacity, as well as the forging of nuanced global architectural alliances, solidified two interconnected worlds and at least two generations of architectural minds willing to appease public and private commissions for attractive buildings designed to represent law, order, and unending power.

Pre-Civil War, Thomas Walsh became established as the county architect. Yet, postwar, he served as architectural designer and superintendent of the jail after the state-approved construction of the Four Courts in February of 1869 at an estimated cost of $300,000 to $320,000. Work began a month later. A two-phased plan consisted of constructing the police department and court system, located in the north front, and the jail housed in the south rear. The three-story building (estimated 60 to 90 feet high) included a basement and attic levels with "a five part pavilion style front, reflecting French Renaissance ideas, complete with mansard and dome roofing." Although originally designed with a combination of brick and stone, it later changed to limestone given the availability of local supply to complete the project. Particularly key to the building of the Four Courts was the jail, which had walls that rose to 45 feet and were framed by large windows estimated to be 40 feet tall and 20 feet wide, completely covered with iron bars. As for the jail cells—separated into four groups—an estimated 152 total could confine between 450 and 500 prisoners. These were "8 by 10 feet and 9 feet high, each cell furnished the prisoner with a bed, toilet, sink with running water, heat source, ventilation, table, and chair."[3] A brick wall, some 16 feet in height, surrounded the courtyard behind the jail. Six entrances permitted access to the jail, which boasted marble-tiled floors—a historical rarity for most penal facilities.

The county willingly raised funds for this unprecedented architectural design. In doing so, it gathered finances by levying a property tax, raising $95,000, while also authorizing the "sale of county jail bonds in the amount of $345,000 bearing an annual rate of 8%."[4] Selling to the banking house Taussig and Gimpp at a 7 percent discount yielded a share of an estimated $320,850 to the court. In turn, they offered to sell their 5,000 shares in Iron Mountain and Southern Railroad stock, which had been secured before the Civil War. A winning stock bid by local railroad financier Hudson E. Bridge—with 50 cents on the dollar at $250,000—enabled the court to proceed with financing a new carceral vision along with selling off the original jail property for $105,641.

Through these varied transactions, a global world of architectural designers (in tandem with an array of investors operating through the fusion of money, legacy making, power, and close networks) gave rise to variations of “Neo Classical” and “Second Empire” architecture that was implemented and socially sanctioned all over carceral America, including in Missouri. Yet, the real story—both invisible and lost in public understanding, let alone memory—is that the initial invested legacy of these architectural pioneers occurred in direct relationship with the state, both financially and socially. These pre- and post-Civil War transactions thus emboldened the building of America’s early jail/asylum/penitentiary environments in several cities and counties across the nation.

The old Four Courts building was located at Twelfth Street and Clark Avenue in St. Louis, long since torn down and lost to local memory. Sadie stayed locked within this city jail for close to four years. Trapped in state hands, she had to navigate state power—even coming close to the “death watch” for causing the death of Sergeant Jenks years before. His body would have similarly passed through the halls of the Four Courts being moved onward to the morgue for the coroner’s inquest, where legal proceedings were completed in order for his family to take claim of Peletiah’s body and conduct his burial. Equally pertinent to the location of the Four Courts is its close proximity to several local press houses. This meant that news circulated regularly far and wide about many iconic murder cases, including Sadie and Peletiah’s fateful encounter. Moreover, interaction between local reporters, police, and infamous prisoners held within the city jail meant that Sadie gained significant journalistic attention and public notoriety as a female prisoner and murderess. At the end of 1883, a new life forcibly began to evolve for Sadie in Thomas Walsh's architecturally applauded design. Her fate remained uncertain. Like other incarcerated individuals, she garnered significant interest while she moved between unfamiliar cells and mandates, while the state determined the necessary justice for murder. Eventually, the state relocated her from St. Louis to Jefferson City, forcing her to go from the city jail to the penitentiary. Sentenced to ninety-nine years for second-degree murder, twenty-five-year-old Sadie Hayes—marked in prison records as 5 foot 2 inches in height, married, and with relatives left behind in St. Louis—arrived to serve prison time at the Missouri State Penitentiary on January 29, 1887.[5]

A week before Sadie's arrival and confinement within the caged interiors of the MSP, a young female killed a fourteen-year-old in Kansas City over an allegedly stolen item. Although marked and publicly read as a woman in local and growing national news, the arrival of a teenage murderess, Maggie Redd, to Jackson County Jail immediately overturned all assumptions of adult-only crimes or confinement in the spring of 1887. Histories of penal evolution rarely acknowledge the carceral reality of teenagers who were locked behind bars as prisoners alongside adults. Yet, Maggie was forced into the twelve-cell jail originally designed by local architect, Asa Beebe Cross, thirty years beforehand. In 1859 he physically fulfilled the need for a Jackson County Jail to accommodate the growing rate of crime in Kansas City. Far from the high cost of jail construction in St. Louis, Cross was able to complete the facility at a considerably cheaper cost of $11,000. Externally, the jail projected a smaller image of carceral power but enabled the holding of prisoners as crime continued to persist.[6]

Records remain silent on how an eighteen-year-old accused of murder fared within county hands while

Emil Boehl, *The Four Courts Building*, 1907, photograph. Missouri Historical Society, N11200.
Public domain.

Andrew O' Reilly, *Four Courts and the City Morgue*, August 9, 1888, photograph. Missouri Historical Society, N10374. Public domain.

held among jailed adults. The severity of Maggie's crime forced her youth to be overlooked and prison life therefore became far more paramount for the state. Once in Kansas City police hands they moved her promptly to Asa Cross's Jackson County Jail. Her case moved swiftly through the courts, and within two months, she was sent to serve a three-year sentence in Jefferson City for first-degree murder.[7] She was forced to serve the latter years of her teenage life mired in an adult carceral world, deprived of her freedom owing to the senseless fatal stabbing of a young boy over a red silk scarf/handkerchief in an alleyway. Architect John Haviland's iconic Missouri State Penitentiary was fifty years in operation. Whether Maggie intended to kill John Nye or not, the swift enforcement of justice against an armed teenager reveals that the state meant to prevent any unchecked outbreaks of violence among others, whether young or old, could wage in any semblance of freedom to kill, and or to become inspired by. Given that Maggie's incarceration began in April of 1887, a decade after locals voted to allow penitentiary prisoners to serve a total of three-quarters of their given sentence, it is interesting to note that she was granted her freedom on July 4, 1889—America's symbolic day of liberty.

Closely following Maggie's release, another spate of teenage violence erupted on the streets of St. Louis, this time owing to eighteen-year-old Lulu Thomas who was charged with assault to kill following a violent incident on October 13, 1889. She pulled out a knife and stabbed her friend, Martha Chambers. Shortly thereafter, she was arrested and transferred to the Four Courts city jail, where Sadie had been held for many years prior. Given the extreme yet non-fatal nature of her crime as well as her young age, Lulu spent less time negotiating the power structures of city holding and a month after the alleged assault, in November of 1889, she was sent to the Missouri State Penitentiary to serve a two-year sentence.[8] Generational changes in crime, law, and punishment according to age were in continual motion in the late-nineteenth century. As such, Lulu not only joined scores of imprisoned men, but she was displaced in the women's wing with convicted adult women and girls. This included Sadie, who still remained in the MSP upon Lulu's arrival (Maggie had, by this point, left to restart her life far beyond prison walls).[9]

Less than a month after Lulu's transfer to the penitentiary, an elderly man, Terry O'Brien, left his home in Kansas City to fetch a pitcher of beer. As he exited a saloon, balancing a filled pitcher and facing winter weather, two women allegedly attacked and robbed him. Seeing O'Brien distracted—and perhaps even intoxicated—the two females purportedly knocked him down with a stone, stole 15 cents from him, and used a knife to cut open his vest lining, taking at least $15 hidden inside. By the middle of December 1889, Lizzie Collins and Hattie Watson were arrested for this crime, forced into Jackson County Jail, and later charged with "highway robbery," having been found "guilty of robbing an old man" who was out alone and entirely defenseless. Two months later, on February 26, 1890, they were both sent to state penal confinement together. However, their paths would soon diverge once they entered the Jefferson City hold to serve their respective sentences.[10] Both were convicted and forced to serve five years for first-degree robbery, yet their carceral time within the Missouri State Penitentiary played out in vastly different ways. Hattie served the full three-quarters of her sentence, while Lizzie—along with two other convicted men—was pardoned by Governor D.R. Francis, and sent back to Jackson County on June 30, 1891 for mental health reasons.[11]

A month prior to Lizzie Collins's forced return to Kansas City, a nineteen-year-old was stabbed multiple times in an alleyway and left for dead because of a love triangle gone wrong. "Black Bottoms" resident Amanda Umble went out on the night of May 15, 1891, looking for her boyfriend. Finding him out with another woman, Effie Jackson, she confronted the pair and, moments later, Amanda and her lover William Jackson fled as Effie lay bleeding in the open street. One week later, Effie died. Although Amanda initially evaded capture, within days she was arrested and placed into local police custody. Over the next month, both Lulu Thomas and Lizzie Collins were released from the MSP, as Amanda was simultaneously filtered into the powerful clutches of Missouri carceral state power.

Within a year spent in Jackson County, trapped in Asa Cross's labyrinth of penal power, Amanda attempted to end her jailed life with morphine pills. This proved useless, however, as quick actions kept her alive. One year later, reformers—both Black and white—made a deal with the governor to have her spared from execution, reducing her sentence to serving fifty years at the Missouri State Penitentiary.[12] In the summer of 1893, Amanda Umble entered the MSP, joining a long list of women, girls, and convicts of varying backgrounds who had passed through its hold, including Sadie Hayes.[13] Both Amanda and Sadie served time incarcerated together at the MSP. Yet archival records leave untold any closeness—whether they would have shared jail cells, a friendship, or whether the two were perhaps enemies behind bars.

Another woman, Mary Wesley, entered the Missouri State Penitentiary one month after Amanda's arrival at the facility in the summer of 1893 following her involvement in a murder outside Flynn's saloon in St. Louis. Mary faced criminal charges in connection with the stabbing and subsequent murder of Mamie Bowman in the spring of 1893. Whether intentional or not, Mary pleaded that the stabbing was committed in self-defense. Mamie, once stabbed, was taken to the Old

Jackson County Jail Interior, 1859. Courtesy of Jackson County Historical Society.

Missouri State Penitentiary Grounds, Administration Building, 1904–1906. Courtesy of Missouri State Archives.

City Hospital, where police brought Mary—her alleged assailant—to her bedside to verify identification. When asked why the incident occurred, Mamie replied that it was over nonsense; she died just a couple of hours later.[14] Two days later, a twenty-four-year-old Black woman repeatedly contended that she had gone out to help her brother in town off the river from work. Yet, knowing his excessive drinking habits, she feared his getting arrested by the police and went out to find him.

Mary Wesley's brother, likely an imagined ghost in the eyes of the public, was nowhere to be found. He never appeared during her time in the city jail, where tensions and fights among female prisoners drastically increased, regularly making local news, nor did he ever emerge during her sentencing and transfer to the by then five-decades old MSP. Mary was originally sentenced to ten years for the crime. After five years, however, her life ended unexpectedly in the fall of 1898 under mysterious circumstances.[15] In essence, the MSP—one of many penal institutions that secured John Haviland's architectural fame in America—became a legalized tomb for Mary Wesley, as it was for so many other prisoners; albeit a temporary grave until she was transferred to (and more than likely buried in) the African American burial space, Greenwood Cemetery in St. Louis. In yet a rather curious and unending link to the carceral past, Mary died at MSP the same year Sadie Hayes was granted a pardon by Governor Lon F. Stephens and released on Thanksgiving Day, November 24, 1898.[16]

When Sadie left that cold day in November, fifteen years after Sergeant Peletiah's murder, she was not the last to be released among the seven women and girls explored within this essay. In fact, it was three more years until Amanda Umble—serving a commuted fifty-year sentence at the MSP—was pardoned. She was freed after eight years of captivity, just as twenty-three new women and girls were transferred into the prison; no less than thirty-one female prisoners entered the same year of her release.[17] Amanda's pardon also came seven years after the death of Jackson County Jail architect Asa Beebe Cross—the man who designed what became a waystation that she was filtered through in Kansas City enroute to the MSP—from apoplexy in August of 1894.[18] Moreover, undoubtedly rare among carceral narratives, Amanda was met with flexibility by the state both for good behavior and the fact that, at the age of twenty-nine, she was the oldest female prisoner confined to serve a term of service. She received a gubernatorial pardon from Governor Alexander Monroe Dockery on July 4, 1901, in the first year of a brand-new century.[19]

Conclusion

Sadie, Maggie, Lulu, Lizzie, Hattie, Amanda, and Mary all served prison time in the female wing of the Missouri State Penitentiary. For the first time, their long untold stories are woven together to provide new revelations on the architecture of confinement, showing how far women and teenage girls could go in the complicated worlds of the nineteenth century. This essay puts their herstories in direct conversation with the foundational architects of the state carceral spaces in which they once forcibly lived.

Their testimonies provide a chilling realization of the human dramas of violence and crime as well as the spaces that states and nations invested in, designed, and built to ensure an active future of incarceration. Each female represented a nightmare for city officials, while also doubling as a financial piece in a larger enterprise, connected to a growing carceral empire amassed through negotiations and backroom deals made among the elite, powerful, and politically interconnected. Global architects who designed and collectively built many American jails and penitentiaries were vital in constructing a carceral system with staying power that was fully aligned with the evolution of cities and nearby counties invested in a world of law and order.

Each building, cellblock, jail cell, each limestone, ashlar, iron bar, and piece of glass approved and installed in America's jails and penitentiaries represented a social and political investment in human warehousing. As these carceral spaces—designed to lock away and maintain full surveillance over alleged criminals—continued to be commissioned and completed, people were thenceforth moved into (and between) spaces built to contain people temporarily and even long term. By bridging the history of female crime with the history of the architects who built and gave legacy, purpose, business need, and functionality to these often-grandiose jails, we can open the long-sealed doors of learning.

There remain many tentacles to the American carceral past: forgotten investors, the architectural world, the mind of designers and their carceral creations. Completion of a jail or penitentiary became a crucial tool in containing people and in growing a carceral future that fueled an appetite for human warehousing. Delving into the architecture of confinement and the evolution of the American carceral past is as much about the people forcibly moved within these carceral spaces as it is the architects and buildings they once erected. The Missouri State Penitentiary, Four Courts, and Jackson County Jail became three key spaces designed to promote a generational legacy of incarceration through new and so-called "modern" or "humane" spaces. Each of them also emerged at three key points in historical time: the 1830s (following Missouri's statehood), the 1850s (mid-century/pre-Civil War), and the 1870s (post-Civil War/the year in which St. Louis legalized prostitution as a social experiment)—which reveals a far more intentional future of carceral institutional building.[20]

To appease societal and state needs, architects designed revolutionary ideas while leaving indelible marks on society, the state, their profession, and each other. Indeed, the architectural origins of carceral America are far more generationally entwined (and global in their foundational influences) than previously thought. Those driven and willing enough to follow through beyond making a mere sketch—realizing a physical building ready for state use and public interaction—were not just American architects. Although Thomas Walsh and Asa Beebe Cross were born in 1826, Walsh advanced early in his training; starting as an apprentice in Ireland at thirteen, he later mentored Cross. Each left architectural variations but also carceral imprints on America, following directly in the footsteps of the architectural carceral legacy forged by British architect John Haviland, America's foremost architect of penal design. Walsh was likewise influenced in designing St. Louis's Four Courts by his own native context—namely, the Four Courts in Dublin, Ireland.

Contained within the city jails and penitentiaries of the American past are the secrets of many hidden worlds; some reveal the consequences of everyday choices and moments that sometimes proved fatal. These buildings became some of the most powerful architecturally driven investments in American history. They also comprised physical investments that emerged across the nation in the early- to mid-nineteenth century, concealing corruption within while being wielded as potent instruments of power and enduring symbolic reminders of land, money, modernity, and a future ever invested in fighting crime. Over time, these globally inspired buildings became the containers of future criminals from forthcoming generations, enabling legacies of cruelty and violent obedience to be inflicted on jailed women, girls, boys, and men behind meticulously designed cells and limestone walls.

1
"A Devilish Deed: Sergeant Jenks, the Police Veteran Killed by A Colored Cyprian," *St. Louis Globe-Democrat*, October 9, 1883, 4.

2
David J. Simmons, "The Four Courts Building: Walsh at The Crossroads of His Career," *The Society of Architectural Historians Newsletter, St Louis and Missouri Valley Chapters*, XXI, no. 2B (Summer 2018), 2.

3
Simmons, "The Four Courts Building," 3.

4
Simmons, 3.

5
Sadie Hayes, Reel S218, Vol. N, Page 26, Prison Intake Registry, Missouri State Penitentiary Database.

6
Jackson County Historical Society Blog: https://www.jchs.org/, accessed October 7, 2024.

7
Maggie Redd, Reel S218, Vol. N, 49, Prison Intake Registry, Missouri State Penitentiary Database.

8
"Arraigned the Indicted: Nolle Prosequies and Pleas of Guilty in the Criminal Court To-day", *St. Louis Post Dispatch* (November 16, 1889), 2.

9
Lulu Thomas, Reel S219, Vol. P, 124, Prison Intake Registry, Missouri State Penitentiary Database.

10
Hattie Watson, Reel S220, Vol. Q, 9, Prison Intake Registry, Missouri State Penitentiary Database. (Listed online as "Hathie").

11
Lizzie Collins, Reel S220, Vol. Q, 9, Prison Intake Registry, Missouri State Penitentiary Database.

12
Sowande' M. Mustakeem, "'Armed with A Knife in Her Bosom': Gender, Violence and the Carceral Consequences of Rage in the Late 19th Century," *Journal of African American History* 100, no. 3 (Summer 2015): 385–405.

13
Amanda Umble, Reel S221, Vol. S, 134, Prison Intake Registry, Missouri State Penitentiary Database.

14
"Mary Wesley and Her Victim," *St. Louis Post Dispatch* (April 15, 1893), 7.

15
Mary Wesley, Reel S221, Vol S, 143, Prison Intake Registry, Missouri State Penitentiary Database.

16
Sadie Hayes, Reel S218, Vol. N, 26, Prison Intake Registry, Missouri State Penitentiary Database.

17
Mustakeem, "'Armed with A Knife in Her Bosom,'" 385–405.

18
"Death of Major A.B. Cross: Kansas City's Best Known Architect and Builder At Rest," *Kansas City Journal* (August 19, 1894): 3.

19
Amanda Umble, Reel S221, Vol. S, Page 134, Prison Intake Registry, Missouri State Penitentiary Database.

20
James Wunsch, "Protecting St Louis Neighborhoods from the Encroachment of Brothels, 1870–1920," *Missouri Historical Review* 104, no. 4 (July 2010): 198–212.

⁂

rl Goldberg

DOUBLE IMPRISONMENT: NARRATIVES OF TRANS CARCERALITY

"A glance at the new art of punishing clearly reveals the supersession of the punitive semio-technique by a new politics of the body."

—Michel Foucault, *Discipline and Punish*[1]

"Who doesn't desire more freedom, to move in a vaster space, to open everyday life to the unexpected? Who wouldn't wish to be delivered from constraints?"

—Anne Dufourmantelle, *In Praise of Risk*[2]

Why is it that transness comes to be figured, in texts dealing with carcerality, as *double imprisonment*? Asked otherwise: what kinds of rhetorical and narrative tropes underpin transness such that it becomes mired not just in the literality of trans incarceration—a trans person being confined in prison—but also in the *metaphor* of carcerality—of transness, as a term, indexing the experience of being "imprisoned" in a body? And how does this slippage between metaphoric confinement and the material bear on the theory and practice of architecture?

The language of being trapped in a body—and related variants like imprisoned, caught, and stuck—has been endemic to descriptions of trans embodiment since before the mid-century; it was famously generalized and eternalized in Harry Benjamin's *The Transsexual Phenomenon* (1966) as the most basic definition of the transsexual: those "who feel that their minds and their souls are 'trapped' in the wrong bodies."[3] This definition—the first in the history of institutional Western trans medicine—served multiple purposes, including drawing out the tension in transness as a problem of disjunction between psychic and bodily architectures, a kink in Cartesian mind-body dualism. As Benjamin's book discusses, the etiology of transness was unclear; it remained to be determined whether it was best conceptualized as a problem at the site of the mind or the body. Benjamin's definition elegantly split the difference as diagnosing neither mind nor body but the uneasy *relation* between the two, the phenomenological experience of orientation to the body schema itself. But in his theorizing of trans phenomenology as "trappedness," Benjamin simultaneously found that the language many transsexuals used indexed, more properly, not just trappedness but *imprisonment*.

Theorizing imprisonment as a metaphor for trans experience underscored the urgency and out-and-out powerlessness transsexuals felt in their bodies. It also offered a shorthand way of describing their experiences of immiseration and bare life—that is, Giorgio Agamben's concept of life stripped of everything save its biological facticity. There are few experiences that speak more clearly to bare life than imprisonment—and the use of the metaphor reinforces the ways in which transsexuals felt painfully eager to make great sacrifices in order to medically transition:

> Especially for the older transsexuals, the urgent need to relieve their gender unhappiness can be powerful and impressive. 'Would you want the operation,' I frequently asked, 'if there could never be a chance for any sex relations with a normal man?' Some hesitated to answer, then said they would have to think it over. Those were the younger ones in whom the sex motive predominated. But others

> replied unhesitatingly, 'Yes.' They admitted they might lose something of their future happiness, but the gain would still be much greater than the loss. 'I will feel free for the first time in my life,' said one forty-year-old, referring to her 'imprisonment' in a male body.[4]

In an earlier chapter in *The Transsexual Phenomenon*, Benjamin cited "Each Day I Live a Lie," by Lorraine Channing, taken from the then-contemporaneous transvestite magazine *Turnabout,* which begins, "Each day I live a lie. Mine is a life of deceit, for I am forced to wear a mask, to be an actor on a stage not of my own choice. I cannot do ... cannot act as I would like or as I feel. Yet, I am not evil. I am not criminal." It concludes:

> Would that I were as other women are! Yet I am not a woman either in body or in the life they lead. I *am* a woman in my soul, in my fantasy. In the deep recesses of my being, I am like them. Inside me, I am one of them. How can I be *more* in their likeness?
>
> That is what I want, yearn for, seek more than anything. Now I live only incompletely. I am in a prison—the prison of my body, the prison of a society which does not understand.
>
> Until I can become more like other women—if I ever can—I must live a lie, day after day. Physically I am a man; mentally and emotionally I am a woman.
> I am a transsexual.[5]

Benjamin's book, the first medical treatise on transsexuality, quickly became the standard for practitioners working in the emerging field of transsexual medicine. As clinicians at Johns Hopkins, the University of

Minnesota, and UCLA attempted to theorize what a transsexual was, and how to medically and psychologically treat these patients, Benjamin's formulation rapidly became essential to the diagnostic criteria that were broadly adopted. Insofar as his framework received attention and popularity not only from clinicians and prospective patients, but also from lay readers, the most basic definition of transsexuality came to hinge on articulations of "confinement." As Channing wrote, the prison she occupied was twofold—spanning her body and a society that was both unsympathetic and unaware of the dire extent of her struggle. Interestingly, Channing describes this prison as singular, "a prison." The lack of a conjunction here, a word that might clarify the relationship between "the prison of my body" and "the prison of a society which does not understand," suggests the ways in which the scrim between body and society is virtually non-existent, separated only by a feeble comma. While one might read this comma as a natural boundary between these two different modes of incarceration, the ambiguity in Channing's account of trans experience puts pressure on the ways in which one might understand themselves to be "doubly imprisoned."

Sandy Stone has famously described how Benjamin's book, as "the standard reference," was taken up by transsexuals visiting gender clinics. She notes that "when the first transsexuals were evaluated for their suitability for surgery, their behavior matched up gratifyingly with Benjamin's criteria. The researchers produced papers which reported on this, and which were used as bases for funding."[6] This led to a recursive process, wherein prospective trans patients relying on the language of Benjamin's text to access care were, at the same time, participating in the iterative reproduction of this language within theoretical and popular writing on transness. Even if some trans people did identify with incarceration as an adequate and accurate phenomenological description, the metaphor's rapid spread across the clinical landscape and its legibility across various architectures—including the newsroom, the university, the clinic, and the prison—came to forcefully interpellate others (for whom this articulation was perhaps less correct or less meaningful) into its use.

The language of being *trapped in a body* has a denser philosophical history encompassing not just transsexuality, specifically, but the very ordinary condition of human embodiment—Plato, Socrates, and Augustine, for instance, all theorized figurations of the body as the soul's prison. That is to say, being "imprisoned" in a body and the distinctive architectural problems this proposition raises is not unique to the experience of being trans. Based on this figuration, to be "doubly" imprisoned is to be incarcerated while also facing the existential condition of being "in" a body. One might say, then, that all incarcerated people are doubly imprisoned, faced with the architectural imprisonment of the correctional facility as well as the universal existential condition of being embodied. Yet the language of being imprisoned in the body seems to have less of a hold on majoritarian discourses of the body, confined instead to other non-normative experiences of embodiment wherein the body seems to draw attention to itself as in some way obstructive: in the case of madness, anorexia, or disability, for instance. In the context of transness, it retains a strange status because it operates as a metaphor that is allegedly meant to "explain" transness, but also fails to reckon with the fact that trans people as a population are literally overincarcerated—that for some incarcerated trans people, the metaphor doesn't get us very far. Its explanatory potential is diluted insofar as it is largely phenomenologically homogenizing while plastering over the reality of trans incarceration.

How, then, do we go about reconciling the figurative carceral resonances of Benjamin's metaphor with the literal relationship trans people have with the carceral system and its vast, disorienting architectures? In the United States there is a long historical precedent for this affiliation between transness and incarceration. Anti-cross-dressing laws dating to the nineteenth century—many of which were not repealed until after the mid-century—criminalized and pathologized trans life in public spaces. The afterlives of these policies have led to today's overincarceration of trans people, many of whom are sex workers, trans femmes, migrants, HIV+, unhoused, and/or of color. "Evidence shows that trans populations disproportionately experience social hardships that typically qualify as risk factors for victimization and criminal offending, such as discrimination-based socioeconomic inequalities, including barriers to housing, employment, and healthcare," Federica Coppola writes. She continues, "Furthermore, trans people are commonly targeted by the discriminatory enforcement of criminal laws, such as drug laws, illegal immigration laws, and anti-prostitution statutes that often force trans people into criminalized and overpoliced survival economies. Research statistics similarly highlight the overrepresentation of trans youth in court for status offenses."[7] We can draw out, from Coppola's description, the ways in which trans discrimination happens quite visibly at the level of architecture and institutions, from the street to the court to the shelter to the school, and how these structural outcomes can appear to lead naturally to carceral confinement, or curtailed life chances.

While, for Harry Benjamin, the promise of transsexual medicine was, at least in part, a humanist one—keeping some people out of prisons who would otherwise be criminalized[8]—that promise has not held. Trans people are today tremendously overrepresented in prisons, and the metaphor of transness as phenomenological incarceration continues to cast an ambiguous pall on articulations of trans experience. But there's more to the metaphor of being imprisoned in one's body—it is not simply a phenomenological category error that metaphorizes, rather than engages with, the material conditions of trans life. We can think, too, in the context of what Mieke Bal calls an *architecture of loneliness*, produced by the language of being imprisoned in a body. What happens when we trace this question through metaphor as an architecture that, much like the architectures of carcerality Foucault described—the prison, the hospital, the school—are problems in the social domain? To borrow and echo a slew of questions asked by Joan Lubin and Jeanne Vaccaro,

> What is the relationship between subject position and spatial positionality? Are adjacent spaces microcosmic or symptomatic of their total environment? How do the relays between taxonomy, hierarchy, and infrastructure organize the architecture of expertise? When we find our spatial metaphors for power relations literalized in architectural space, do they confirm or confound our analysis? Does it lend our metaphors concretion or prove their insuperable figurality?[9]

At least in the language of being "imprisoned" in a body, trans incarceration would seem to "lend concretion" to the metaphor. At the same time, the wager of transsexuality—of changing one's sex, of seeking an alignment between mind and body that is not confining—is that there exists the possibility of freedom, however incomplete. "What would a 'self' do," Anne Dufourmantelle asks, "who wasn't bolted shut from the inside?"[10] We'd be wise, here, however, in considering Lubin and Vaccaro's first question—*What is the relationship between subject position and spatial positionality*?—which draws attention to a trend in trans theorizing that equates transness with the capacity for subterranean movement, for undermining stasis. Through such a reading, trans uniquely offers the potential and flexibility, the *fugitivity* of moving across, or through, or beyond; the prefix does an astonishing amount of load-bearing work. When trans does not, or cannot signify in these ways, or when fugitivity—like being imprisoned—is no longer a metaphor but a reality (through, say, existing under conditions of literal confinement), how then is this sense of movement (becoming untrapped, un-imprisoned) unsettled?

Trans or not, all selves are bolted shut from the inside, constrained by the all-too-human conditions of embodiment. Yet in prison, selves are, rather famously, bolted shut from the outside, too. To be trans in prison is, perhaps, to be doubly imprisoned—but not in the metaphoric sense as I've considered here, which is to say, not in the sense of being imprisoned in one's body *as* a trans person. Rather, transness has historically posed architectural challenges to confinement, which often results in compounded punishment and increased vulnerability. As Tait Sanders explains,

> In one sense, the trans person literally has no place, since the carceral setting itself is built upon cisnormative gendered systems, with one prison for men who meet the legal requirements to be deemed men, and another for women who do not. In another sense, the architecture of the prison archive reifies trans by demanding an origin (Derrida and Prenowitz, 1995: 57)—the sex assigned at birth, or the root of cisnormative rule of law.[11]

The problem, according to those involved in the day-to-day organizing and management of prisons, is uncertainty about where trans people fit, how to fit them into a rigidly gender-segregated space where their presence is understood most immediately through the calculus of institutional, not personal, risk. To be doubly imprisoned, then, might in fact mean being housed in units that put trans people at greater risk, and limit the possibilities of pursuing desirable or meaningful expressions of gender and sex.

Perhaps the most longstanding and broad conversation that juxtaposes transness and architecture is shaped around "bathroom bills"—namely, federal and state legislation determining which gendered restrooms are most appropriate to trans people, and whether restroom access in binary architectures ought to be determined by sex assigned at birth or self-identification. This dominant discourse about trans people is likewise concerned with exclusion, but less frequently with confinement—unless architectural exclusion is presented as a foregone chronology, one initial step on the inevitable path to confinement. As has been pointed out *ad nauseam*: bathroom bill legislation is, in practice, difficult to enforce. Without the presence of some Kafkaesque gatekeeper able to admit or deny entry—not unlike, say, a Berghain bouncer—bathroom access ends up being socially or self-policed through the rhetoric of exclusion and the threat of violence. This is a rhetoric that disseminates like buckshot; it has wider psychosocial implications than the architecture of the bathroom cubicle would have us believe. Trans people who pass—who are unreadable as trans—are often able to access the appropriate restroom and relieve themselves undisturbed, their presence rarely disrupting the ordinariness of the space. Still, trying to intellectualize or rationalize one's way out of an ideology like TERFism (trans-exclusionary radical feminism)—which is not rational but rather stirred and roused by pure phobia—is a losing game.

Aside from Lucas Crawford's *Transgender Architectonics: The Shape of Change in Modernist Space* (2015), little attention has been invested in bridging the gap between trans studies, which so often focuses on the subjectivities of trans genders and sexualities, and architectural theory. Crawford's text theorizes transness as an access to movement, either across architectures or across the architectures of modernist literature. The trouble with considering trans architecture as one ontologically grounded in liberatory possibility and movement is that any significant, materialist encounter with trans architecture thematizes the frequent *im*possibilities of movement through physical space, whether that be in historical anti-cross-dressing laws, or contemporary bathroom bills, targeting of sex workers, housing discrimination, or immigration policy. Accounting for trans incarceration offers one of the best examples of how restriction is inseparable from trans architecture. Critical carceral studies stakes out a broad ethical position: that carcerality is not just about the physicality of the prison; the physical architectures of the prison are merely one manifestation of biometric systems of control and power that characterize modernity and extend far beyond prison walls. The problems of carcerality, in this framework, are not to be (re)solved with minor adjustments to a fundamentally debased and dehumanizing way of warehousing impoverished people nor by removing from sight those who might cause harm—though carceral studies frameworks also recognize that reform is crucially necessary for those currently suffering confinement.

The purpose of gender-based segregation is risk management and, as an organizing principle, it too has a history. "It was not until well into the 19th century, when prisons reoriented to 'treatment' and 'rehabilitation', that gender segregation became a key tool in correctional efforts," Ren-yo Hwang writes. "It was then deemed necessary to separate 'the sexes' to modify prisoner behaviour in accordance with gender norms. Women's prisons were designed to transform 'fallen' women into better wives, homemakers and domestic servants, whereas men's prisons sought to transform deviant men into productive workers and citizens."[12] But incarceration is a strange, ineffectual way of managing risk insofar as it creates more risk—an ouroboros of risk. We know that incarceration does not do what it claims, on its face, to do—rehabilitate, provide resources for those returning to society, and offer meaningful opportunities for people while they are incarcerated. Since it fails to deliver on this charge, confinement is little more than a way of managing perceived risk to those who are not incarcerated while, at the same time, exposing incarcerated people to various forms of risk and retributive violence.

The language of risk unlocks additional questions about metaphor: if gender is portrayed as the site of risk for the most vulnerable inside, then gender comes to operate *as* risky. But more troublingly, through this unequal exposure to risk, gender becomes perceived as something aggressive. Gayle Salamon writes about this beautifully in her book *The Life and Death of Latisha King* (2018) where, in her account of King's murder, Salamon offers a phenomenology of transphobia. King was murdered at age fifteen, by a classmate, for her gender expression. The defendant's lawyers employed a gay panic defense—though such a defense was illegal in California—on the basis of the defendant feeling threatened by Latisha's gender. Salamon writes, "What we see in this case, and in many instances of violence against gender-nonconforming and transpeople, is that violence justifies itself by characterizing non-normative gender as itself a violent act of aggression and reading the expression of gender identity *as itself a sexual act*."[13] In a similar way, "high risk" incarcerated people are portrayed as high risk because non-normative gender is perceived as aggression. Risk management then is less about protecting those most vulnerable—incarcerated queer and trans people—but, instead, a series of policies and decisions that "fail to consider the significant ways in which vulnerability is institutionalized, and to a great extent endemic to criminal justice processes."[14] For this reason, something like the gender-responsive K6G—the first self-segregated gay and transgender unit, founded in 1985 at the Los Angeles County Men's Central Jail—fails even at the point of conception. "The trap of K6G," Hwang writes, "is in its ability to be an absolute diversion from attending to the mechanics of sexual and gendered violence that undergird the very inception and cultures of perpetual domination that are the mainstay of carceral institutions."[15]

To return to narrative: the trans metaphor of being imprisoned in a body becomes a problem not simply because it's historically oblivious, or phenomenologically inaccurate for many. Rather, the metaphor itself becomes an architecture of confinement, a prison house of language. But that isn't simply a narrative concern—it's a coalitional one. Narrative does something. Surely the figuration of trans as a double imprisonment manufactures what Mieke Bal refers to as an *architecture of loneliness*. In the context of Bal's term, *architecture* can be understood in at least two ways: first, in thinking about the material architectural realities that incarcerated trans people face, which differ from non-trans people in many ways, chief among them, institutional anxieties about gender segregation and how to determine where trans people might be housed; and secondly, metaphorically, in creating an alienated narrative architecture that cleaves the experiences of imprisoned trans people from imprisoned non-trans people. This schism produces two imbricated discourses about incarcerating, diverting attention from the need for carceral abolition onto a singular focus on gender segregation. The violent substrate on which all incarceration is built thus remains an untouched foundation.

Loneliness is not just a problem of affect, of feeling bad or disaffected or estranged. To be trapped in a metaphor and trapped in a prison are not the same thing. Both point us, in their own ways, to the need for relation, for the kinds of coalition able to see where transness is architecturally excluded, or made to appear as "risky"—in housing, education, employment, and citizenship—and the need to displace the metaphor. "Metaphor invests a space of meaning that didn't exist beforehand," Anne Dufourmantelle reminds us.[16] What coalitional thinking can emerge in this site of displacement? What can be built?

1
Michel Foucault, *Discipline and Punish: The Birth of the Prison* (Random House, 1977), 103.

2
Anne Dufourmantelle, *In Praise of Risk* (Fordham University Press, 2019), 49.

3
Harry Benjamin, *The Transsexual Phenomenon* (Julian Press, 1966), 17.

4
Benjamin, *The Transsexual Phenomenon*, 126.

5
Benjamin, *The Transsexual Phenomenon*, 80–81. Benjamin cited the piece in its entirety in *The Transsexual Phenomenon*. In that same issue of *Turnabout*, the magazine reprinted a piece, "Advice to a Transsexual" by Harry Benjamin, which originally appeared in the December 1963 issue of *Sexology*.

6
Sandy Stone, "The Empire Strikes Back: A Posttranssexual Manifesto," *Camera Obscura* 10, no. 2 (1992): 150–76.

7
Federica Coppola, "Gender Identity in the Era of Mass Incarceration: The Cruel and Unusual Segregation of Trans People in the United States," *I·CON* 21, no. 2 (2023): 650–651.

8
As Benjamin wrote, "The desire to change sex has been known to psychologists for a long time. Such patients were rare. Their abnormality has been described in scientific journals in the past in various ways; for instance, as 'total sexual inversion,' or 'sex role inversion.' Beyond some attempts with psychotherapy in a (futile) effort to cure them of their strange desires, nothing was or could be done for them medically. Some of them probably languished in mental institutions, some in prisons, and the majority as miserable, unhappy members of the community, unless they committed suicide. Only because of the recent great advances in endocrinology and surgical techniques has the picture changed" (22).

9
Joan Lubin and Jeanne Vaccaro, "The Sexological Floorplan: Trans Study and the Incorporation of Sexology," *Transgender Studies Quarterly* 10, nos. 3–4 (2023): 350.

10
Dufourmantelle, *In Praise of Risk*, 49.

11
Tait Sanders, et al., "Trans Architecture and the Prison as Archive: 'Don't Be a Queen and You Won't Be Arrested,'" *Punishment and Society* 25, no. 3 (2023): 749.

12
Sarah Lamble, "Outrage: Trans Incarceration," *The Architectural Review*, March 29, 2022, https://www.architectural-review.com/essays/outrage/outrage-trans-incarceration, accessed January 6, 2025.

13
Gayle Salamon, *The Life and Death of Latisha King: A Critical Phenomenology of Transphobia*, (NYU Press, 2018), 5.

14
Jess Rodgers, Angela Dwyer, and Nicole Asquith, "Cisnormativity, Criminalisation, Vulnerability: Transgender People in Prisons," *Tasmanian Institute of Law Enforcement Studies Briefing Paper* 12 (2017): 4.

15
Ren-yo Hwang, "Trans of Color Entrapments and Carceral Coalitions," *WSQ: Women's Studies Quarterly* 51, nos. 1–2 (n.d.): 143.

16
Dufourmantelle, *In Praise of Risk*, 171.

⁂

Isabelle Bonzom

ART IN AND FOR CARCERAL SPACES

Painting with Architecture

Painting on a wall is painting on an architecture in a real space. By surrounding the viewer, the painted walls embrace the visitor who wanders through this space or the person who lives within it. This is not about invading the viewer's gaze by completely covering a wall. It's about suggesting rather than imposing, weaving a dialogue and creating in line with the volume of the building. My aim is to bring the space to life while seeking circulation, rather than freezing an image on a wall. My murals are designed to integrate themselves into the site.

As an artist working on site-specific projects, I was commissioned in 2000 to create murals at the prison of Saint-Malo, in the region of Brittany, western France. The directors of the Bureau of Prisons at the French Ministry of Justice were initially looking for a street artist to decorate one wall in a prison courtyard, but when they heard about my approach, they decided to give me *carte blanche* and commissioned me to create an ensemble of paintings in the detention area. The Ministry of Justice together with the Ministry of Culture were interested in my conception of mural art as pictorial punctuation in real space, which serves to reinforce the relationship between painting, architecture, and the viewer. They appreciated my pictorial language and themes, which explore transitions and use the healing power of art to relieve isolation and suffering. They understood that my paintings harmonize with the surrounding architecture and position the viewer at the heart of the artistic experience. They thought that my approach would be relevant to the prisoners' wellbeing. The art project they commissioned from me was part of the prisoner reintegration program.

A Tailor-made Project

First, I visited the prison. I met the people who work and live there. Then, I conceived a mural project to suit the architecture: the structure, the light, and the existing colors. The building was well-maintained and the paintwork had been refreshed: vanilla on walls, red on doors and bars, gray on gates, black on railings and locks. I also considered the routines and movements of the people who use the space—whether guards, incarcerated individuals, teachers, etc. I wanted my paintings to be present, not omnipresent. So, when I looked at the floor plans, I made sure that the paintings would be visible from various viewpoints, yet not overpowering. I created a pictorial pathway in relation to how people ambulated. To do that, I walked a lot inside the prison and moved around to determine where to place the paintings, how they would evolve. I made the models from plans and pictures I had taken. Finally, I painted freehand with oil paint directly on the walls of the detention area, in between the cell doors. I worked at the prison for three weeks. Ultimately, these paintings were staggered punctuations made for the site.

Saint-Malo is a seaside town whose entire history is linked to the coast. For the murals, I chose the theme of the sea. Although it may seem banal in such a city, the sea speaks deeply to the incarcerated people there. It remains unseen to them because of their incarceration. My murals deliberately did not represent the sea but only suggested its presence by focusing on what people, animals, and craft can do in the aquatic environment.

I painted figures structured around the notion of evolution. Built in the 1930s and inspired by religious architecture, the Saint-Malo prison features cells arranged in staggered rows along a nave. I organized a progression of murals linked to the specificity of that space. On the ground floor, I painted divers, boats, and animals evolving underwater. On the first floor, I painted similar subjects, only on the water's surface. On the top floor, my characters moved above the water level. The layout of the three-dozen painted figures in the detention area created visual breathing spaces. Figures could be followed from one floor to the next, inscribing this transformational narrative as a living part of the building. For instance, a female swimmer was preparing her dive on the top floor and entering the water on the first floor. In this way, I aimed to convey a continuum of human motion through the mural's relation to the detention area. Even if I was a woman working in a male prison environment, I was focused on the representation of the body, showing the precariousness and strength of the body, whether male or female. I wished to express vitality and dignity.

Psychotherapist and art critic Paola Cocchi wrote that "this wall that Isabelle Bonzom didn't hide or cover with paint, she managed to divert it to the point of dematerializing it."[1] Cocchi explained that the images I painted "induce the experience of passage, of metamorphosis as a test of life and a creative initiation." She added:

> The effectiveness of Isabelle Bonzom's approach lies in playing with the implicit and the implied, making them present without describing them. It's not the underwater landscape that the paintings are going to imitate, it's the prison landscape that the images are going to change. It's not about making the prisoners believe they're in Tahiti, but about helping them open up and experience a mental space.

As part of this project, I also led a workshop during which some of the incarcerated persons volunteered to create their own paintings based on the same general theme as my main project. None of those incarcerated men had ever touched a paintbrush and made art. Each created a painting inscribed in a circle evoking a porthole. They painted in the stairwells and opposite the parlor. Although individual, these paintings were designed by the group for the collective space and the community. This workshop was a great way to empower people who felt deprived of any agency in their current living situation.

From Defined Space to Infinity

This mural project was made possible by an agreement between the French Ministries of Culture and Justice. Marnix Bonnike, visual art advisor of the Regional Cultural Affairs Office in Brittany, stressed that my paintings at the prison, instead of conveying the traditional metaphor of "windows onto the world, were actually doors, access points and passages which forge points of view or sources of debate." According to Georges Camps, Regional Director of Penitentiary Services in Brittany, "Isabelle Bonzom's murals are exemplary as they reevaluate the prisoners' relationship to learning, to fighting against exclusion and to improving the living environment." Joël Gard, Head of the Socio-Educational Unit, considered this artistic project "a means of asserting a freedom that is not individual and demanding, but supportive and constructive." Two years after completion of the murals, a study was conducted by the French Bureau of Prisons' Rehabilitation Department. The report indicated that my mural paintings, which were entirely integrated into common spaces, had improved relations between residents and staff as well as between prisoners of various ages, races, and social backgrounds.

Isabelle Bonzom, *Plunge*, 2000, oil/wall, jailhouse of Saint-Malo (Brittany, western France). Courtesy of Isabelle Bonzom / Adagp.

My work sought to stimulate incarcerated individuals' creativity, intuition, and respect for themselves and others. According to prison residents and guards, my paintings brought comfort, connectedness, and peace. Dominique, a prisoner, noticed that "it's possible to evolve" and he added that those murals had succeeded in "exciting our minds to build other horizons and move from defined space to infinity." Another incarcerated man, named Sergio, remarked that "the wall comes to life." "We regain confidence," Sergio said. For his part, Maurice asserted that "the paintings bring a little bit of happiness." He recounted: "As often as I can, I walk the corridors to look at the paintings. It's a real spiritual escape. A pleasure for the eye and for the soul. I almost feel like living normally."[2]

A Sea of Possibilities

For the Saint-Malo prison, I created paintings which emphasized harmony and action. Like subliminal images, they suggested a realm of possibilities and opportunities. They instilled a sense of openness. Through optic and tactile sensations, they developed cognitive functions, intuition, daydreaming, and creativity. As art critic Cocchi observed, "prison is a static place *par excellence*, yet Isabelle Bonzom has managed to suggest that within the prison itself we can transmit a logic of rebuilding oneself, an apprenticeship in autonomy and freedom." Philosopher Baldine Saint Girons noted that "Isabelle Bonzom's pictorial promenade for men in prison is an admirable project. Healing through the imaginary, the paintings allow us to grasp the possibilities of evolution and reversibility in any situation. The paintings inscribe themselves in the space they traverse, oceanizing it, liberating it according to their own dynamic."[3]

My site-specific artwork at the Saint-Malo prison was a profound experience for me and for the people who lived or worked there. It reflects the impact of art on our behaviors and living spaces, especially those where suffering, anxiety, and dysfunction exist.

1
Unless explicitly stated, all the following quotations are taken from the catalog *Peintures murales d'Isabelle Bonzom et des détenus à la maison d'arrêt de Saint-Malo* (Ministères de la Culture et de la Justice, 2001), http://isabelle-bonzom.org/cataloguesaintmalo.html, accessed November 26, 2024.

2
L.D. Maurice, Post-project interviews with incarcerated persons in Saint-Malo prison, 2001.

3
Baldine Saint Girons, *Corps à corps, terre à terre: Peinture d'Isabelle Bonzom* (Ville des Herbiers, 2003), 17.

Isabelle Bonzom, *Preparing for the dive, through the safety net*, 2000, oil/wall, jailhouse of Saint-Malo (Brittany, western France). Courtesy of Isabelle Bonzom / Adagp.

Individual promenoir, Melun central prison, 1930, photograph.
Courtesy of Henri Manuel / Fonds Manuel / ENAP – CRHCP, M-09-025.

SITE

SITE SITE

SITE II SITE

SITE SITE

SITE

SITE

SITE

SITE II SITE

SITE

SITE

SITE SITE

SITE II SITE

SITE SITE

SITE

⁂

Chris Etienne

SITE

Humans are malleable creatures poured into a mixture of culture, circumstances, and personal catastrophe; like wet concrete, we're placed into nondescript molds until we harden and cement our sense of self. We are defined by borders, city blocks, neighborhoods, and, more often, buildings. We may live on the same vast planet, but our experiences in school, at work, in our places of worship and homes encompass our existence and become our world. The buildings we navigate through aren't simply rooms and empty hallways, they are anchored mementoes that we inscribe with heartfelt moments and hardships. Whether we are recalling the echoes of laughter reverberating in the halls of a childhood home or the faint smell of a favorite meal simmering in the kitchen, the gentle reminders of past events in the buildings we've occupied are enough to quicken heartbeats and send us down a rabbit hole of past emotions and experiences. Unfortunately, just as wholesome spaces can conjure up positive memories, toxic locations can trigger traumatic ones. There is an architecture to trauma that you can find present both in poor communities and carceral spaces. For individuals raised in low-income housing, one of the most unsettling things about our prison system is the whispers of familiarity that you will find tattooed in cell blocks. The smell of industrial paint on porous stone, the presence of bars on windows, and the weight of patrolling eyes watching you all serve as faint reminders of public housing conditions.

The presence of incarceration is etched into the structure of poor communities because prison is the expectation; for many, it has become the final destination in the journey of their lives. The first command on arrival in prison is to strip, but the second lesson in shedding attachments to the outside world is what resonates with you the most. You're taught to cast aside your pride and follow orders, to exchange your name for a sequence of numbers, and to accept your position as a "less than" in the Department of Corrections' pecking order. Once escorted into your housing unit, you'll encounter casualties from the carceral system's war on poverty. Society's outcasts overpopulate our carceral sites; the unhoused, those battling addiction and undergoing severe mental illnesses, are the primary residents of the prison-industrial complex. Some are granted escape through potent medication and spend the majority of their sentence in a drug-induced stupor; others succumb to their frustrations until violence becomes their universal means of communication. The trauma and hostility from these experiences don't dissipate once you transition out of that environment. Reminders of incarceration are present in the communities you re-enter. The labels that are placed on you and the barriers you encounter all serve as traumatic reminders that make it difficult to distinguish your incarceration from the free world. Thus, you feel perpetually trapped in a prison site.

⁂

Anna Arabindan-Kesson and Jessica Womack

CONTAINMENT OR CONTAMINATION: VISUALIZING THE PLANTATION HOSPITAL IN THE AMERICAS

In the introduction to his book *A Treatise on the Diseases of Negroes, As They Occur in the Island of Jamaica*, published in 1820, Scottish physician James Thomson relays advice he was given when graduating from medical school in Edinburgh. "I was strongly advised," he writes, "by my friend the late Dr. W. Wright, if my situation in life ever led me to the West-Indies, to institute inquiries into the nature of the disorders to which the negroes are liable, as affording a subject rich with materials."[1] Thomson, who traveled to Jamaica around 1814, worked in Saint Thomas in the Vale Parish, in what was formerly called Middlesex County, where he carried out a range of medical duties, including experimenting with inoculation and dissection on enslaved people. The book he published describes the range of illnesses and treatments he observed in enslaved communities, demonstrating that, indeed, plantations and the people enslaved on them were "a subject rich with materials."

Thomson's book describes the work he undertakes on the plantation and the interactions he has with enslaved healers and patients. Although he rarely mentions where the work takes place, from the descriptions he has compiled there is the suggestion that the plantation had some kind of hospital, where he was able to observe and manage the patients he saw. Thomson's book is one of many manuals, which offer encyclopedic descriptions of medical management on the plantation and, quite often, document experiments that colonial physicians carried out on enslaved people in the interests of expanding knowledge about disease. Like these other texts, it reveals the centrality of the plantation to the development of medicine, both in the Americas and in Europe. Here was a space where medical practitioners could test out and refine their skills.[2] Underpinning these accounts is a premise that the plantation offered doctors forms of unmediated access and bountiful return. In other words, the language of these publications and the kinds of survey-like, observational studies they provided, reinforce the visual conventions by which the plantation typically comes into view in conventional visual representation: as a place of oversight and control. Yet what also becomes clear from texts like Thomson's is the dissonance between the viewpoint he describes—the all-seeing medic who observes from a distance—and the intimate encounters he has with enslaved people in the process of detailing his observations. The threat of contagion, or contamination, is always near.

The plantation's relationship to medicine takes different forms in the eighteenth- and nineteenth-century British colonial world.[3] But the key connection that Thomson makes here seems to be this: the plantation was built to ensure clear oversight and maximize extraction, and this spatial logic could also greatly aid the practice of medicine, especially in its reliance on observation and diagnosis. The reality, and perhaps perils, of proximity between different forms of life—namely, between the enslaved and those who exploited them—remains unacknowledged, just as it often does in plantation accounts. To explore these relationships further, this essay begins with a discussion of the visual conventions—the ways of seeing—that shaped plantation imagery and the broader connections these conventions had to medical discourse in the eighteenth- and nineteenth-century Americas. From there, it examines the rise of plantation hospitals and the forms of observation and control they afforded. It concludes with a discussion of the ways enslaved people refused these architectures of confinement and considers other forms of healing that took place on the plantation, beyond these practices of observation and control.

Colonial expansion transformed the Caribbean through the dispossession and genocide of Indigenous communities, deforestation, clearing of undergrowth, and burning of roots.[4] Through this process, the plantation was established as a site of transplantation; maintained by displaced people, it also sustained the growth of cash crops that were brought to the Caribbean, along with other kinds of vegetation and plants required for the subsistence of its inhabitants.[5] The cultivation of islands like Barbados and Jamaica from the seventeenth century onward were forms of landscaping that translated aesthetic theory into spatial practice. The plantation became a recurring subject for artists traveling through the British Empire, especially in the eighteenth and nineteenth centuries. Patrons who owned plantations commissioned representations of their property—both human and non-human. Views of plantations were included in topographical accounts of the Caribbean, to encourage interest and investment in the area. In the nineteenth century, as debates about abolition in the British Caribbean colonies become louder and more urgent, plantation scenes such as James Hakewill's *A Picturesque Tour of Jamaica*, or William Clark's *Ten Views in the Island of Antigua* offered sanitized, agreeable views of well-managed estates, depicting industrious enslaved laborers as evidence of the colonies' good order and management, and as proof of slavery's benefits.[6] As Krista Thompson has shown, these earlier views of the plantation—using the strategies and conventions of the picturesque—continued to frame representations of post-slavery Jamaica and the Bahamas, thereby naturalizing the plantation's organization of human and non-human life.[7]

The picturesque genre and the plantation both revolve around the idea of oversight: seeing clearly and making space for modes of visual surveillance is central to their construction. While the picturesque is a representational mode and the plantation a physical space, the aim of both is to gain a certain kind of visual acuity. In the case of the picturesque, the ability to see clearly allows for interactions with place that are premised on control and possession as the means for enforcing—or reinforcing—one's connection to, and movement through, the natural world. The picturesque plantation, created through clearance, is represented as a site that offers an uninterrupted view over the lives who were forced to sustain its industrial extraction.

The logic of the plantation, and its representation, can also be intimately connected to the rise of medical discourses—in particular medical topography—in the British Empire during the eighteenth century. As part of the tropics, the Caribbean was already understood to be a place of potential benefit and potential danger. Medical topographies encouraged forms of "environmental diagnosis,"[8] as Emily Senior has termed them, encouraging readers—and viewers—to understand topographical features and climate through the language of health and wellbeing. How a landscape looked could reveal much about its health, and "healthfulness," for those who might live and work within it. Tropical landscapes might harbor disease, or disease-causing agents, and this threat could be decreased by the clearing of forests and undergrowth. These landscape management activities were crucial to the organization of the plantation, as they afforded unobstructed sightlines over the land, and so they were considered integral to the plantation's economic success while also yielding other health benefits. The plantation became, in the language of medical topography and environmental diagnosis, a "therapeutic landscape"—one that promoted wellbeing and enhanced the healthfulness of the natural environment.[9] As a cleared space then, the plantation also offered the illusion of a landscape (theoretically) rid of disease and a space of (relative) immunity and protection from the tropics' more hazardous elements.

Moving Down into the Plantation Hospital

Observe the plantation depicted in James Hakewill's watercolor of the *Holland Estate, St. Thomas in the East, View from the Change of Air House*, a property owned by G.W. Taylor. The decorative floor tiling, garlanded porch, and fine horses led into the composition by an enslaved laborer reinforce the assumed wealth and privilege of the unseen person taking in the vista. Shaded on this porch, the convalescent is offered respite from what are presumably the warmer plains below, a "change of air" to aid in recovery. Here in the shade, one might be surrounded by cooler, fragrant, breezes—notice the garlands wrapped around the pillars. The excellent ventilation—an open porch—is precisely what allows their all-encompassing view over the land and its enslaved laborers. The convalescent referred to in Hakewill's drawing is obviously white, someone who—despite their ill-health—remains in control of their surroundings. While they are situated in the plantation estate, contained but not confined by the structure of the porch, their distance from the workings of the plantation keeps them (relatively) safe from potential disease and contamination. Their elevated position demonstrates the carefully arranged sightlines of the picturesque, with its ample opportunities for taking a view. This position also establishes the sightlines needed for the plantation to function, demonstrating how its reliance on clearance also "cleared" the land of potential threats—both medical and otherwise.[10]

James Hakewill (1778–1843), *Holland Estate, St. Thomas in the East, View from the Change of Air House*, circa 1820–2, watercolor; image: 10⅞ × 16½ in. (27.7 × 41.9 cm); sheet: 12¼ × 16½ in. (31.2 × 41.9 cm), Yale Center for British Art, Paul Mellon Collection. Public domain.

MAS·IN·THE·EAST·JAMAICA
YLOR ESQ.R M.P.

As a cleared and clear space, the plantation sustained a fantasy of unobstructed access and control—over both land and life. It was a fantasy that hinged on encoding a certain amount of distance between the observer and the observed, approximating a form of spatial immunity. But how did this "immunity" work in the context of the plantation hospital, where proximity was paramount? Plantation hospitals were strategically placed: often located close to the overseer's house and to the enslaved quarters, but not too close to the plantation house in the event of contagion.[11] So, unlike the elevated position shown in Hakewill's watercolor, hospitals were incorporated into working life on the plantation. Located at ground level, the spatial experience of oversight had to be approximated through other means.

Public hospitals in the British Caribbean were used almost exclusively for the treatment of European and white Caribbean inhabitants, although there were enslaved workers at these hospitals "assisting" white doctors and nurses.[12] There is also evidence of medical establishments run by "doctresses," such as Mary Seacole and her mother.[13] Mary's mother had practiced on a plantation and learned European medical techniques from military doctors. Both Mary and her mother were also able to serve urban Black communities in Kingston, Jamaica. According to Richard Sheridan, "laws and ordinances calling for suitable slave hospitals and lying-in wards were enacted in the 1790s."[14] These laws came into being during a period known as "Amelioration," and coincided with increased demand in England for the improvement of colonial plantation management. These new provisos were a response to increasingly vehement calls in the United Kingdom for slavery's abolition and, before 1807, planters' concerns about the rise in price of enslaved people.[15] But it is also important to note that this legislation followed the events of the Haitian Revolution; the revolutionaries' successful overthrow of the French plantocracy brought a new and "threatening" reality of Black freedom and sovereignty to the Caribbean, with which planters had to contend. These measures, an attempt to ward off the restriction of planters' commercial interests and potential uprisings, instrumentalized the language of care. For example, legislation required planters "to provide improved food, clothing, health care, and working conditions for enslaved people."[16] In Trinidad, Governor Thomas Picton enacted an ordinance in 1800 that required planters "to lodge, clothe, and maintain them sufficiently, as well in health, while able to work, as in time of sickness, age and infirmity."[17] The ordinance also required plantations to ensure there was a hospital on the estate in proportion to the number of enslaved laborers, with one or more female attendants present to oversee patient care.

In his "manual" on Caribbean diseases and plantation management, physician and poet James Grainger is careful to include a description of the kinds of architectural structures required for adequate medical management of the enslaved. "Every plantation ought to have a large sick house, and if it were floored, so much the better." He goes on, "every plantation should have a proper hut for the reception of yawey [yaws, written here as "yawey," is a bacterial chronic skin infection causing painful ulcers and lumps] patients: This ought to be to *[sic]* leeward, and at a distance from the sick house, which should be built near the dwelling house, but to leeward of it."[18] Grainger's ideal hospital is a four-chambered structure, arranged around a central courtyard/ bath area. As well as a kitchen, living accommodation for nurses and a ward for general ailments, he envisages a surgery, a treatment room, an area for patients with venereal diseases, with each section housing excellent ventilation and latrine facilities. He suggests the entire structure is fenced-off and enclosed with borders of botanical herbs and citrus fruit, to ameliorate odors and for medicinal use.

We have few images of plantation hospitals, at least of how they looked internally. A hospital at Orange Valley Plantation is one example we do have. Archaeologists have found a well-ventilated, spacious structure divided into two halves, most likely meant to segregate women and men. The hospital was two-storied with large rectangular and Palladian windows, built to ensure excellent ventilation, along with a paired hipped roof—used in the Caribbean to prevent hurricane damage. The hospital is

Eighteenth-century slave hospital, Orange Valley, Jamaica, photograph, Lucinda Lambton. All rights reserved 2024/ Bridgeman Images.

"notable for its Palladio-inspired symmetrical Georgian architecture, its aesthetics are unusually pleasing for a building designed to serve a strictly utilitarian purpose and the needs of an enslaved population generally accorded only the bare rudiments of life."[19] The space of the Orange Valley Plantation hospital, and the description Grainger offers, approximate the sense of openness that Hakewill depicts in his *Change of Air* house. They also give us an idea of how planters and doctors might have imagined the relationship of the hospital to the rest of the plantation. Open, accessible, yet also contained, these examples demonstrate the multiple uses of the hospital: a site for the confinement of potentially contagious diseases, a site for medical observation and treatment, and a site for maintaining the conditions of working life on the plantation.

However, many descriptions of plantation houses in the British Caribbean and United States suggest they were often dirty, poorly ventilated, and badly lit. Following his visit to Jamaica, Richard Bickell wrote in 1825, "Their hot-houses, or hospitals are, generally speaking, filthy receptacles; they are very happily styled hot-houses, for they are hot enough; as the hospital is, on most estates, a confined room, very often an earthen floor."[20] For anti-slavery activists, the shameful medical facilities and the (mal)treatment of sick enslaved people that occurred there were the main testaments to the violence of slavery. For those who supported slavery—such as Hakewill—however, the commercial benefits of the plantation could be reinforced in images that demonstrated its benefits in other ways. As such, notwithstanding the quality of care it actually provided, the very existence of the plantation hospital could be used to argue for slavery as an inherently benevolent institution. Its architecture and the practices it facilitated demonstrated yet another aspect of the plantation's beneficial "effect" on "diseased" landscapes—in containing and eliminating infection, the hospital ensured well maintained estates and people.

It was in planters' best interests to provide good healthcare. Ill-health had a negative impact on the labor force and, consequently, on the plantation's profits. In an institution where enslaved people were considered a financial investment, their wellbeing was crucial for maintaining optimal productivity. After the abolition of the slave trade, the numbers of enslaved people on estates could not be boosted by communities forcibly brought across the Atlantic from West Africa. So, to ensure the population of enslaved people grew through reproduction, more effort was also made to maintain the health of pregnant women and newborns. James Thomson considered it imperative that "lying-in" hospitals also be built on plantations:

> As to the question regarding the propriety of having a lying-in hospital on every property there can be no doubt, and it ought to be enforced on every occasion: The superior accommodations, the quiet so necessary for the mother and infant, the cleanliness which can be observed towards them, regular diet, and the dressing of the *Umbilicus*, are objects of the first importance. I would recommend that the lying-in room be separated from the hospital for the sick.[21]

It is not easy to read a text like this. While, on the one hand, it provides an account of maternal health practices, these descriptions of care are also part of the economic "calculus" of the plantation—the minimum "care" needed, ultimately, to ensure maximum profit. We can also see how "care" converges with the visual logic sustaining the plantation. Keeping healthy mothers and newborns away from the potential contagion of the sick hospital, and away from their plantation kin, ensured doctors and planters were able to monitor and watch over their bodies. While the convalescent in the *Change of Air* house was free to look down across the plantation, surveying the view from a stance of power, enslaved Black people were subjected to surveillance even under the pretense of a "caring" architecture like the plantation hospital. In other words, despite the discrepancy between the *Change of Air* house (set high up, at a remove from the landscape) and the plantation hospital (sited at ground level), both offered white viewers, at least, a similar view—one premised on oversight and control.

This inequity is reinforced by the other "uses" of the plantation hospital. It was common for hospitals to be places of confinement for enslaved people who had been captured or punished. As Richard Bickell describes, "The hot-house is often the place, where the Negroes are also confined in the stocks; so that it is both hospital and gaol."[22] The plantation hospital, then, was quite literally a carceral space, used both to confine diseased bodies and those whose behavior threatened to disrupt the workings of the plantation. Confinement here also meant the detention of those who might perpetrate actions—such as running away or feigning illness to avoid work—or even ideas that might be contagious, spreading across enslaved communities and potentially causing other kinds of outbreaks.[23] As Sheridan describes, hospitals were built with barred windows and locked doors to prevent escape.[24]

The confinement of enslaved patients in plantation hospitals ensured they were subjected to more intimate modes of surveillance. But this intimacy, while collapsing the physical distance encoded in the plantation picturesque, also maintained the sense of oversight the logic of the plantation required. Rather than labor practices, it was physical behavior and bodily functions that were monitored and controlled in the hospital. Bodily examinations and medical procedures could be used to "assess" and "measure" while treatments could be prescribed either as curative or punitive. Despite their proximity to the unwell and the contagious, white doctors and overseers continued to maintain the illusion of distance based on the visual dynamics of observation and diagnosis, confinement, and control. This notion of "objectivity" becomes more significant in the context of the plantation hospital as laboratory. The proximity to enslaved patients, inmates, or "subjects," was one of the reasons why doctors like James Thomson traveled to the plantations of the Caribbean. Here, they had access to new bodies and new diseases that enabled them to learn about, experiment with, and publish on new kinds of treatments.[25] Thomson, for example, includes descriptions of medical "interventions" in his treatise, including forced inoculations of children and skin biopsies. While acknowledging these interventions had physical effects on enslaved people, the aim for Thomson and his colleagues was to draw out the implications of these findings for readers, to direct them to the medical "returns"—financial and intellectual—that plantation hospitals could provide.

The plantation hospital was crucial to the apparatus of the plantation in that it continued and reinforced its operational and visual logics. It is also where the fantasies of distance and objectivity encoded in these operations began to come undone. Thomson's treatise for example, also includes anecdotes in which his medical "mastery" appears to break down. There are unfamiliar physical conditions and local practices that he simply did not understand. For example, in discussing treatments for the effects of Gonorrhea he writes "few drops of the juice of the wild ... parrotweed [in the poppy family] is a favourite country remedy, and, from many trials I have made of it, seems worthy of confidence."[26] This nonchalant aside reminds us of the reliance of many plantation doctors on enslaved healers to explain the curative properties of local plants. Thomson also learns of new treatments and practices from enslaved communities—such as inoculation—who brought this knowledge with them across the Atlantic: "It is somewhat singular that the practice of inoculating for the small-pox has been known from the remotest ages in many parts of Africa."[27] Enslaved people used this knowledge to leverage payment from doctors as they experimented with inoculation against smallpox. Thomson explains:

John A. Waller, *Slaves in Barbados*, engraving, 1820, from John A. Waller, *A voyage in the West Indies* (Sir Richard Phillips and Co., 1820), 20. Public domain.

"They term it buying the small-pox, from the circumstance that the parent of the child, from whom matter is taken, always expects a small remuneration from the person to whom the disease is communicated."[28] These brief examples demonstrate the importance of enslaved healers in the management and function of the plantation hospital as they were required to be in attendance onsite and often managed patient care. The work of enslaved nurses, doctresses, and healers ranged from mixing and administering medicines, supervising diets, and tending to the sick to assisting with the activities of daily life and carrying out medical procedures. The plantation hospital required, and facilitated, this strange proximity between enslaved people and white overseers or doctors—it was precisely this intimacy, not the illusion of sovereignty suggested by visual representations, that allowed it to operate at all. While medical care was used as a form of control on the plantation, the practice of medicine was also wholly contingent on the labor and knowledge of the enslaved.

Despite its carceral uses, the plantation hospital was also a place of respite, where some enslaved laborers chose to feign illness to avoid the arduous labor of field work.[29] However, doctors also describe how difficult it was to confine enslaved people, especially when they were forced to stay close to others being punished for various offenses. Enslaved people—as is true of many patients today—objected to hospital food and vile tasting medicines, and they resented being housed in a place of death.[30] Thomas Cooper observed that enslaved people disliked being "separated from the kindness of their friends and would prefer being in their own houses, even though in a miserable state."[31] Being admitted to the hospital took them away from kinship, support systems, and familiar modes of treatment. Some enslaved laborers simply refused to be admitted or confined, choosing instead to continue to work while sick.[32] In different ways, enslaved people attempted to undermine the systems of oversight and "care" that were facilitated by the plantation hospital.[33]

John A. Waller, another British colonial doctor who traveled through the British Caribbean, includes a unique depiction of enslaved life in the book he published after his voyage. The drawing shows an enslaved community on an unnamed Barbados plantation, organized like a stage set: a hilly backdrop elevates the architecture of the plantation, offering key vantage points over the scene below. In the mid-ground, a plantation manor commands an extensive view over the sugar works while the domestic architecture of various groups of enslaved people dominates the print's foreground. Perhaps the hospital is among these buildings. Certainly, there is more to say about Waller's drawing and the strange figures, drawn in profile, arranged across its foreground. For the purposes of this essay, however, it is the cutaway view of an enslaved family's home in the print's center that draws the eye. The house, like an anatomical dissection, is sliced open so we can look inside. Reinforced by the small figures in the foreground, this is a viewpoint that brings us down from the typically elevated vista of the picturesque, grounding us in the interior workings of the plantation. Perhaps such a view resembles the kind of unfettered access doctors like Thomson hoped to find on the plantation. Yet, in creating this image, Waller draws attention to other forms of sustenance and care that might have been taking place away from the watchful gaze of plantation management. Inside the house, two people—a young man kneeling and a woman wearing an ornate headwrap—tend to a fire. Ceramic vessels line walls and tables, a cloth curves against the wall, a bed is waiting in the next room. The home is full of materials that were instrumental to enslaved people's practices of physical and spiritual care: ceramics were used to hold food, water, and medicine as well as to sustain rituals.[34] Cloths and quilts provided cover against the elements and also served as bandages and supports.[35] Meanwhile, the plantain trees growing outside were often used for various medical remedies. These small vignettes—even though they are produced by colonial artists—offer different sightlines into the world of the plantation, visualizing alternative forms of care and other material practices of healing beyond the forms of control exercised in the plantation hospital. Taken together, the practices evoked in this image demonstrate other ways of "tending to [B]lackness"[36] that continued alongside the operations of plantation oversight, and that can continue to direct us now.

1
James Thomson, *A Treatise on the Diseases of Negroes, as They Occur in the Island of Jamaica: With Observations on the Country Remedies* (Alex Aikman Jnr., 1820), 1.

2
For more on this see Londa Schiebinger, *Secret Cures of Slaves: People, Plants, and Medicine in the Eighteenth-Century Atlantic World* (Stanford University Press, 2017).

3
For more on this see: Rana A. Hogarth, *Medicalizing Blackness: Making Racial Difference in the Atlantic World, 1780–1840* (University of North Carolina Press, 2017); Richard B. Sheridan, *Doctors and Slaves: A Medical and Demographic History of Slavery in the British West Indies, 1680–1834* (Cambridge University Press, 2009); Suman Seth, *Difference and Disease: Medicine, Race, and the Eighteenth-Century British Empire* (Cambridge University Press, 2018); Sean Morey Smith and Christopher Willoughby, *Medicine and Healing in the Age of Slavery* (LSU Press, 2021); Jim Downs, *Maladies of Empire: How Colonialism, Slavery, and War Transformed Medicine* (Belknap Press, 2021); Deirdre Cooper Owens, *Medical Bondage: Race, Gender, and the Origins of American Gynecology* (University of Georgia Press, 2017).

4
Jill H. Casid, *Sowing Empire: Landscape and Colonization* (University of Minnesota Press, 2005), 7–8.

5
Casid, *Sowing Empire*, 8; Beth Fowkes Tobin, *Colonizing Nature the Tropics in British Arts and Letters, 1760–1820* (University of Pennsylvania Press, 2005), 32–55; Juliane Braun, "Bioprospecting Breadfruit: Imperial Botany, Transoceanic Relations, and the Politics of Translation," *Early American Literature* 54, no. 3 (2019): 643–71.

6
James Hakewill, *A Picturesque Tour of the Island of Jamaica* (Hurst and Robinson, 1825); William Clark, *Ten Views in the Island of Antigua: In Which Are Represented the Process of Sugar Making, and the Employment of the Negroes, in the Field, Boiling-House and Distillery* (Thomas Clay, 1823).

7
Krista A. Thompson, *An Eye for the Tropics: Tourism, Photography, and Framing the Caribbean Picturesque* (Duke University Press, 2006).

8
Emily Senior, *The Caribbean and the Medical Imagination, 1764–1834: Slavery, Disease and Colonial Modernity* (Cambridge University Press, 2018), 62.

9
Julie Collins, *The Architecture and Landscape of Health: A Historical Perspective on Therapeutic Places 1790–1940* (Routledge, 2020); Allison Williams, *Therapeutic Landscapes* (Routledge, 2017); Wilbert M. Gesler, "Therapeutic Landscapes: Medical Issues in Light of the New Cultural Geography," *Social Science & Medicine* 34, no. 7 (1992): 735–46.

10
For more on Hakewill see Tim Barringer, "Picturesque Prospects and the Labor of the Enslaved," in *Art and Emancipation in Jamaica: Isaac Mendes Belisario and His Worlds* (Yale Center for British Art, 2019).

11
Dr. Collins, *Practical Rules for the Management and Medical Treatment of Negro Slaves in the Sugar Colonies* (J. Barfield, 1803).

12
Sheridan, *Doctors and Slaves*; Hogarth, *Medicalizing Blackness*, 133–58; Stephen C. Kenny, "'A Dictate of Both Interest and Mercy'? Slave Hospitals in the Antebellum South," *Journal of the History of Medicine and Allied Sciences* 65, no. 1 (2010): 1–47; Richard F. Veit et al., "'Not Unmindful of the Unfortunate': Finding the Forgotten through Archaeology at the Orange Valley Hospital for the Enslaved," *International*

Journal of Historical Archaeology 27, no. 1 (March 1, 2023): 51–80

13
Mary Seacole, *Wonderful Adventures of Mrs. Seacole in Many Lands*, Black Women Writers (J. Blackwood, 1857).

14
Sheridan, *Doctors and Slaves*, 272.

15
Sheridan, *Doctors and Slaves*, 276.

16
Veit et al., "'Not Unmindful of the Unfortunate,'" 58.

17
Sheridan, *Doctors and Slaves*, 273.

18
James Grainger, *An Essay on the More Common West-India Diseases* (T. Becket and P.A. De Hondt, 1764), 71.

19
Veit et al., "'Not Unmindful of the Unfortunate,'" 62.

20
Richard Bickell, *The West Indies As They Are: Or, A Real Picture of Slavery: But More Particularly as It Exists in the Island of Jamaica. In Three Parts. With Notes* (J. Hatchard and Son, 1825), 52; Fanny Kemble, *Journal of a Residence on a Georgian Plantation in 1838–1839* (Harper & Brothers, 1864), 52.

21
Thomson, *A Treatise on the Diseases of Negroes*, 14.

22
Bickell, *The West Indies As They Are*, 52.

23
For more on confinement and punishment see also Hogarth, *Medicalizing Blackness*.

24
Sheridan, *Doctors and Slaves*, 270.

25
Owens, *Medical Bondage*; Harriet A. Washington, *Medical Apartheid: The Dark History of Medical Experimentation on Black Americans from Colonial Times to the Present* (Knopf, 2008).

26
Thomson, *A Treatise on the Diseases of Negroes*, 54.

27
Thomson, *A Treatise on the Diseases of Negroes*, 62.

28
Thomson, *A Treatise on the Diseases of Negroes*.

29
For more on this see Sharla M. Fett, *Working Cures: Healing, Health, and Power on Southern Slave Plantations* (University of North Carolina Press, 2002), 169–93.

30
Sheridan, *Doctors and Slaves*, 272.

31
Thomas Cooper, *Facts Illustrative of the Condition of the Negro Slaves in Jamaica* (1824), 27.

32
Sheridan, *Doctors and Slaves*, 284–87.

33
For more on this see especially Fett, *Working Cures*; Todd Lee Savitt, *Medicine and Slavery: The Diseases and Health Care of Blacks in Antebellum Virginia* (University of Illinois Press, 2002); Smith and Willoughby, *Medicine and Healing in the Age of Slavery*.

34
Fett, *Working Cures*, 84–108; Herbert C. Covey, *African American Slave Medicine: Herbal and Non-Herbal Treatments* (Lexington Books, 2007); Albert J. Raboteau, *Slave Religion: The "Invisible Institution" in the Antebellum South* (Oxford University Press, 2004).

35
Katie Knowles, "Fashioning Slavery: Slaves and Clothing in the U.S. South, 1830–1865," Thesis, Rice University, 2014; Helen Bradley Foster, *New Raiments of Self: African American Clothing in the Antebellum South* (Berg, 1997).

36
Huey Copeland, "Tending-toward-Blackness," *October*, no. 156 (May 1, 2016): 141–44.

⁂

Katie Chizuko Solien

DOMESTICATING BARRACKS: CARCERAL CONSTRUCTIONS OF THE AMERICAN WEST

The word *barrack* falls into the unique category of words that have the ability to move between noun and verb. Barrack refers to "a building or set of buildings used especially for lodging soldiers in garrison," "a structure resembling a shed or barn that provides temporary housing," or "housing characterized by extreme plainness or dreary uniformity."[1] As reflected in its etymological roots, barracks must precariously negotiate their own permanence since the duration of their intended stay or use is never clear. As this definition indicates, *barrack* implies a military encampment: typologically marked by banality and transience, they are often hastily constructed in anticipation of conflict. This spatial ambiguity was reflected in the construction of barracks intended to hold two very different groups of people—Japanese-American incarcerees[2] and veteran homesteaders—under drastically different circumstances during World War II and the postwar period.

Following the attack on Pearl Harbor, thousands of barracks were built in order to contain more than 120,000 Japanese Americans incarcerated in a wide-sweeping impulse fueled by racial hysteria and justified as "military necessity."[3] On February 19, 1942, President Franklin D. Roosevelt signed Executive Order 9066 which permitted the Secretary of War to "prescribe military areas in such places and of such extent as he ... may determine, from which any or all persons may be excluded, and with respect to which, the right of any person to enter, remain in, or leave shall be subject to whatever restrictions the Secretary of War or the appropriate Military Commander may impose in his discretion."[4] While Japanese Americans were not specifically mentioned in the Executive Order, they were the only racial group targeted and removed from the West Coast Exclusion Zone. Within roughly fourteen weeks, the government had hastily constructed what they referred to as "Relocation Centers." These areas were laid out as typical military encampments far away from urban centers, sited in remote areas of the American West including California, Arizona, Utah, Idaho, Wyoming, Colorado, and Arkansas.

Following the war's conclusion, the same structures were recycled as part of a congratulatory incentive orchestrated by the government's Bureau of Reclamation, a federal agency that intended to draw veteran family men to homestead the American interior. *Homestead*, like barrack, is another word that can operate as both verb and noun, implying—both linguistically and physically—an operational intention in its establishment. Defined as the home and adjoining land occupied by a family, a house, or an ancestral home,[5] *homestead* blurs the distinction between land and house, occupation and ownership. These paradoxical definitions of barrack and homestead provide convenient metaphors for the Japanese-American carceral experience and the following reoccupation of the land and structures by veteran homesteaders. The former's experience was marked by haste, conflict, and precarity, while the latter became an extension of prewar expansionist idealism intended to develop and settle the American West. Understanding the logistical networks that orchestrated Japanese-American incarceration during World War II enables us to relate this carceral history to an overarching narrative of American expansion and development. Following the barracks, and the tangible traces of these architectures still embedded in the landscape today, serve to connect the mythic construction of the American West with its carceral underpinnings.

Spatial Politics of Drawing and Assembly

Ahead of its deployment, construction documents for the carceral barrack were drawn and produced in sets, which included plans, elevations, and wall sections featuring architectural details. These plans rigorously considered the smallest moments of assembly, such as the electrical circuitry, the door jambs, window dimensions, and foundation footings. The barracks were timber-framed structures measuring 120 feet long and roughly 20 feet wide.[6] Unexplained in the margins of the construction documents were careful decisions made along the way with a sensitivity toward resource and labor efficiency. The structures were clad in pine boards and insulated only by tar paper held in place by thin wooden battens. Although variances in small details can sometimes be identified in photos of barracks from one camp to the next, these changes highlight the barracks' adaptability and reflect ways in which the barracks were easily adjusted to suit their respective camps. Their construction was purposefully simple and required little specialized training or tools. Its singular dimensions, able to be divided as necessary, maximized programmatic flexibility. The low-sloping roof with little to no rake[7] at the gable or eave minimized the length of timbers required for its assembly. As seen in the floor and electrical plans of the barracks, throughout the camps the structure was divided into six units of varying sizes by partial-height walls and furnished with just one woodstove and a lightbulb. Typically, one

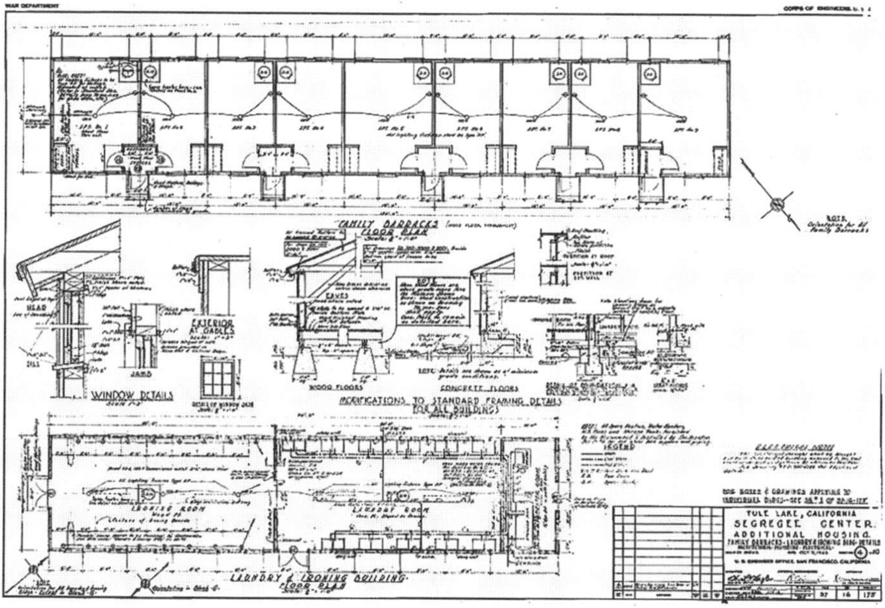

Family barracks, laundry, and ironing building details, Tule Lake Relocation Center, Newell, California. Records Group 210, National Archives, Cartographic Division. Washington, D. C.

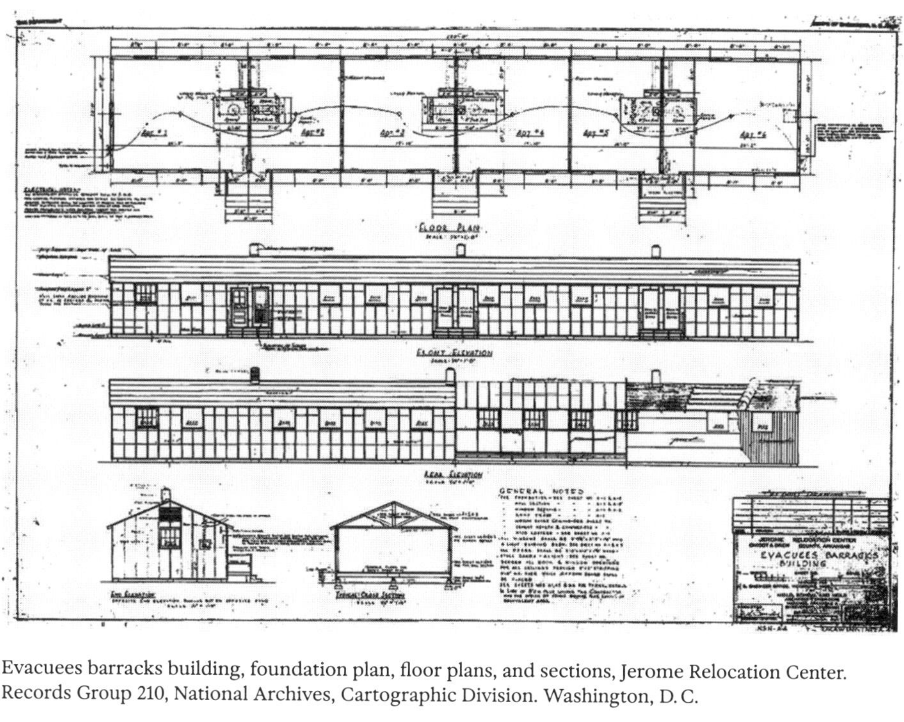

Evacuees barracks building, foundation plan, floor plans, and sections, Jerome Relocation Center. Records Group 210, National Archives, Cartographic Division. Washington, D. C.

family would occupy one of the six units with a group of unmarried individuals sharing the smaller units at either end of the barrack.

Although appearing shed-like, barn-like, or perhaps even house-like, it is critical to note the design and specificity of the carceral barracks used to contain Japanese Americans in order to grasp the nuance and spatial politics of these structures. The specific signature of the architect or engineer, while visible, is illegible in the documents' scan, but its presence reminds us of the human touch behind these seemingly benign and architecturally normative plans. These drawings indicate ostensibly neutral details concerning dimensions, materials, and assembly methods. However, in doing so, they also render how much livable area one person, or one family should be afforded—thus putting a square footage on the right to space (or lack thereof).

At the start of the war, the U.S. Army Corps was tasked with the construction of the camps. This early involvement in spatial organization reverberated in the layout of the barracks and the camps themselves. Each camp was organized differently based on their respective sites, but all of them resembled the same general framework of a military base. Barracks were laid out in blocs, with each bloc including a mess hall, latrine, and a recreation building. One bloc was typically made up of twelve to fourteen barracks, and each camp contained between twelve to seventy-five blocs. The singular barrack that was drawn into the construction set produced over 6,000 carceral barracks[8] built across the ten Relocation Centers. The militaristic scalar dynamics of the carceral barrack are not tangible in the standalone structure drawn on the page but instead emerge through its seemingly infinite potential for expansion and duplication. Methods in architectural drawing fail to register the scale of this sprawling architectural project. Stripped down to its basic instructions of assembly, the impact of confining 120,000 people is made suddenly ambiguous.

To take on the immense task of constructing the carceral camps, the government relied on preexisting relationships and ongoing contracts already involved in the war effort. This included Morrison–Knudsen, a construction company who built two camps while simultaneously engaged in the construction of active military bases and infrastructure along the West Coast. Included in their corporate newsletter in 1942 was a memo titled *IT CAN'T MUST BE DONE !!* which announced, "[There is] the impossible task of building a reception center Camp in 30 days, capable of housing several thousand Japanese ... Details of the contract are still unknown, but work has started." It continues to propose a slogan for the project, "[our job] is not to question why, ours [is] but to do or die."[9] While providing limited details, men were called to take up arms with hammers and saws to support the war effort on the home front.

Rather than training every laborer in all aspects of the construction process, the barracks were erected on-site in an assembly-line fashion. One team of men would set the foundation posts and move on, only to be followed by another team who would construct the floor, followed by another whose task was to raise the exterior walls—and so on and so forth until the structures were finished. Allegedly, some teams were able to assemble a single barrack in under an hour.[10]

These large-scale construction processes, practiced across each camp and confinement site, were celebrated as "new methods now being employed in shipyards."[11] The companies that were turning out warships with unprecedented speed were also tasked with applying the same construction techniques to the barracks and internment camps. An "architectural draft" refers to the technical drawings that are used in the design and construction of a structure. They represent a moment when an idea is translated into an intention or a plan for construction. To draft is to draw; but, in yet another ironic linguistic twist, it also refers to compulsory enlistment into military service. The barracks were drafted onto the page and again into service to contain and defend the nation from an unfounded threat of espionage or sabotage. These shared logistics of assembly blurred the lines between the weapons and war machines sent to the battlefield and the carceral barracks being assembled on the home front.

Domesticating Barracks

The design and construction of the carceral barracks involved architects and engineers who optimized the structure in terms of both spatial and resource efficiency, but this same role was replicated and expanded at a bureaucratic scale. The War Relocation Authority (WRA) was formed and exclusively tasked with the bureaucratic management and administration of the camps. In its inception, President Roosevelt originally appointed Milton Eisenhower as the director of the WRA, after he had effectively served within the U.S. Department of Agriculture.[12] When it became clear that the Japanese Americans were not just going to be temporarily evacuated, processed, and subsequently approved to return home for the duration of the war, Eisenhower resigned from this position. His appointed replacement was Dillon S. Myer, who, like Eisenhower, had previously worked within the Agricultural Adjustment Administration, in the Department of Agriculture, and as chief of the Soil Conservation Service.[13] Eisenhower cautioned his successor, advising him to only take the position "if you can do the job and sleep at night"—a challenge Myer accepted.[14]

The sheer scale of the project led to direct collaboration between the WRA and the Bureau of Indian

Affairs, the Department of Agriculture, the National Forest Service, The Public Land Office, the U.S. Fish and Wildlife Service, and the Bureau of Reclamation. Dillon and Eisenhower were two key figures here, each reflecting an organization of agents with deep roots in larger government agencies and clear agendas relating to land and resource management and development. The government agencies driving this carceral project seamlessly extended their jurisdictions from managing natural resources to managing human resources.

Japanese Americans incarcerated in the camps were able to earn meager wages through a variety of jobs that assisted in the day-to-day operation of the camps. This included working in the hospital, mess halls, and schools, but it also entailed laboring on nearby infrastructure, irrigation, or agricultural projects. With most able-bodied American men drafted or enlisted, Japanese-American labor was critical to the continued development of these projects. Eisenhower hoped that, "It would give these [Japanese American] citizens a measure of assurance and trust should we afford them an opportunity to do their part in the war effort, with the possibility that recognition of this contribution eventually may be accorded by the American public."[15] This sentiment mirrored that of prewar social programs like the Works Progress Administration (1935) and the Civilian Conservation Corps (1933). While these programs had not been geared toward Japanese Americans before the war, they blurred the lines between economic relief and social engineering, continuing the practice of using labor as a tool for shaping national identity. Through these men and their shared agendas, the WRA successfully reproduced the same idealistic social policies from New Deal liberalism that they had previously championed.

To these men, the camps presented an opportunity where, despite the unfortunate incidence of war, Japanese Americans could assimilate and demonstrate

Incarceree posing with a parasol in front of Heart Mountain. Photograph taken by Yoshio Okumoto in 1943. Courtesy of Heart Mountain Wyoming Foundation.

their patriotism through self-government, education, and public service. The overarching governing apparatuses reflected in the WRA considered this labor as a means of restoring American ideals and patriotism in incarcerees. This network of governing agencies and the deployment of military encampments became the base on which the WRA built its carceral program. These camps were almost exclusively sited on municipal- or federal-owned land,[16] landscapes which—in their barren and undeveloped state—seemingly lacked cultural or local specificity. These encampments—intended to contain Japanese Americans for the foreseeable future—thus provided a new, blank slate for the cultivation of an inherently American idealism.

The political players in the WRA who organized and orchestrated the Japanese-American incarceration project aspired to assimilate the incarcerees, but instead the landscape internalized their experience. The barracks, intended to assert order and assimilate the community, became a vehicle through which to demonstrate resilience and reassert identity. Changes made to the carceral barrack and to the landscape by incarcerees operated beyond the bureaucratic imaginary. In a photograph taken by Yoshio Okumoto, a young man incarcerated at Heart Mountain Relocation Center, a woman with a parasol poses in the foreground with the rows of barracks looming behind her. The landscape appears dusty, sparsely covered in sagebrush and patches of grass until it meets the long rows of barracks, each covered in black tar-paper siding. Their shapes overlap and merge into one mass to form a thick, dark boundary at the horizon line. Here, the barracks articulate a division between the carceral landscape and the open sky above it. The only interruption in the dense overlay of barracks is a string of laundry hung alongside the length of one of the structures. The white sheets appear in stark contrast, gently fluttering against a tar-paper backdrop. The routines of daily life prompted the first adaptations to the barrack, but more robust and ambitious renovations were to follow.

Initial adaptations by incarcerated Japanese Americans were responses to the immediate environment, whether that be climatic or social conditions. This included changes to the structures to shield themselves from sun or surveillance. Curtains were hung in the windows; pergolas constructed in scrap wood and, eventually, trees and gardens were planted alongside the barracks. These adaptations to the barrack's exterior led them to take on another appearance altogether. Pergolas over front steps and window boxes introduced a notion of domesticity to an otherwise barren structure. Some modifications were modest in scale and complexity, while others appeared altogether foreign against a carceral backdrop that exemplified a bleak homogeneity. Spread out from California to Arkansas, each camp took on a different appearance that reflected the landscape, the individuality, and the expertise of the incarcerees that lived there, along with the local resources made available to them.

Bonnie Clark's book *Finding Solace in the Soil* provides a detailed look into the archaeological surveys completed at the site of Amache Relocation Center[17] by her and a team from the University of Denver. Clark reminds us that "the soil is an artifact"[18]—one that reflects the ingenuity and resilience of its past inhabitants. The archaeological surveys collected data on pollen and plant remains, identifying which plants were likely introduced at Camp Amache. They were able to determine over twenty different non-native plants including flowers such as canna lily, roses, morning glory, and petunia, as well as crops including squash, gourd, and melon, along with various edible and ornamental herbs and ground cover plants.[19] These findings were accompanied by almost the same number of native plants,

Incarceree adaptations to barrack at Tule Lake Relocation Center, Newell, California. Photograph taken by the War Relocation Authority on November 3, 1942.

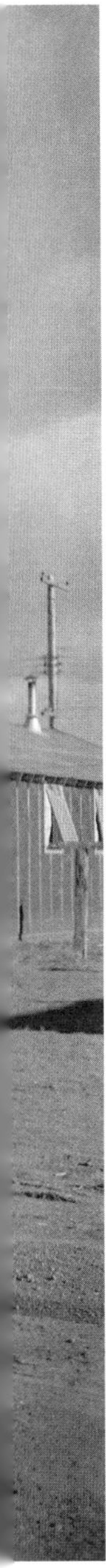

Incarceree adaptations to barrack at Rohwer Relocation Center, McGee, Arkansas. Photograph taken by Charles E. Mace for the War Relocation Authority on June 16, 1944.

Japanese-American incarceree and their victory garden, planted alongside their barrack. Photograph taken by Yoshio Okumoto at Heart Mountain Relocation Center in Cody, Wyoming, 1944. Courtesy of Heart Mountain Wyoming Foundation.

also likely introduced to the landscape by incarcerees. Although it's unclear where exactly each of the seeds came from, their remnants are still scattered in the soil. These plants represented an ecological melting pot, as seeds were brought with incarcerees from their former homes and later exchanged between the camps to create greater biological diversity.

Planted against the periphery of the barracks, these gardens took the stark geometry of the structure and dissolved its edges into the landscape. In other cases, the vegetation was decorative, softening the harsh lines of the carceral barracks and the camp. These adaptations transformed the landscape and the carceral structures, reclaiming them as something that challenged the expectations of the carceral project. The gardens lining the barracks extended the boundaries of one person or one family's personal space. Given the spatial limitations of their barracks, gardens allowed incarcerees to claim the space between barracks as their front or back yards. By using residual building resources from the camp's construction, incarcerees were able to circumvent the carceral logics projected onto them. The construction of the camps by the WRA and the U.S. Army, which capitalized on rapid, assembly line logistics, poses a stark contrast to the gradual adaptive measures implemented by the incarcerees. Eventually, the carceral landscape became a patchwork shaped by the simultaneous habits of individual members and groups within the larger community. Through this, incarcerees embedded themselves—their agricultural acumen, cultural differences, and other layers of embodied knowledge—into the surrounding environment.

Mythmaking Constructions

As the war drew to a close and the threat of espionage and foreign invasion subsided, the U.S. government and the WRA had to repeat their removal efforts—this time evacuating Japanese Americans out of the camps and back to wherever they came from or were able to go to. After Japanese Americans had been dispersed, the Bureau of Reclamation began the process of relocating the barracks and resumed their interest in establishing communities of homesteaders in the American interior. Having provided land for three of the camps, the Bureau of Reclamation—which still exists and continues to operate under the Department of the Interior, overseeing water resource management—was a major benefactor in the land development undertaken by Japanese-American incarcerees. While *reclamation* is often understood as the process of returning or reasserting ownership of something, in environmental science its definition also refers to the cultivation of wasteland or land formerly submerged under water. This "reclamation" not only used Japanese-American bodies and expertise to construct irrigation and other agricultural infrastructure. Ultimately, the overarching governing apparatuses were engineering a particular type of agrarian landscape that could be proliferated throughout the American West—one expertly prepared for white farmers to settle on. While Japanese Americans had effectively labored on agricultural projects, successfully developing the area into a productive and arable landscape,[20] the resuscitation of these prewar homesteading programs demonstrated that the Bureau of Reclamation's interest was in introducing white American homesteaders rather than permanently settling Japanese-Americans.

These barracks were raffled for $1 to any veteran homesteader that would retrieve and move the structure themselves. Three lotteries took place over the course of three years in highly publicized events that were broadcasted and well-attended by hopeful homesteaders.[21] In the Klamath Basin, Oregon, the former site of the Minidoka War Relocation Center, winning families were quickly brought to the top of a hill to be photographed looking at their future homestead. These photoshoots were typically used as propaganda to bring more homesteaders in from either coast. In one photograph, commissioned by the Bureau of Reclamation, a couple looks out across an expansive landscape presumably ripe for development. The man in the photo points his finger toward the distance where the sky bleeds into the horizon line of the landscape, seemingly extending the topography to infinity. The couple, directing their attention left—or, compositionally speaking, west—mirrors a scene not unlike John Gast's *American Progress*, gesturing toward the allegorical idealism of pioneering and Manifest Destiny.[22]

These photographs and documents still exist in the archives today. Typically, they belong to various divisions of the federal government that championed the homesteader programs, while other collections are held by municipal libraries, public universities, or private institutions. Although the connection to America's carceral history is often ambiguous it is never truly erased. In another vignette, photographed and archived by the Bureau of Reclamation, a different couple poses while looking over the Klamath Basin. This time they face the opposite direction, their sightline traveling in the direction of Minidoka War Relocation Center where the long forms of the barracks haunt the edge of the image. Within these archival collections, invisible traces of the Japanese-American carceral experience coexist alongside other supposedly neutral bureaucratic documents, such as construction drawings of canals, laterals and structures, water-right and farm-unit maps, as well as photos of finished and in-progress infrastructural projects. The fragmentation of the material that records this experience—Japanese-American incarceration, the major infrastructural development of the interior, and the homesteading programs that followed—demonstrates a lack of consensus on who this history belongs to and what narratives are allowed to be included in the recollection of American expansionism. What all these documents share is that they operate as evidence of ownership and development. The collections from these federal archives reflect a vision of homesteaders championing the American West and, in the dislocation of this history from the Japanese-American experience, further frays its connection to the carceral project.

Barracks occupied by homesteaders eventually underwent their own alterations, but not until they were demolished and deconstructed or uprooted and transported. While the ownership and use of these barracks may have changed, and their value as raw building material eventually led to their deconstruction, many remain on the same site as their original homesteads. Despite the inspiring invocations of homesteader exceptionalism orchestrated and promoted by the government, the traces of Japanese-American incarceration are embedded in the history of these structures. Disfigured, relocated, and re-clad, they continue to exist. In Cody, Wyoming, where Heart Mountain Relocation Center was located, barrack fragments have been traced to locations over 200 kilometers away from the encampment, but most were relocated within sight of Heart Mountain.[23] Some have been converted into barns or sheds while others were fortified and made into almost unrecognizable conventional homes. Their resemblance to their carceral forerunners can be captured in the pitch of the low-slope roof, the doorways, the dimensions and spacing of windows, and other architectural details loyal to the construction drawings that inspired them.

Japanese-American incarceration during World War II is something of an inconvenient truth in American history. As is all too often the case with shameful pasts, its legacy has been neatly bookended into a regrettable chapter of history worthy of our sympathy, but ultimately not to be dwelled on. The barracks, scattered today across the landscape, persevere against their own ephemeral intentions. By attending to the socio-spatial construction of the barrack, and following the narrative arc of its domestication and dislocation, a tangible link is forged between its carceral origins and the subsequent homesteading projects, thus providing an alternative reading to the persistent erasure of the American West's carceral history. The barracks were a tool that operated as an extension of New Deal politics and those that championed it. While formally indistinct and functionally flexible, the structures were designed to disappear both into the landscape and overarching narratives of American exceptionalism. By disentangling the organizing logics of extraction at work in the barracks—extraction of resources, of human capital, and of buildings themselves—we are able to recuperate the Japanese-American internment experience as more than just a shameful episode in U.S. history. Instead, through this loophole, the Japanese-American incarceration project is tied back into the physical and mythic construction of the American West.

1
"Barrack Definition & Meaning," Merriam-Webster, https://www.merriam-webster.com/dictionary/barrack, accessed January 7, 2025.

2
There is ongoing discussion regarding the best way to refer to the period of Japanese-American exclusion during World War II. Historically, the language used by government officials to refer to displacement is often

made ambiguous in order to mask its severity or legal foothold. This essay will use terms such as incarceration, incarceree, and carceral experience to refer to the military encampments created to contain Japanese Americans during the war. The ten Relocation Centers (as they were referred to by the government at the time) are typically referred to as "camps" today. This preference follows an ongoing debate over how to aptly refer to the experience since euphemisms such as removal, exclusion, detention, evacuation, etc. fail to register the punitive, unjust, and racially charged nuances of the experience. The forced relocation is commonly referred to as "internment," which is defined as the legally permissible detention of "enemy aliens" during wartime. While the U.S. government frequently referred to the Japanese Americans residing within the West Coast Exclusion Zone as "enemy aliens," only about 8,000 were *Issei*, or first-generation immigrants from Japan, while the remainder of the 120,000 incarcerees were *Nisei*, or second-generation naturally born American citizens. With this in mind, this essay refuses the usage of "internment" as the vast majority cannot be considered "aliens" unless referring to racial difference.

3
Headquarters Western Defense Command and Fourth Army. Office of the Commanding General, and J.L. DeWitt, *Japanese evacuation from the West coast, 1942: Final Report (1943)*, iiv–ix. In 1943, a 618-page report—titled *Final Report on the Evacuation of Japanese from Certain Military Areas in Western Defense Command*—was produced by the Western Defense Command on behalf of General John L. DeWitt. The report sought to justify the evacuation as well as establish a defense against the anticipated legal challenges to come, specifically in *Korematsu vs. U.S.* In the second line of DeWitt's "Letter of Transmittal to the Chief of Staff" he asserts plainly, "The evacuation was impelled by military necessity." Part I of the *Report* echoes this sentiment in its title, "EVACUATION – ITS MILITARY NECESSITY." This phrase is repeated twenty-four times throughout the report and is often associated with internment given the irony that no person of Japanese ancestry living in the United States was ever convicted of espionage or sabotage for the duration of the war.

4
"Executive Order 9066, February 19, 1942," General Records of the United States Government, Record Group 11, National Archives.

5
"Homestead Definition & Meaning," Merriam-Webster, https://www.merriam-webster.com/dictionary/homestead, accessed January 6, 2025.

6
Eric J. Sandeen, "The Japanese American Relocation Center at Heart Mountain and the Construction of the Post-World War II Landscape," in *Politics and Cultures of Liberation: Media, Memory, and Projections of Democracy,* edited by Frank Mehring, Hans Bak, and Mathilde Roza (Brill, 2018), 290.

7
The rake refers to the depth of the depth that extends past the façade. Functionally, a deeper rake protects the structure from water damage or sun exposure.

8
This estimate was calculated by counting barracks from Relocation Center site plans provided by the National Parks Service. This number only includes barracks used for residential purposes. Auxiliary structures at each of the Relocation Centers such as storage spaces, administrative offices, schools, meeting houses, etc. were also retrofitted barrack structures.

9
"IT CAN'T MUST BE DONE !!," *Em Kayan magazine*, May 1942, 15.

10
Sandeen, "The Japanese American Relocation Center," 290.

11
Em Kayan magazine, 15.

12
Brian Niiya, "Milton Eisenhower," *Densho Encyclopedia*, https://encyclopedia.densho.org/Milton%20Eisenhower, accessed January 7, 2025.

13
Richard Drinnon, *Keeper of Concentration Camps: Dillon S. Myer and American Racism* (University of California Press, 1989).

14
Dillon S. Myer, *Uprooted Americans: The Japanese Americans and the War Relocation Authority during World War II* (University of Arizona Press, 1971), 3. According to Myer, "I was sure that I could sleep, and so agreed to accept the position if he felt that I was the one to do it, although it was not something I would have chosen for myself."

15
Cited in Connie Y. Chiang, "Imprisoned Nature: Toward an Environmental History of the World War II Japanese American Incarceration," *Environmental History* 15, no. 2 (April 2010): 240.

16
Bruce Babbit, *Report to the President: Japanese-American Internment Sites Preservation* (Washington, D.C.: Department of the Interior, January 9, 2001). The report includes a table which lists each of the camps and the jurisdiction/ownership of the land they were located on. The National Park Service, the Bureau of Land Management, and the Town of Granada, CO, all contributed property to host encampments. Three camps were located on land owned by the Bureau of Reclamation. The land for the two camps in Arizona was acquired from the Gila River and Colorado River Indian Reservations under the pretense that, in lieu of rental payments, the land would be cultivated upon its return.

17
Officially named Granada War Relocation Center by the WRA, incarcerees referred to the camp as Amache after its postal designation. This continued preference is reflected in this paper.

18
Bonnie Clark, "Cultivating Community," in *Legacies of Space and Intangible Heritage*, edited by Fernando Armstrong-Fumero and Julio Hoil Gutierrez (University Press of Colorado), 9.

19
Clark, "Cultivating Community."

20
Clark, "Cultivating Community," 9.

21
Robert Wilson, "Landscapes of Promise and Betrayal: Reclamation, Homesteading, and Japanese American Incarceration," *Annals of the Association of the American Geographers* 101 (2011): 435.

22
Originating in the nineteenth century, Manifest Destiny refers to a set of beliefs grounded in American expansionism and exceptionalism. While not explicitly associated with a specific policy, it was defined by a moral and even divine assertion of republican government. It is considered one of the earliest expressions of American imperialism.

23
Sandeen, "The Japanese American Relocation Center," 294.

⁂

Sarah Lopez

THE ARCHITECTURE OF IMMIGRANT DETENTION

The intentions of immigrant detention centers are legally distinct from prisons. An immigrant detention center is defined as an administrative center used to process cases that determine if and when a person can join legal pathways to residency or citizenship, or if they are deported. A prison is a place of punishment. This distinction was established in 1892 with the Geary Act, an extension of the Chinese Exclusion Act, which forced Chinese laborers to carry internal resident permits. Failure to do so would result in detention and deportation. Tracking the congressional debates of this period, historian Kelly Lytle Hernández illuminates in *City of Inmates* how forcibly removing persons from the United States (which involved detaining and deporting) was defined as *administrative* in part so the rights and punishments associated with criminal prosecution would not apply.[1] This 120-year-old definition was again confirmed in 2009 by then ICE administrator Dora Schriro: "Immigration proceedings are civil proceedings and immigrant detention is not punishment."[2] Being in the United States without proper authorization is legally understood as a technicality and thus processed as a civil issue.

Yet the political right's clarion call describes newcomers as *illegals*. One could easily connect such illegality with punishment: it seems purposely to evoke criminality. Xenophobic and so-called "anti-immigrant" discourse is reflected in, and strengthened by, the architecture of migrant immobilization, which exists on a seamless continuum with prison design. In fact, whether one is comparing schematics or reflecting on the actual experience of being locked inside, one would be hard-pressed to tell detention centers and prisons apart. This invites questions: where, between physical infrastructure and subjective experience, does imprisonment happen? And to what extent do the formal and material properties or systems of detention design influence social outcomes, human experience, and policy itself?

The architecture of immigrant detention, I argue, not only impacts the experience of arrival for newcomers to the United States but it also—perhaps surprisingly to those who do not think about architecture as central to Immigration and Customs Enforcement—influences immigration legislation itself.[3] This argument requires us to broaden the definition of "architecture" from the specific material and formal characteristics of a building to the spatial systems that support a building's construction and future management.

Key to what Sean Anderson and Jennifer Ferng call the "detention-industrial complex,"[4] in part driven by a rotating door of government immigration officials who also work for prison corporations, are building contracts and buildings themselves. Building contracts between the federal government, counties and cities, and private corporations involve long-term guarantees of future revenue—in some cases the government promises to pay corporations for a minimum number of migrant detainees per facility for years, independent of the number of people actually detained. The large upfront capital investments necessary to build new facilities and the high cost of operations and maintenance are only justified through long-term gains; private corporations thus have great incentives to ensure long-term detention practices. Money is locked and situated. Once built, buildings' inertial properties get to work; the buildings outlast the administration that produced them. Building contracts and building industries thus shape the form and experience of immigration enforcement for decades beyond the actual moment of their conception and realization. Thus, the philosophical and architectural ideas that were implemented at one specific time act as a force against human interpretations of the same space at another. There is feedback between material worlds and social practices that is influential, not deterministic. Detention centers carry an inertia into the collective future of how U.S. society welcomes its newcomers.

In the U.S., it is private prison corporations (not the government) that instantiate their vision of detention infrastructure, and they do so *quickly*. In the 1990s, companies like Corrections Corporation of America (now rebranded as CoreCivic) and GEO Group promised government savings through *faster* construction; buildings were erected in two to three years rather than five to six.[5] In the 2020s, GEO Group's website announced large-scale Texas facilities that were erected in an astonishing one to two years. The fast construction of ever-larger facilities means that people with stakes in the decision and design have less time to react. Building permanent and semipermanent structures this quickly both impedes citizens and activists' ability to engage with (and express resistance to) new facilities whose construction is a means of detaining more people and normalizing the prison form as the material solution.

Corporations also allowed the government to finance facility construction in new ways by using financial accounts whose budgets, according to Douglas McDonald, were not subject to public vote, thus potentially minimizing democratic engagement.[6] In the early 2000s and 2010s, two of the largest corporations, CoreCivic and GEO Group, lobbied Congress. In 2004, the federal government instated the Department of Homeland Securities Appropriations Act which allocated money to fund 8,000 immigrant detention "beds" (irrespective of

La Salle County Regional Detention Center, Encinal, Texas. The private prison corporation, Emerald Companies, broke ground on this female and male detention facility in 2002. Photograph by author, 2015.

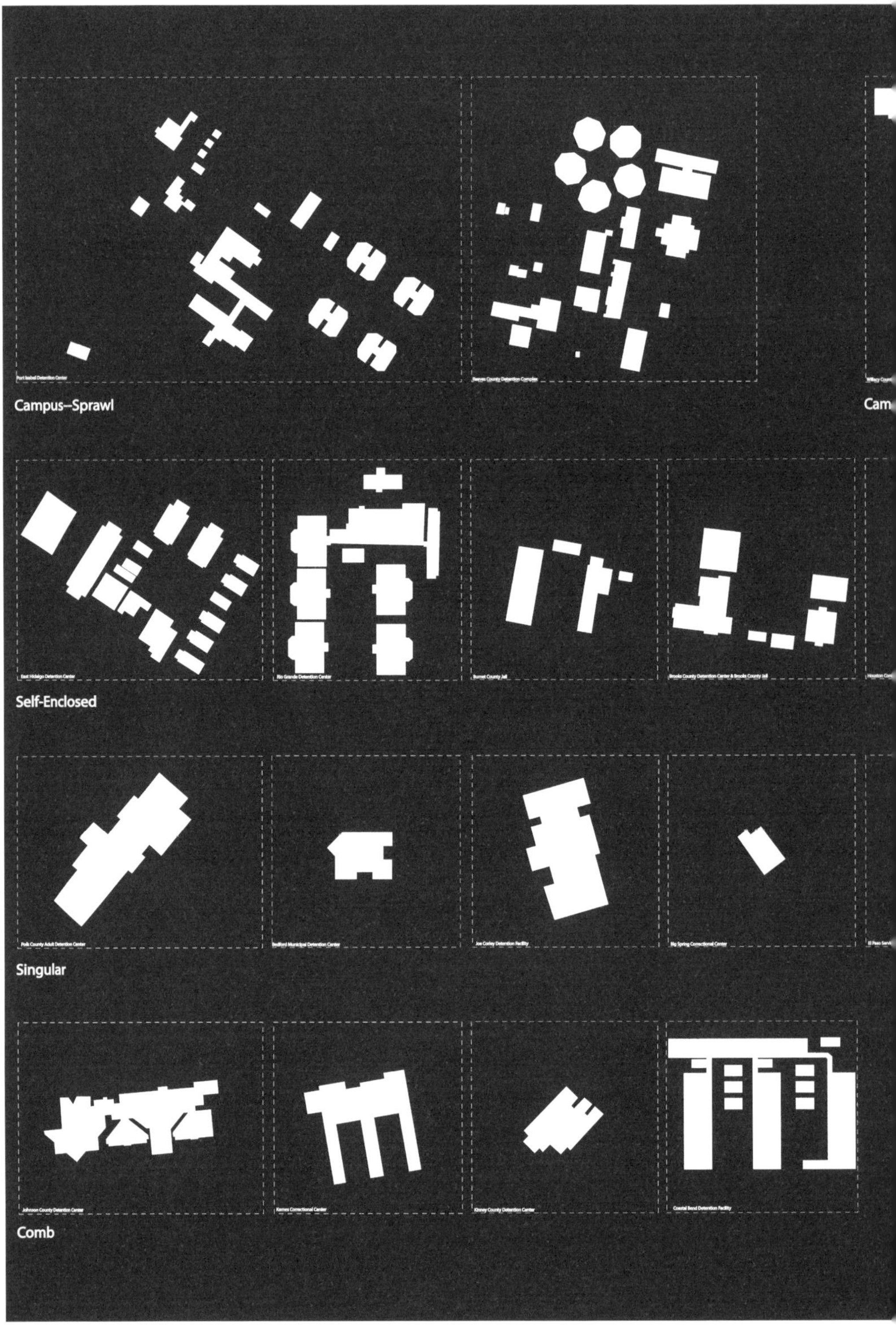
Port Isabel Detention Center
Reeves County Detention Complex
Campus–Sprawl
East Hidalgo Detention Center
Rio Grande Detention Center
Burnet County Jail
Brooks County Detention Center & Brooks County Jail
Self-Enclosed
Polk County Adult Detention Center
Bedford Municipal Detention Center
Joe Corley Detention Facility
Big Spring Correctional Center
Singular
Johnson County Detention Center
Karnes Correctional Center
Kinney County Detention Center
Coastal Bend Detention Facility
Comb

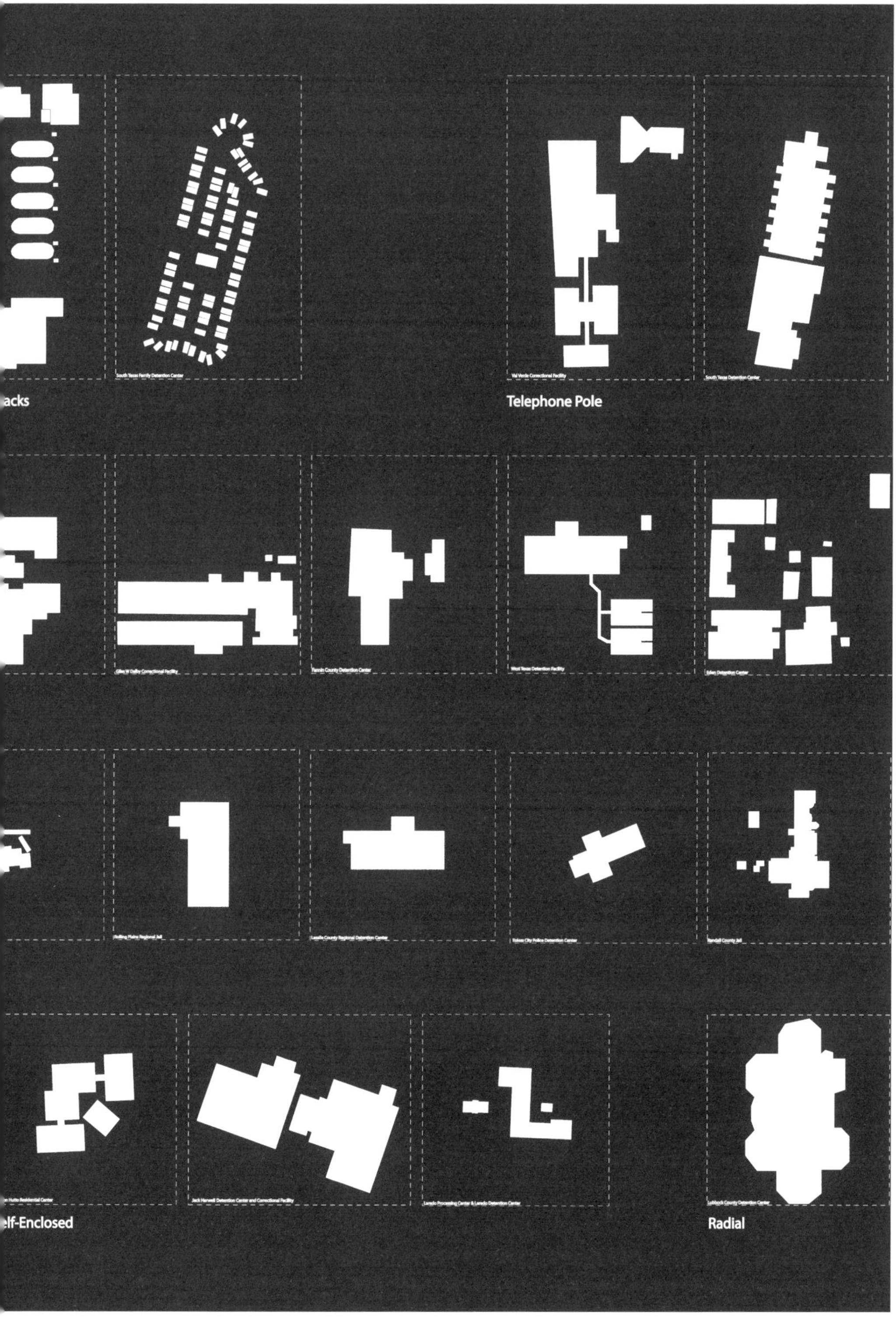

The footprints of Texas immigrant detention centers (past and current) are here clustered by formal prison “type.” Drawing by Sarah Dubicki.

the number of people detained)—a bed allotment they keep increasing. How centers are built and financed should not be understood as the logistical execution of immigration policy. Rather, construction itself influences the transparency, accessibility, social outcome, and implementation of immigration policy.

My research seeks specifically to explore this by casting light on the immigrant detention infrastructure of Texas. Texas has long been a place of experimentation and expertise when it comes to defining and hardening borders and immobilizing migrants. But in recent decades, Texas's detention infrastructure has increased massively. Before the 1980s, Texas had only three main immigrant processing stations, in El Paso, Laredo, and Port Isabel—all major cities near the Mexico–U.S. boundary. Since the 1980s, at least eighteen large-scale detention centers for the federal government have been built in increasingly remote localities. And this tally does not include the county and city jails that may detain migrants, nor the Criminal Alien Requirement (CAR) facilities run by the Federal Bureau of Prisons (BOP) to incarcerate so-called criminal aliens. As of September 2024, when ICE published an excel spreadsheet matrix that lists all the facilities they contract, Texas was detaining over 11,000 individuals.[7]

While private prison corporations have been involved in all aspects of the design and management of facilities since the 1990s, setting a new course for the spatial and political reality of detention centers, specific information about how they design and what they design is primarily unavailable to the public. Nor is such information available from the U.S. government; ICE does not typically include information about architects or general contractors on internal compliance reports that audit facilities, or on facility websites that might detail the number of people detained and facility square footage. One exception to this was an ICE commentary about the opening of a facility in Texas that was purposefully designed as a "civic" facility in response to a damning 2009 internal audit of ICE performance.[8] In 2012, ICE announced its "first-ever designed-and-built civil detention center" in "the entire history of immigration detention."[9] Even in this case, when ICE held an architectural competition to design a new model of detention, the winning firm—Argenta Architectural—did not publish any information on their website about Karnes

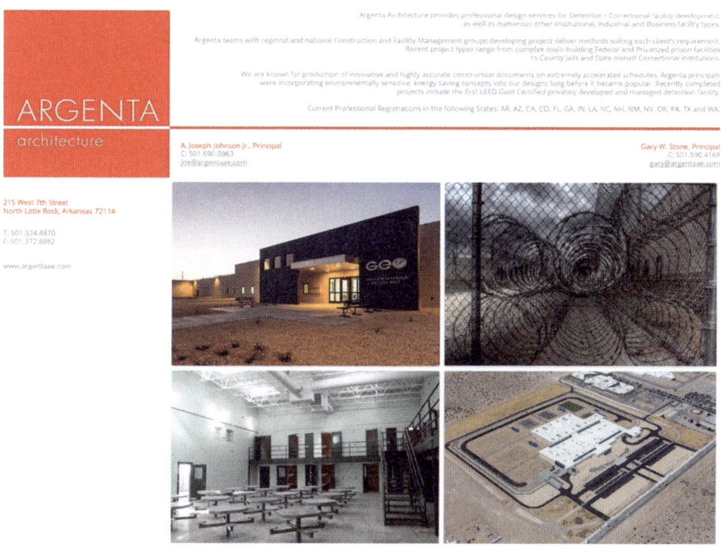

Argenta Architectural in Little Rock, Arkansas, advertised their involvement with detention design on their business website, but did not publish information about their award-winning design for a more humane facility for women and children. Screenshot, 2015.

specifically, but did demonstrate their involvement with correctional facilities using photographs of completed GEO Group projects; the office and principal architect did not respond to my requests for interviews. I have also been unsuccessful at securing architectural plans or building details for privately run detention centers through Freedom of Information Act requests.

We know, though, that the 1990s and 2000s was a period when U.S. carceral architecture in general was adopting increasingly punitive design elements. During this period, the *Justice Facilities Review*, an annual publication of the American Institute of Architects on "justice architecture," sounded an alarm bell in relation to broader trends in carceral architecture. Juries composed of three architects and three practitioners from the judiciary, corrections, and law enforcement fields repeatedly described prisons as increasingly "non normative environments."[10] By the end of the 1990s the jurors warned: "Feelings were that once a facility is toughened, there may be no going back–it is difficult to rescind philosophical and architectural decisions."[11] Twenty years later, not only have these ideas not been rescinded, but non-normative technologies of design and management have expanded to create disorienting, dislocating spaces of maximum human deprivation.

The AIA jurors in particular identified a number of features that they felt marked the "hardening" of facilities: small dark cells, caged recreational spaces, an absence of natural light (replaced by "borrowed light," where skylights and clerestories are used to channel indirect light in lieu of windows), heavy reliance on concrete floors, and crude signage.[12] The jury identified the design of the "indirect supervision concept" where video surveillance and visitation, one-way glass, and non-overlapping circulation spaces for both employees and inmates meant that the incarcerated are watched but physically isolated. All these features are evident in the three Texas immigrant detention facilities I have been able to personally visit (The T. Don Hutto Residential Center, the LaSalle County Regional Detention Center, the South Texas ICE Processing Center). They can also be seen in the dozens of photographs of other Texas detention facilities that are available on the internet.

Private prison corporations have assumed the lead in designing "the hardening of facilities" under the auspices of efficiency. A top manager of JE Dunn Construction, which has built several prisons and detention centers in Texas, described the driving factor behind detention design as "cost per bed," a slight modification of the "cost per square foot" calculus used to build houses. And decisions about how to save money and build fast often happen in-house. In 1992, Geo Group—one of the largest corporations, which boasts responsibility for the construction of seventy "facility construction and renovation" projects related to detention in eighteen U.S. states and eight countries worldwide—initiated a design/build component into their corporate structure.[13] Green, efficient, and standardized design practices are their stated principles and non-citizen populations their guinea pigs as they test new low-cost technologies of immobilization.

These low-cost technologies result in single-story facilities that are effectively one large mass broken up with interior masonry partitions and covered with a flat roof. Designing discrete buildings for offices, dormitories, courthouses, and separate yards—as is evident in the archival photographs and aerial images of the early facilities, such as Port Isabel, which was erected in the 1960s—would cost more. Ever-larger dormitories that house fifty to one hundred men (rather than cells with two to eight persons) minimize wall construction and maximize bodies. These technologies are also evident in facility management, where non-citizens are hired to work, cook, and clean at the facilities in which they are incarcerated for between $1 to $3 a day.

In terms of design, private prison corporations make hard and important decisions so that ICE does not have to. In 2007, ICE published a Design Standards manual—I have not been able to find a more recent version—to "establish operational directions and architectural relationships for ICE spaces."[14] Plans, photographic illustrations, and dimensions describe ICE offices; details like window size and placement are articulated. But the ICE Design Standards are incomplete: they do not detail the parts of the building where migrants are to be housed. Where "Detainee Living Zone" is meant to be on the plan, it is filled with these words: "Contractor Responsibility."[15] On the face of it, this is absurd: the design of the detainee living quarters exacts the greatest influence over the daily lives of non-citizens in ICE custody. Companies like GEO Group, who must refer to this manual for detailed information about ICE's "organizational" requirements, find that it is their responsibility to fill in the gaps in the architectural plan in order to complete the real-life building. This lacuna at the heart of the architectural program severs the awesome power of the government to detain from the physical environment in which that power is exercised. ICE has made a crucial design decision: to abdicate its hand and role in design itself.

In addition to design, location plays a key role in how these facilities are experienced. Triangulating facility locations with nearby towns, cities, and immigration support services reveals a science of remoteness, whereby distance is maximized between different groups of people: migrants, loved ones, visitors, townspeople, judges, personnel, activists, doctors. Video visitation and even video court hearings are on the rise. Security personnel are minimized through non-overlapping circulation floor plans. Unlike an earlier generation of Texas facilities, sited close to or within cities, today's facilities are on average 105 miles from cities with *pro bono* legal services.[16]

While the siting of detention facilities has an ambiguous impact on the cost of detention construction (land in rural localities is cheaper, but the labor and expertise needed to build is more expensive and it is hard to secure experienced employees), siting can have a damning effect on the people incarcerated. Remote facility locations may increase one's time in detention. Immigration lawyers argue that legal representation greatly increases one's chance of winning asylum and reducing sentences. As Alison Mountz notes, by limiting migrants' access to services, press, and legal support, as well as family and friends, "geography is used to deny access to rights."[17] Furthermore, migrants are relocated from New York or Florida to Texas, resulting in what Nancy Hiemstra calls a "chaotic geography" of migrant detention whereby migrants lose representation after they cross state lines and are relocated far from airports.[18]

There is one detention center in Texas that sheds light on these spatial systems and that the ICE Design Standards uses as a specific example of detention design. ICE published the The South Texas ICE Processing Center (formerly known as the Pearsall Immigration Detention Center) plan in their manual to illustrate government standards. I have been able to interview formerly detained persons who described their time inside the facility. Through my research, it became clear that the dislocation produced by the physical infrastructure itself—both its design and its remoteness—is exacerbated by an overlay of managerial cruelty: imposed tedium, enforced lack of privacy, deprivation of sleep and light, and willful disregard for shared humanity.

The South Texas Detention Center, better known as "Pearsall," was built in 2005 near a town of some 9,500 people approximately 60 miles from San Antonio. GEO Group's 238,000-square-foot facility can immobilize up to 1,904 people. In the nineteenth and twentieth centuries, prison architecture was stabilized around a few key layouts replicated in nearly every facility: the barracks, telephone pole, radial, self-enclosed, singular, and comb layouts. For the sake of this discussion, these names are less important than the fact that many of the aerial views and detention footprints found in Texas's immigrant detention landscape cohere with these archetypal prison layouts. And GEO Group's Pearsall facility is no exception. Pearsall has a telephone pole layout, which

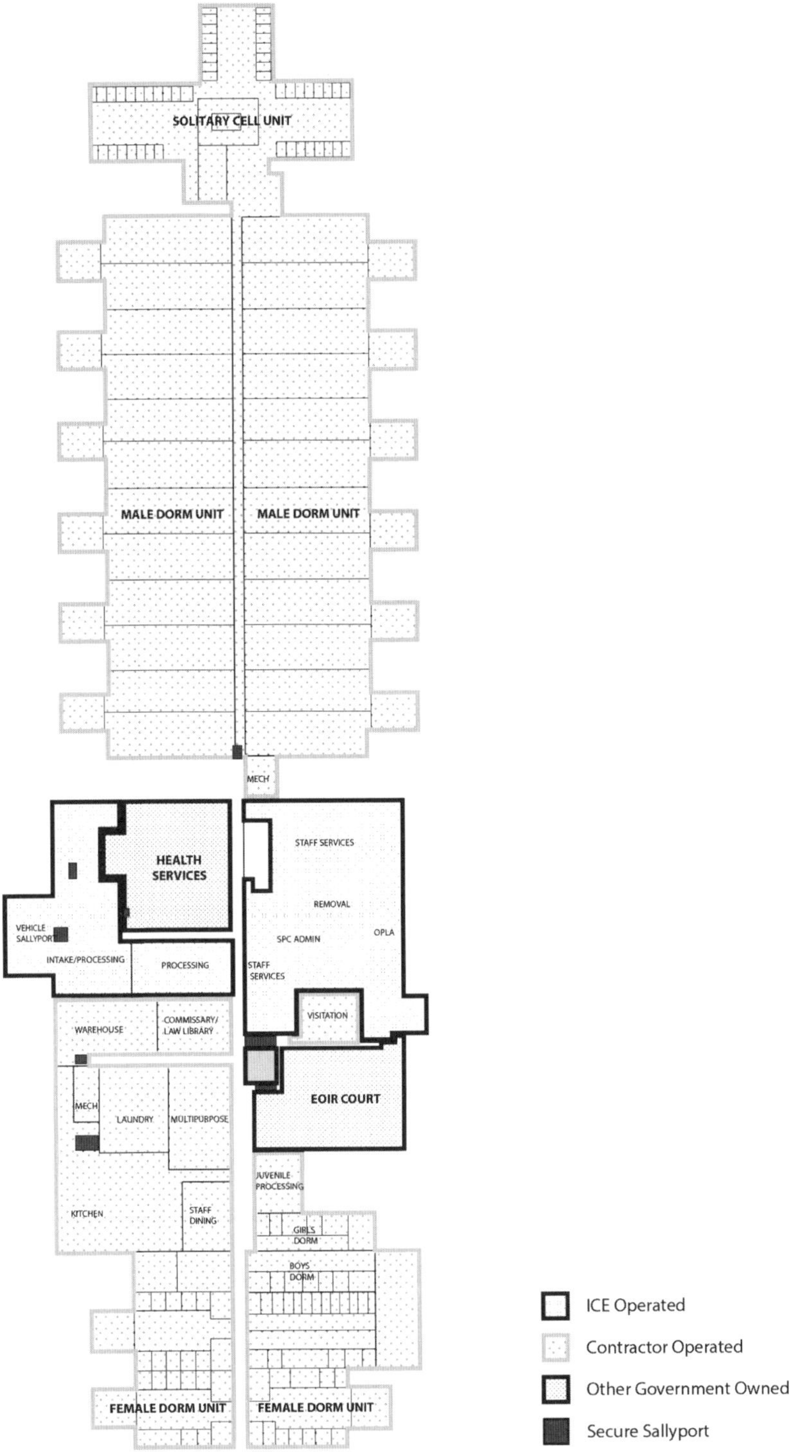

South Texas Detention Center, Geo Group Inc., Pearsall, Texas. This schematic rendering is based on the only publicly available architectural drawing of an immigrant detention center found in the 2007 ICE *Design Standards* manual. Drawing by Anjulie Palta.

means a central spine controls interior organization and circulation. In plan, Pearsall's facility classifies and categorizes men, women, and juveniles into separate wings (even though in practice the facility is all male). Along either side of the main circulation or "pole" are large dormitories, each housing a hundred men. At the end of a phalanx of dormitories, three nodes comprised of individual cells are used for solitary confinement.

Miguel, an asylum seeker fleeing Panama, was detained for four months and living at an immigrant shelter in Texas when we met. He described the "detainee living quarters" by drawing a large rectilinear room with two long tables in the middle surrounded by bunk beds. Toilets, sinks, and showers are depicted at one end surrounded by a half-wall that ensured the men's continuous surveillance (by both male and female guards). There was a small square room at the other end that had basketball hoops fastened to the wall. Miguel explained that a hundred men (from all over the world) slept; ate breakfast, lunch, and dinner; went to the bathroom and showered; prayed and played basketball; or paced in this pod twenty-four hours a day, seven days a week, with few breaks or exceptions. The pod has no skylight or windows. The outdoor space is a caged "rec room" with a narrow clerestory at the top that is covered with concertina wire.

The role that management played in the men's sense of dislocation became clear when Miguel explained a string of letters at the bottom of his diagram. Whenever he would start to learn his podmates' names and stories—in other words, as soon as they would begin to form bonds of friendship or camaraderie—the guards would call all the people by their bed numbers and reshuffle them into new pods. In four months, Miguel was reshuffled four times. The tension and fear would start all over again: *Who am I sleeping next to? What will happen tonight?*

This description aligns with another man I spoke to who was incarcerated in Pearsall for ten months. Muhammad Nazry Mustakim (Naz) was born in Singapore but brought to the United States as a child; he was a long-time green card holder. Before he was locked up in Pearsall, Naz lived in Waco, Texas, with his wife Hope. To see him for a one-hour "no touch" visitation, she drove

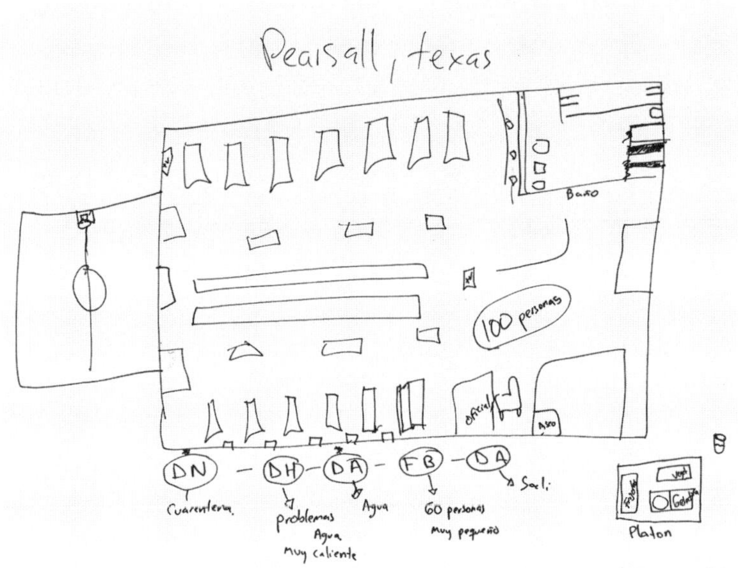

Cognitive drawing by Miguel, Austin, Texas, 2015. A migrant drawing of his dormitory or "pod" in Pearsall, where he spent four months alongside ninety-nine other men. Drawing facilitated by Jessica Carey-Webb and Sarah Lopez, 2015.

for eight hours round trip across the state. Within the facility, Naz described his "detainee living zone" as a pod that contained fifty bunk beds and housed a hundred men. Despite ICE's mandate that "for at least one hour per day, detainees must have the opportunity for outdoor exercise or an indoor equivalent during inclement weather," Naz's "outdoor" recreation space was indoors. Naz told me: "You really don't get to see the outside, you don't get to see the grass or whatever" unless you crouched toward the ground to peer through a "very small drain hole for the water to flow out of the rec area. If you look through that you were able to see the grass on the other side." Naz also experienced the systematic reshuffling as a challenge: "Each time I moved to a different dorm I always looked for a familiar face so I could feel comfortable in there."

After Naz returned home, the phonic landscape of Pearsall stuck with him:

> When I came home, I had real PTSD for like a week, coming back at nighttime. Whenever my wife would, like, try to wake me up, I had nightmares of them trying to take me, to put me back in there. I was in trauma and covered in sweat and stuff. When I was in detention sometimes some officers would wake us up by banging on our beds, by kicking on our bunk beds making such a loud noise.[19]

U.S. citizens pay taxes that finance places like Pearsall. Most will never see these facilities, though. Even if they wanted to, gaining access is difficult. Detention is thus largely a black box occasionally punctured by investigations spearheaded by legal advocates and activist organizations such as the ACLU ("Justice Free Zones," "Warehousing Migrants") and Detention Watch Network.[20] From their accounts, as well as those of persons formerly detained, we know that detention (a federally sanctified and locally enacted arm of U.S. immigration policy) is designed to deprive humans of dignity. Still, even when (and if) the veil of detention is pierced, incarcerating unauthorized people in detention centers run by private corporations is now mostly accepted as the status quo.

An uptick in public condemnation over the treatment of migrants in detention did not persuade President Biden to include immigrant detention (and thus ICE) in his 2021 executive order to phase out contracts between the BOP and private prison corporations. Since the time of this order, the proportion of immigrant detention infrastructure owned and managed by private prison corporations increased from 80 to 90 percent.[21]

And, days after Donald Trump was re-elected to office in 2024, the stock prices of CoreCivic and GEO Group surged. Having their "best weekly gains" since he was first elected in 2016[22], the corporations know that a Trump presidency means big contracts, little oversight, and fast implementation. Projecting future yields for these companies is a calculation based on the number of facilities that can be contracted and built in four years. How radically huge can the infrastructure of immigrant detention become? And, if a modest estimate of three, or ten 400,000-square-foot facilities are built in the next four years (some 1,200,000 or 4,000,000 square feet) what will that mean for how people are processed in the United States for decades to come?

There are several cold ironies at play in these recent transformations—as hope for migrant rights becomes increasingly hard to justify. Economists on the political right and left have demonstrated, again and again, that people who come to the U.S. from other countries (both unauthorized and authorized) are a net positive for the economy in the U.S., and for business, even taking into account, for example, the "tax" of undocumented peoples on local public schools or emergency rooms.[23] This fact is ignored by the caustic chants that stand in for discourse, beating a drum of associations between migrants and criminality, between migrants and weakness. But, more importantly, the neoliberal argument about net gain or net cost is not the right question to be asking. As political and civic culture strays increasingly far away from human rights and human dignity as its guiding values, we must double down and articulate rights, dignity, and freedom as core values that guide decision making about how and when to take away a primary and fundamental freedom of movement. Newcomers to the

United States arrive for an infinite number of reasons: asylum seekers scarred by the trauma of war, children brought on the backs of parents, farmers searching for options other than fallow fields, young men who simply want a better economic forecast. For those who cross without prior authorization—whether they seek out Border Patrol to commence their asylum application or get caught in the glaring light of active officers—the U.S. demonstrates its position by swiftly taking away their right of movement and locking them in metal cages.

A critical way to think through values is to turn our attention to the work that architecture does—on individuals, on societies, and on systems. This work, the work of architecture, is material, political, social, and cognitive. At the very least, citizens in countries that use detention facilities to enact immigration legislation must think critically about how building is related to time, and how the enduring legacy of any building is out of step with the relatively short tenure of political leadership. What long-term decisions about human experience, public messaging, environmental stewardship, and basic freedoms are made through building detention centers that mirror prisons? Activists who have been fighting immigrant detention for decades have inherently understood this, as they have worked to dismantle the detention landscape through hyper-localized campaigns to shut one facility down at a time. They have won major gains in California, Washington, Illinois, Maryland, New Jersey, and Oregon, where efforts have led to the termination of Intergovernmental Service Agreements between counties and corporations. Legislation to ban private prison corporations altogether has been passed in California, Illinois, and Washington. Such state laws create useful voids and slow down the rate of incarceration as some facilities sit empty. Such individuals—those working for immigrant shelters like Casa Marianella or those campaigning with Grassroots

Leadership—understand that architecture is not benign. And, as a part of laying the foundation of an alternative infrastructure of immigrant detention, we can join them in imagining a different status quo for what welcoming newcomers would look like, and what spatial systems would be needed to support it, at our southern border and beyond.

1
Kelly Lytle Hernández, *City of Inmates: Conquest, Rebellion, and the Rise of Human Caging in Los Angeles, 1771–1965* (University of North Carolina Press, 2017).

2
Dora Schriro, *Immigration Detention Overview and Recommendations*, Homeland Security, Immigration and Customs Enforcement, October 6, 2009, https://www.nytimes.com/interactive/projects/documents/immigration-detention-overview-and-recommendations, accessed January 6, 2025.

3
Sarah Lopez, "From Penal to 'Civil': A Legacy of Private Prison Policy in a Landscape of Immigrant Detention," *American Quarterly* 71, no. 1 (2019): 105–134.

4
Sean Anderson and Jennifer Ferng, "The Detention-Industrial Complex in Australia," *Society of Architectural Historians* 73, no. 4 (2014): 469–74.

5
See James Austin and Garry Coventry, *Emerging Issues on Privatized Prisons: National Council on Crime and Delinquency* (Bureau of Justice, February 2001), 11; and Douglas McDonald, "Public Imprisonment by Private Means," *British Journal of Criminology* 34 (1994): 29–48.

6
McDonald, "Public Imprisonment by Private Means," 30–31.

7
Immigration and Custom Enforcement and Removal Operations (ERO) division facilities matrix. https://www.ice.gov/about-ice/ero, accessed January 9, 2025.

8
Dora Schriro, *Immigration Detention Overview and Recommendations*, Homeland Security, Immigration and Customs Enforcement, October 6, 2009.

9
Immigration and Customs Enforcement, "ICE Opens Its First-Ever Designed-and-Built Civil Detention Center," March, 13, 2012, www.ice.gov/news/releases/ice-opens-its-first-ever-designed-and-built-civil-detention-center, accessed January 6, 2025.

10
American Institute of Architects, *Justice Facilities Review*, "History of the Justice Facilities Review," public.aia.org/sites/jfr/SitePages/History%20of%20the%20JFR.aspx, accessed July 15, 2016.

11
American Institute of Architects, *Justice Facilities Review*, Jury Comments, 1997–98, iv.

12
American Institute of Architects, *Justice Facilities Review*.

13
Geo Group website, www.geogroup.com/Design_Build_Finance/Lease, accessed November 12, 2016.

14
U.S. Department of Homeland Security, U.S. Immigration and Customs Enforcement, Office of Detention and Removal Operations, *Contract Detention Facility Design Standards for Immigration Customs Enforcement*, May 14, 2007, 8, cams.ocgov.com/Web_Publisher/Agenda07_20_2010_files/images/O00110-000775A.PDF, accessed January 6, 2025.

15
U.S. Department of Homeland Security, *Contract Detention Facility Design Standards for Immigration Customs Enforcement*, 273–75.

16
Newspapers, facility websites, and watchdog reports were used to approximate the history of facility construction. This average calculated the distance between migrant detention centers in use in 2016 and cities with a population of at least 300,000.

17
Alison Mountz, "Mapping Remote Detention: Dis/location through Isolation," in *Beyond Walls and Cages: Prisons, Borders, and Global Crisis*, ed. by Jenna M. Loyd, Matt Mitchelson, and Andrew Burridge, (University of Georgia Press, 2012), 98.

18
Nancy Hiemstra, "You Don't Even Know Where You Are: The Chaotic Geography of US Detention," in *Carceral Spaces: Mobility and Agency in Imprisonment and Migrant Detention*, ed. by Nick Gill, Deirdre Conlon, and Dominique Moran (Routledge, 2013).

19
Muhammad Nazry Mustakim (Naz), interview by the author, December 2015.

20
See American Civil Liberties Union, *Warehoused and Forgotten: Immigrants Trapped in the Shadow of Our Private Prison System*, June 2014, www.aclu.org/sites/default/files/assets/060614-aclu-car-reportonline.pdf, 4; Detention Watch Network at www.detentionwatchnetwork.org, accessed January 6, 2025.

21
Eunice Hyunhye Cho, "Unchecked Growth: Private Prison Corporations and Immigration Detention, Three Years Into the Biden Administration," August 7, 2023, https://www.aclu.org/news/immigrants-rights/unchecked-growth-private-prison-corporations-and-immigration-detention-three-years-into-the-biden-administration, accessed January 6, 2025.

22
Aparna Narayanan, "These Prison Stocks Jump Again After Trump's Hardline Border Move," *Investor's Business Daily*, November 11, 2024: https://www.investors.com/news/trump-stock-winners-core-civic-geo-group-biggest-week-since-2016/, accessed January 6, 2025.

23
For a summary of many different institutional and organizational studies on this question, see Julia Gelatt, "Explainer: Immigrants and the U.S. Economy," the Migration Policy Institute, October 2024: https://www.migrationpolicy.org/content/explainer-immigrants-and-us-economy, accessed January 6, 2025.

⁂

Regina Chen

THE ARCHITECTURE OF DECARCERATION

"Maps are not just analytical tools. They are visual arguments that contain and convey political statements, meaning, and power."

–Kari S. McLeod, *Our sense of Snow: the myth of John Snow in medical geography*

"You know nothing, Jon Snow."[1]

–Ygritte, from the series "A Song of Ice and Fire" by George R. R. Martin

The Broad Street Pump

When I was in my Urban Planning graduate program, we often shared the parable of Dr. John Snow. The story goes: Dr. John Snow was an obstetrician and anesthesiologist living and working in London in the mid-1800s, when a cholera outbreak occurred that killed thousands.[2] Skeptical of the prepondering "miasma theory" at the time, which proposed that cholera was caused by the "bad airs" of smelly neighborhoods, he began investigating an alternative theory that cholera was carried in the water. Snow worked with the coroner to identify the homes of people killed by cholera and plotted their addresses on a map of the city. As he looked more closely into the pattern of deaths, he saw many clusters around the Broad Street water pump.[3] Walking the neighborhood, he found a sewage pipe that was running into the source of the water pump. And, when he alerted the authorities of the Board of Guardians of St. James's Parish to his findings, they didn't believe him, and so he went back and removed the pump handle himself, ending the outbreak.[4]

Million Dollar Blocks

One hundred and fifty years later, architect and professor Laura Kurgan and criminal justice expert Eric Cadora employed the same methodology to understand a new epidemic: they went to four cities across the country and recorded the home addresses of people going into and coming out of prisons and jails.[5] Like Snow, their research identified clusters in certain neighborhoods—what they would come to term "Million Dollar Blocks"—where governments were spending over $1,000,000 dollars annually incarcerating people from those blocks. But like in London, authorities would remain skeptical and divided about what to do with the findings.

(Telling you what I'm about to tell you)

This essay will position the Million Dollar Block map as the Broad Street map of the twenty-first century. Just as research has definitively connected neighborhood design to community health outcomes, I extend that relationship to rates of incarceration. The long-term legacy of John Snow has been linked to the creation of entire fields of study (such as epidemiology or medical cartography) and broad investments in city wastewater infrastructure. If we truly understood how the development of our cities is connected to mass incarceration, could the long-term legacy of the Million Dollar Block map mirror that of the Broad Street map?

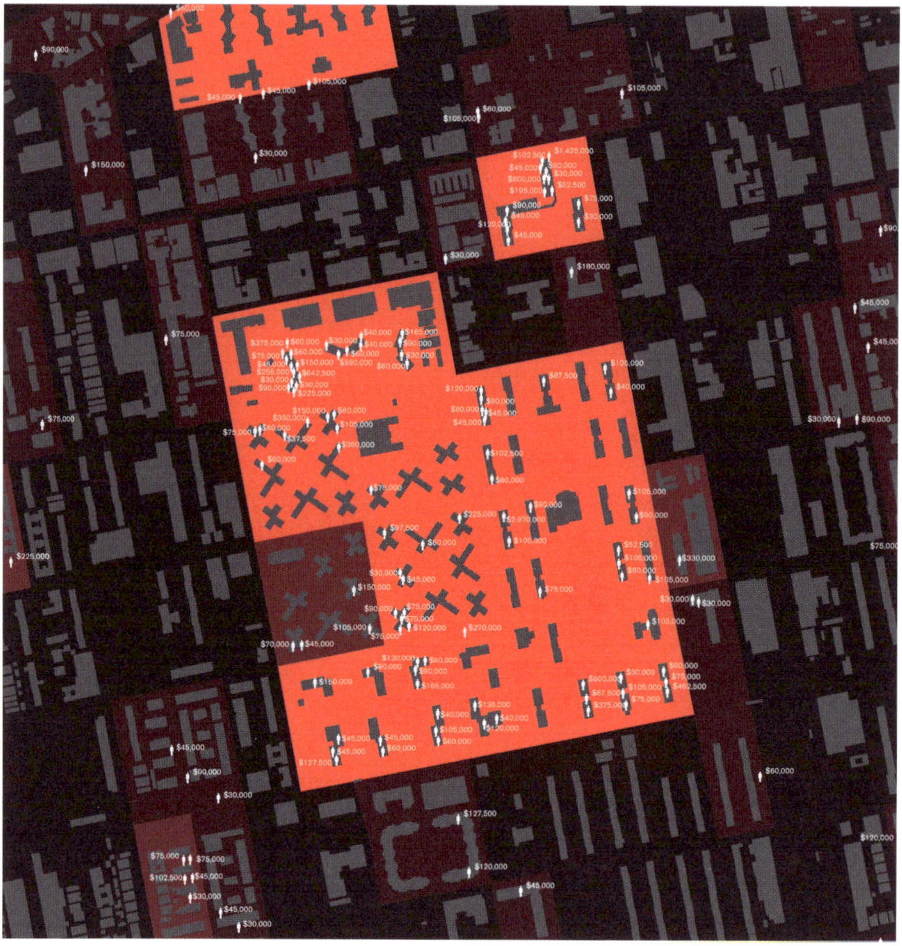

A detailed view of the Brownsville neighborhood. Columbia University, Center for Spatial Research.

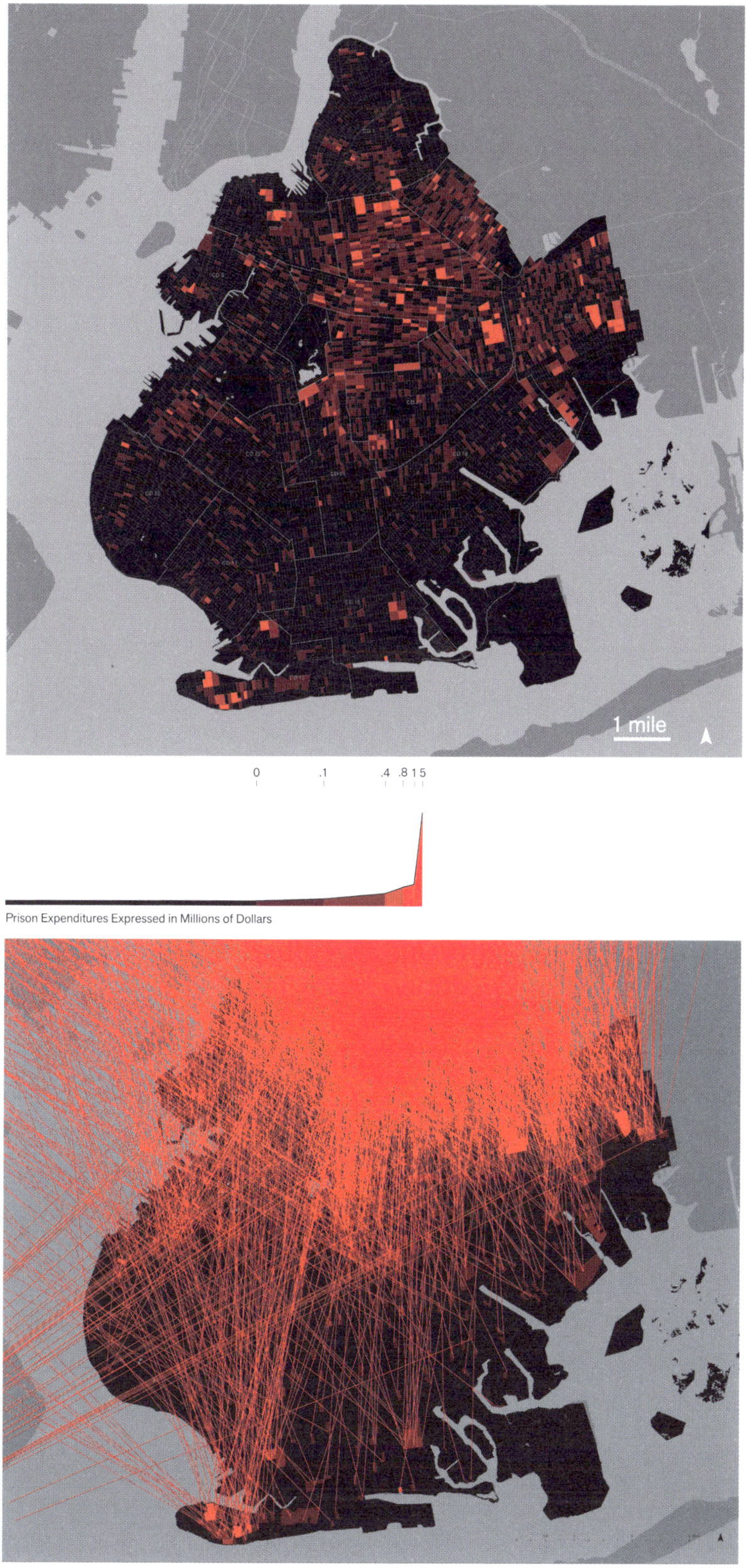

The mass migration of individuals from their homes to prisons in upstate New York. Columbia University, Center for Spatial Research.

Our Neighborhoods and Community Health

Design, Social Cohesion, and Heat Deaths

The year 2020 wrought many global changes, including a growing awareness of the role played by architecture in helping keep us—and in making us feel—safe from airborne infection. Throughout history, pandemics like cholera and the Spanish Flu have spurred inquiries into the epidemiology of disease which have shaped the design and layouts of our cities.[6] One such pandemic, the 1995 heat wave disaster in Chicago, was the basis of a new investigation exploring the fundamental connection between urban design and public health. In sociologist Eric Klinenberg's book, *Heat Wave,* he conducts what he calls a "social autopsy" into the phenomenon. Between July 14 and July 20, temperatures in Chicago consistently reached 105°F with a heat index climbing to 120 to 125°F at different moments in the week.

At the end of the heat wave, epidemiologists concluded that 739 more Chicago residents died that week compared to a typical week in July.[7] Klinenberg details the process of Jan Semenza and his colleagues at the Centers for Disease Control and Prevention (CDC): they identified a random sample of matched pairs (one victim and one control), seeking to analyze the relationship between the risk of untimely heat death and specific personal characteristics.[8] Their research revealed that "city residents were more vulnerable if they stayed at home, had medical issues, were bedridden, lived alone, or lacked air-conditioning, access to transportation, or nearby social contacts."[9]

Klinenberg took the research beyond an investigation into individual risk factors to understand the wider "social environmental" conditions that determined the extent to which Chicago residents were affected by the heat wave.[10] Building on previous research that connected mortality to neighborhood conditions like poverty, low-quality housing, lack of green space, and urban heat island effects,[11] *Heat Wave* further adds risk factors linked to "place-specific social ecology,"[12] including "the quality of public spaces, the vigor of street-level commercial activity, and the centralization of support networks and institutions."[13] Klinenberg's social environmental autopsy of Chicago's heat wave disaster looks beyond demographics or population-level data to draw connections between mortality and the physical condition and design of our neighborhoods.

Klinenberg's research extends the already well-documented relationship between social cohesion and physical health evidenced in Robert Putnam and Jane Jacobs's work. Putnam, in his book *Bowling Alone*, writes that "[p]eople who are socially disconnected are between two and five times more likely to die from all causes, compared with matched individuals who have close ties with family, friends, and community."[14] Jane Jacobs, an urban planner and activist who challenged the top-down ideologies of urban renewal in the 1960s, likewise drew connections between neighborhood density, diversity, and activity, arguing that these factors were integral to community resilience.[15] The ties between physical health, social cohesion, and resilience are well established. Evidence clearly links the design and development of neighborhoods with increased social capital and reduced risk of mortality both at the community and population level (this applies on any typical day as well as in the event of a disaster).

Financial Policies, Redlining, and Wealth Building

The design and development of our neighborhoods are neither accidental happenstance nor the result of population-level practices or preferences. Instead, they are the result of deliberate (or, read in the best light, naïve) top-down, racist practices that entrenched inequity in our neighborhoods via the built environment.

In his book, *The Color of Law*, Richard Rothstein lays out an argument against the idea that segregated neighborhoods were the result of individual, private, or community-level practices, such as personal prejudice, "white flight," real estate steering, bank redlining, income differences, and self-segregation.[16] Instead, he identifies the role of law or government policy in advancing "racially explicit policies of federal, state, and local governments [that] defined where whites and African Americans should live."[17] Such examples include the siting and development of public housing, Federal Housing Administration policies (like redlining), the Low-Income Housing Tax Credit and Housing Choice Vouchers ("Section 8"),[18] the subsidization of suburban developments (which were restricted to white buyers), unfair zoning practices, tax assessments,[19] and law enforcement. These policies predominantly furthered the development of affordable housing in communities of color, reinforcing segregation and limiting the opportunity for its families to access more diverse and affluent neighborhoods.

These discriminatory housing practices have direct links to slavery and the aftermath of the 13th Amendment, as well as Jim Crow era laws and the Great Migration (when approximately 6 million Black families moved from Southern cities to Northern cities in response to acts of terrorism and lynching). Matthew Desmond, in his book, *Poverty, By America,* summarizes these connections, saying:

> American cities had zoning ordinances in the 1920s, but they tended to be the general kind that organized the urban landscape—build your factory here, the shops go there, the people live here—not the kind we have today, which ban certain kinds

> of residences from residential space. Exclusionary zoning ordinances of that sort began appearing in response to the Great Migration. As millions of Black families fled racial terrorism in the South, the cities to which they moved began erecting walls between Black and white neighborhoods via zoning ordinances.[20]

In the wake of the 1866 Civil Rights Act and the 14th Amendment–which (among many other things) granted citizenship to formerly enslaved individuals and extended the bill of rights to provide equal protection under the law to all citizens–housing discrimination, or the effort to prevent Black families from living next to white families, ran rampant. In 1968, a landmark Supreme Court case, Jones v. Mayer, set the legal precedent acknowledging the relationship between housing discrimination and the ideas of racial difference that served as the foundation for slavery. In response to the court case, which barred racial discrimination in the private sale of housing, exclusionary zoning policies entrenched their foothold across America. Desmond summarizes the role of zoning in furthering housing discrimination, saying: "We went from banning certain kinds of people from our communities to banning the kinds of housing in which those people lived–namely, apartment buildings designed for multiple families–achieving the same ends."[21]

In addition to local, individual, and private practices of racism and segregation, our federal government likewise advanced development practices, including those intended to advance equity on the surface, that actually exacerbated segregation and the concentration of poverty in "ghettos."[22] From 1949 to 1974, a series of "Urban Renewal" practices sought to revitalize the urban downtown of cities by tearing down neighborhoods filled with "blight" and constructing miles of highway to bring suburban dwellers back downtown. These interventions largely served to raze diverse neighborhoods and displace communities of color, failing to rehouse the residents it displaced and ultimately furthering the flight to the suburbs for those who could afford it (namely, white families). These practices concentrated poverty in communities of color and excluded Black families from homeownership, hindering the potential for upward economic mobility embodied by the "American Dream," and the passing down of wealth to future generations. Opportunity Insights, an organization emerging from Harvard University, has conducted research which demonstrates that those who live, work, and play in economically diverse neighborhoods have the most opportunity for wealth creation and upward mobilization.

One hypothesis about why this is the case is the influence of social relationships: for example, when children living in low-income families are exposed to families with diverse vocations, this experience can shape their aspirations for their own futures.[23] I myself am the result of diverse social engagements via the Chinese Church where I grew up—families with older children shared the importance of the SAT with my immigrant parents, who then influenced my SAT scores (by bribing me to study). I was accepted into a top-tier university and have had diverse career opportunities that would follow. Our development practices on the whole do not create these opportunities; instead, they have not only concentrated poverty, but have also fundamentally limited the ability of families in those communities to move out of those neighborhoods (unless forced).[24]

I have recently been witnessing the same process in my hometown: a very vocal contingent of residents wants to concentrate higher density housing in the areas farthest away from their single-family homes. Because of the financial mechanisms that make affordable housing feasible, this serves to effectively separate affordable housing from the almost $1,000,000 price point of the median single-family home. At its worst, this opposition is known as NIMBYism—Not In My Back Yard—and is witnessed when residents argue in community meetings for unwanted development to occur somewhere else. In lieu of centering affordable and supportive housing, drug treatment facilities, and crisis centers in the core of our neighborhoods—near accessible transit, schools, jobs, and green space—we further displace and render inaccessible the very services that might impede the prison pipeline.

Mass Incarceration, the New Jim Crow, and Million Dollar Blocks

The racial and economic bias at the core of decades of neighborhood development have resulted in communities that then become targeted by the racial and economic bias present in our policing and justice system. Michelle Alexander, in her book *The New Jim Crow: Mass Incarceration in the Age of Colorblindness*, writes:

> In every state across our nation, African Americans—particularly in poor communities—are subject to tactics and practices that would result in public outrage and scandal if committed in middle-class white neighborhoods. SWAT teams raid the homes of African Americans in ghetto communities, stopping and frisking young men of color in the streets with little or no justification, and arresting African Americans en masse for minor drug offenses.[25]

We have created neighborhoods where we've intentionally concentrated communities of color; exposed those communities to disproportionate amounts of environmental harm (like smoke pollutants and overheating via the urban heat island effect) and inhibited

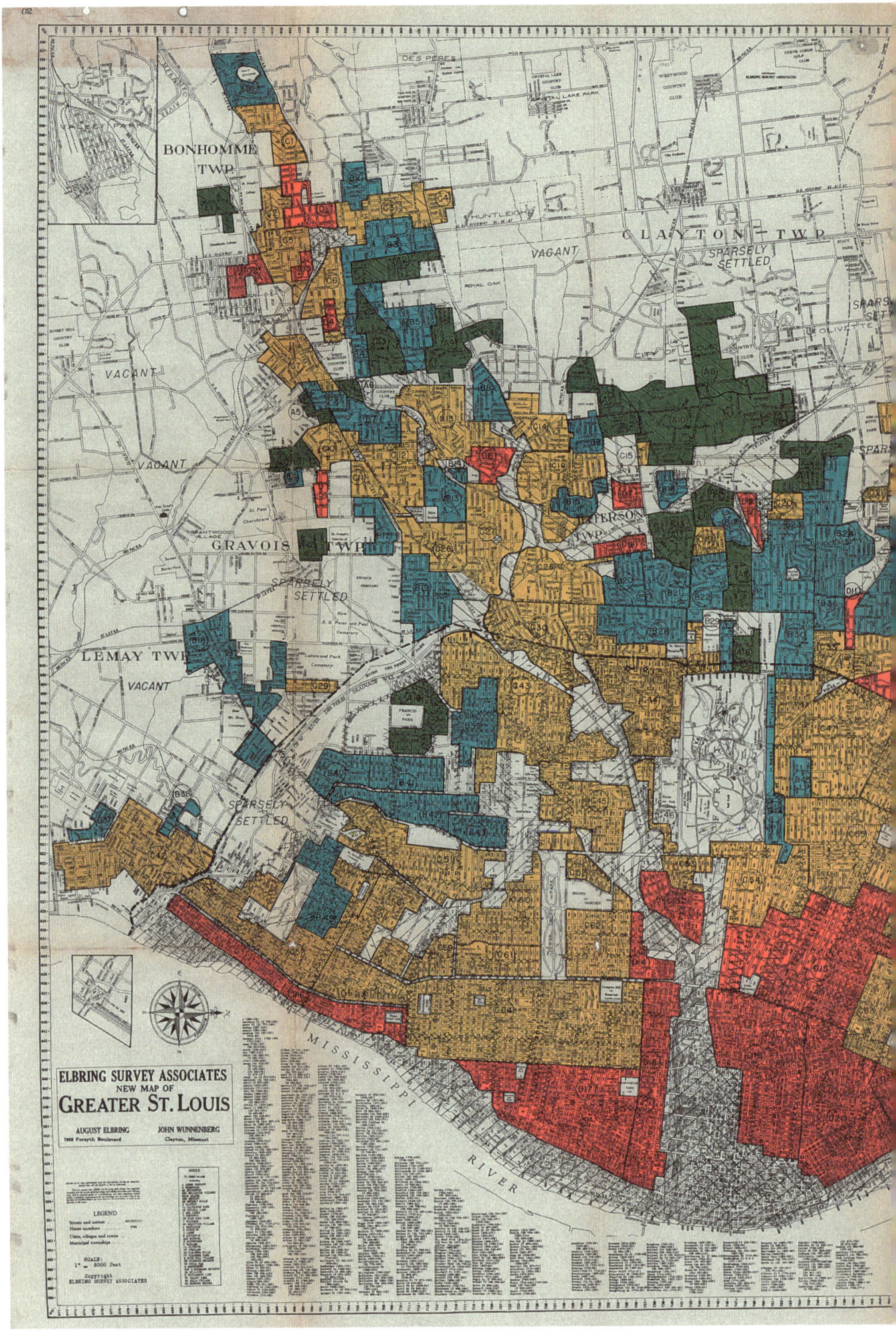

A “residential security map” of St. Louis, MO. Now known as “redlining,” the map categorized mortgage lending risk by geographic location. Image source: Federal Loan Agency, Federal Home Loan Bank Board, Home Owners’ Loan Corporation (July 1, 1939–February 24, 1942). Courtesy of the National Archives.

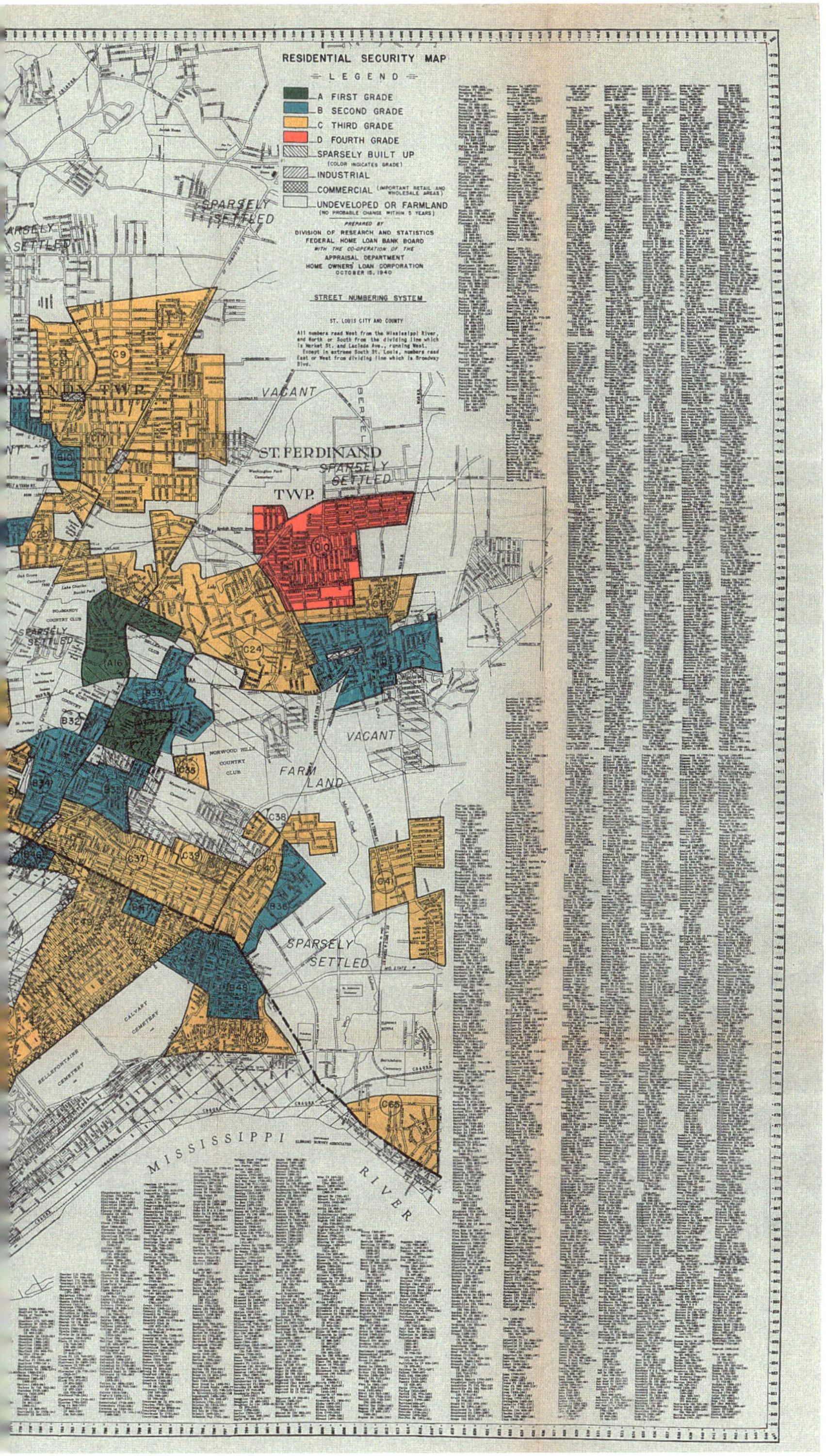

RESIDENTIAL SECURITY MAP
LEGEND
A FIRST GRADE
B SECOND GRADE
C THIRD GRADE
D FOURTH GRADE
SPARSELY BUILT UP
(COLOR INDICATES GRADE)
INDUSTRIAL
COMMERCIAL (IMPORTANT RETAIL AND WHOLESALE AREAS)
UNDEVELOPED OR FARMLAND
(NO PROBABLE CHANGE WITHIN 5 YEARS)
PREPARED BY
DIVISION OF RESEARCH AND STATISTICS
FEDERAL HOME LOAN BANK BOARD
WITH THE CO-OPERATION OF THE
APPRAISAL DEPARTMENT
HOME OWNERS' LOAN CORPORATION
OCTOBER 15, 1940
STREET NUMBERING SYSTEM
ST. LOUIS CITY AND COUNTY
SPARSELY SETTLED
VACANT
ST. FERDINAND TWP.
FARM LAND
NORWOOD HILLS COUNTRY CLUB
CALVARY CEMETERY
BELLEFONTAINE CEMETERY
MISSISSIPPI RIVER

those communities from building wealth. We have then overpoliced and incarcerated those neighborhoods because of the conditions we have forced upon them. Chicago's Million Dollar Blocks research encapsulates the issue succinctly, saying, "we are not simply punishing people for the crimes they commit. We are also punishing them for the places where they live, the schools that failed them[,] and the employers that rejected them. And, without question, we are punishing them for the darkness of their skin."[26]

Disentangling the long history of how our cities were developed can feel complex and overwhelming. However, there exists a precedent for how we understand development legacies, especially their impacts on community health, and how we can leverage public and private attention to address its root causes: the field of public health.

Social Determinants of Health

When I was studying Urban Planning in 2011, everyone was marveling over recent research which suggested that, for the first time in history, there were more people living in cities than in rural areas. It was the idea *du jour*, highlighting the importance of the city planning profession writ large. I wouldn't learn until after I graduated, however, that the true influence of city planning practices would be better captured by the realization that community health was more determined by zip code than genetic code.[27] While a holistic understanding of health has been embraced by Eastern and Indigenous communities since time immemorial, the World Health Organization (WHO) only began focusing on social health practices in the mid-twentieth century. Building on the realization that increased morbidity and mortality were tied to work conditions in the wake of the Industrial Revolution,[28] as well as studies like the Lalonde Report and the Black Report (which determined that health inequalities in the UK and Canada, respectively, were connected to social inequalities including living conditions, socioeconomic status, and education), a new idea was created, defined, and peddled–namely, the social determinants of health.

To understand the basis of the social determinants of health, we must understand that public health practitioners have classified five elements that impact health: genetics, behavior, physical environment, social factors, and medical care.[29] The social determinants of health focus specifically on the "conditions in the environments where people are born, live, learn, work, play, worship, and age that affect a wide range of health, functioning, and quality-of-life outcomes and risks."[30] They are: 1) economic stability; 2) education access and quality; 3) healthcare access and quality; 4) neighborhood and built environment; and 5) social and community context.

The idea behind the social determinants of health can be summarized by the idea that we can only manage symptoms, but we must treat the cause of illness. Put more strongly, healthcare providers acknowledge that, "[i]n fact, social factors can impact health more profoundly than one's access to medical care. Medical care alone often cannot outweigh the impact that social factors have on health."[31] The importance of these social determinants can be seen in acute cases: the aforementioned 1995 heat wave in Chicago (where neighborhoods with more violence saw higher rates of death because elderly and at-risk adults were less likely to be out and about in the neighborhoods and thus less likely to have social connections); in Flint, Michigan (where residents were poisoned by lead in their water); or in ProPublica's ToxMap (which mapped the risk of cancer in relation to industrial pollution).[32]

The WHO established the Commission on Social Determinants of Health in 2005, which included recommendations necessary for addressing global health equity. Today, the effects of the social determinants of health are widely seen and understood. When I bring my children to the pediatrician for their regular check-ups, I am asked about how stable our housing is and whether we have ever had to choose between food and medicine, housing or medical care, because doctors today know that in order for a child to be truly healthy, they must have stable housing. Others are writing prescriptions for their patients to take a walk in the park, via programs like ParkRx, to decrease the burden of cardiovascular disease in communities.[33] In addition, major health insurance companies have begun investing in affordable housing, because the cost of taking care of someone who gets sick is inordinately more expensive than the cost of keeping them healthy.[34]

Mass Incarceration as a Public Health Problem

In addition to our neighborhoods being drivers of public health problems and mass incarceration, there is also a clear linkage between mass incarceration and public health. David Cloud, Andrea Armstrong, et al., elucidate several ways that incarceration contributes to worsening public health outcomes in their essay "Public Health and Prisons: Priorities in the Age of Mass Incarceration." Nearly all major public health concerns are exacerbated in prison: suicide rates (estimated to range from five to twenty times higher than the general population);[35] drug use (reported at 58 percent of those incarcerated in state prisons, with a note that "people are 12.7 times more likely to die from an overdose during the first two weeks following prison release");[36] the burden of infectious diseases (one in ten incarcerated individuals have been diagnosed with Hepatitis C, compared to one in a hundred in the general population);[37] the rates of COVID-19 infections and death rates (3.3 times more likely to be diagnosed with COVID, and 2.5 times more likely to die, ultimately resulting in thousands of deaths of residents and prison staff);[38] and the incidence of women who have "experienced physical or sexual trauma" (75 to 95 percent), notwithstanding the lack of data about conditions affecting women, transgender and nonbinary individuals, and the elderly. The authors link risk factors of noncommunicable diseases to "individual, community, and structural factors preincarceration," as well as pointing toward the fact that "incarceration produces its own risk factors that likely exacerbate health outcomes due to acute and chronic stress from dehumanizing conditions, exposure, to trauma and violence, poor diet, and variable access to physical activity and quality health care."[39]

The American Medical Association has named police brutality as a public health concern, and the American Public Health Association likewise indicated that decarceration would help advance the public's health.[40] In 2010, the Department of Health and Human Services "included incarceration as a determinant of health disparities and identified it as a priority policy area for reform."[41] Other researchers directly name mass incarceration itself as a social determinant of health.[42] Even after release, incarceration continues to drive mental health challenges and drug usage. Additionally, national legislation prevents those who were incarcerated from being eligible for support to access other social determinants of health, such as affordable housing or healthy, low-cost foods. Research over the last ten years has suggested that blood lead level indicators are so closely correlated with crime rates that they can serve to predict the likelihood of violent offences (such as firearm crimes, robbery, assault, or homicide), even after accounting for other sociological factors.[43] Additionally, there has been research showing a 10°F increase in heat was associated with a 9 percent increase in violent crime.[44]

Transformative Justice through the Design of Our Neighborhoods

When John Snow removed the handle of the Broad Street water pump, he did more than just end one outbreak of cholera: he added momentum to the movement of the "great sanitary wakening,"[45] which would invest untold amounts of capital in sewage and water purification infrastructure in cities around the world.[46] We likewise have seen how an understanding of social determinants of health can dramatically change public and private practices, supporting improvements in community health outcomes.

The corollary idea in justice spaces is one of transformative justice. Restorative justice is a name for a process that seeks to address and repair harm between individuals. Transformative justice takes that one step further, trying to address the structural systems that contributed to that harm being enacted in the first place.

Put another way—the Million Dollar Block research is the Broad Street map of our day. Just as we know that cholera is not the outcome of "bad airs" emanating from smelly neighborhoods, we likewise know that blaming crime on "superpredators" is an outdated, racist idea. Our cities are not overrun with young, remorseless "criminals" who "kill, rape, maim, without giving it a second thought."[47] Instead, it is our development policies and design practices—the very way we design our cities—that creates the preconditions of incarceration.

The architecture of decarceration must not look to make trauma-informed prisons, but instead should take the path of public health: treating the cause rather than the symptom. We must shift our attention and our dollars to making investments in our communities that address the socio-environmental conditions that predispose certain neighborhoods to be over-policed and over-incarcerated.

The Architecture of Decarceration

Designing to address our socio-environmental determinants of incarceration would mean designing for social, environmental, and economic healing through connection and restoration. It means more affordable housing, with space for foster families and multi-generational families to support each other during times of crises—heat waves or otherwise. Families would live within a ten-minute walk to a park, affecting both physical and emotional health and improving their ability to deal with stressors.[48] We would design for accountability instead of designing for surveillance, by creating more "third spaces" that allowed people from different generations and social circles to gather. Our neighborhoods would address risk factors for incarceration, such as experiences of poverty, poor education, unstable housing, and unaddressed mental health or drug abuse challenges.

The following three community-based organizations are investing in communities and spaces that: 1) support connection and restoration during crisis events; 2) facilitate intergenerational relationship and accountability; and 3) nurture cultural connection with elders, community, and our land.

Children's Services of Roxbury

Children's Services of Roxbury (CSR) is one of the largest Black-led nonprofits in Massachusetts, founded in 1972 in response to the war on drugs that targeted communities of color and neighborhoods. With a mission of disrupting the cycle of generational trauma, CSR advocates for and empowers communities that have been historically overlooked and underrepresented. They provide culturally competent behavioral and mental health services that help support youth and families in the community, providing wraparound services in behavioral health, early education and childcare, intensive foster care and family support, housing and stability, and youth development. CSR's community center provides a safe space in Roxbury that invests in trauma-informed care and design at a neighborhood scale, creating physical spaces that promote safety, healing, and wellbeing.

A rendering of the entry experience at Children's Services of Roxbury, whose renovation used trauma-informed design principles to serve as a safe place for the community. Rendering by MASS Design Group.

The Treehouse Foundation

It costs the state of Massachusetts $194,000 annually to incarcerate a child—an amount that is roughly equivalent to $530 a day.[49] Yet, stipends for families who take on the care of foster children only range from $32 to $38 per day. Youth in the foster system are significantly more likely than comparable peers outside the system to be impacted by the justice system, with a particularly striking study indicating that youth that have moved families more than five times have a 90 percent likelihood of being arrested.[50] Treehouse at Olmsted Village development will be a model of intergenerational living that supports families with children who have experienced foster care and adoption, young people at risk of "aging out" of foster care, and older adults in its intentional communities. They leverage each individual's resources to provide community-based care instead of institution-based care.

A rendering of the entry stairwell at the Treehouse development in Olmsted Village, showing joyful, calming, and inclusive design rooted in biophilic and healing principles. Rendering by MASS Design Group.

The MILPA Collective

Motivating Intergenerational Leadership for Public Advancement (MILPA) is a movement space led by formerly incarcerated and system-impacted individuals. The mission of MILPA is about Cultivating Future Makers for the Next Seven Generations by creating opportunities for cultural healing, intergenerational leadership, and empowerment through community-driven decision making for healthier communities.

Wholeness as Healing

Growing up, I was always enraptured with the biblical idea of *shalom*. Traditionally it translates to mean "peace," but it actually encompasses a much deeper concept of flourishing—one that pursues societal justice, harmony, and community restoration.[51] Juliet Davis says about the spread of diseases, "Cities themselves have created conditions conducive to the emergence and spread of disease within broader environmental, social, political, and economic contexts."[52] So, too, our cities have created conditions conducive to the emergence and spread of mass incarceration. But we can redesign our cities to address it and invest in restorative, transformative communities, and—in fact—everything we do, from planting a tree to designing great public spaces, helps us to pursue the idea of wholeness as a form of healing in our cities.

1
A well-known catchphrase of Ygritte's from the "Song of Ice and Fire" series, by George R.R. Martin, used here ironically, because our Dr. John Snow did, in fact, know quite a lot.

2
Theodore H. Tulchinsky, "John Snow, Cholera, the Broad Street Pump; Waterborne Diseases Then and Now," *Case Studies in Public Health* (2018): 77–99.

3
Kari S. McLeod, "Our sense of Snow: the myth of John Snow in medical geography," *Social Science & Medicine* 50, nos. 7–8 (2000): 923–935.

4
I have, for the sake of storytelling, simplified this history quite a bit. Kari S. McLeod does an incredible job of bringing together different perspectives and influences of the John Snow "myth" in the paper above, and I highly recommend you check it out.

5
Diane Orson, "'Million-Dollar Blocks' Map Incarceration's Costs," *NPR*, October 2, 2012. https://www.npr.org/2012/10/02/162149431/million-dollar-blocks-map-incarcerations-costs, accessed January 6, 2025.

6
There are a number of research papers that discuss this topic, including, but not limited to "Epidemics, Planning and the City: A Special Issue of Planning Perspectives," *Planning Perspectives* 37, no. 1 (2022): 1–8 or "Pale Rider: The Spanish Flu of 1918 and How It Changed the World" by Laura Spinney, or "Epidemics and Society: From the Black Death to the Present" by Frank M. Snowden.

7
Eric Klinenberg, *Heat Wave: A Social Autopsy of Disaster in Chicago* (University of Chicago Press, 2002), 9.

8
Klinenberg, *Heat Wave*, 79.

9
Klinenberg, *Heat Wave*, 80.

10
Klinenberg, *Heat Wave*.

11
Klinenberg, *Heat Wave*, 81.

12
Klinenberg, *Heat Wave*, 91.

13
Klinenberg, *Heat Wave*, 127.

14
Robert D. Putnam, *Bowling Alone: The Collapse and Revival of American Community* (Simon & Schuster, 2000), 326.

15
Jane Jacobs, *The Death and Life of Great American Cities* (Random House, 1961).

16
Richard Rothstein, *The Color of Law: A Forgotten History of How Our Government Segregated America* (Liveright Publishing, 2017), viii.

17
Rothstein, *The Color of Law*, vii.

18
Rothstein, *The Color of Law*, 190.

19
Rothstein, *The Color of Law*, 171.

20
Matthew Desmond, *Poverty, By America* (Crown, 2023), 114.

21
Desmond, *Poverty*, 114.

22
Richard Rothstein, in his prologue (on page xvi), gives explicit reasoning as to the intentional use of the word "ghetto"–one that I would not do justice to try to replicate here. I suggest you read his book!

23
Chetty Raj, Will S. Dobbie, Benjamin Goldman, Sonya Porter, and Crystal Yang, *Changing Opportunity: How Changes in Children's Social Environments Have Increased Class Gaps and Reduced Racial Gaps in Economic Mobility*, Working Paper 32697 (National Bureau of Economic Research, 2024).

24
Raj et al., *Changing Opportunity.*

25
Michelle Alexander, *The New Jim Crow: Mass Incarceration in the Age of Colorblindness* (The New Press, 2010), 98.

26
Chicago's Million Dollar Blocks, chicagosmillion-dollarblocks.com, accessed February 27, 2025.

27
Ellen Orminski, "Your Zip Code is More Important than Your Genetic Code," *National Community Reinvestment Coalition*, June 30, 2021, https://ncrc.org/your-zip-code-is-more-important-than-your-genetic-code, accessed January 6, 2025.

28
There is much scholarship that touches on this, but one text that stands out is that of Friedrich Engels. Consider reading *The Condition of the Working Class in England*, originally published in 1845.

29
"Social Determinants of Health," *Venice Family Clinic*, https://venicefamilyclinic.org/street-medicine/taking-social-medicine-to-the-unsheltered/venice-family-clinic-approach-to-street-medicine/social-determinants-of-health/, accessed August 8, 2024.

30
Healthy People 2030, U.S. Department of Health and Human Services, Office of Disease Prevention and Health Promotion. Retrieved November 4, 2024, from https://odphp.health.gov/healthypeople/objectives-and-data/social-determinants-health, accessed August 8, 2024.

31
"Social Determinants of Health."

32
ProPublica, "ToxMap," *ProPublica*, https://projects.propublica.org/toxmap/, accessed October 17, 2024.

33
ParkRx America, "Home," *ParkRx America*, https://parkrxamerica.org/, accessed October 21, 2024.

34
Maya Goldman, "Health insurers take on the affordability crisis–in housing," *Axios*, June 5, 2024, https://www.axios.com/2024/06/05/housing-affordability-health-care-insurers-investments, accessed August 8, 2024.

35
Seena Fazel, Taanvi Ramesh, and Keith Hawton, "Suicide in prisons: an international study of prevalence and contributory factors," *Lancet Psychiatry* 12, no. 4 (2017): 946–952.

36
David Cloud, Ilana Garcia-Grossman, Andrea Armstrong, and Brie Williams, "Public Health and Prisons: Priorities in the Age of Mass Incarceration," *Annual Review of Public Health*, 44 (2023): 412.

37
Cloud et al., "Public Health," 414.

38
Cloud et al., "Public Health."

39
Cloud et al., "Public Health," 414–415.

40
Cloud et al., "Public Health," 420.

41
Cloud et al., "Public Health," 410.

42
Karen M. Anderson and Steve Olson, eds., *The Effects of Incarceration and Reentry on Community Health and Well-Being: Proceedings of a Workshop* (National Academies Press, 2020). See especially Chapter 3, "Mass Incarceration as a Public Health Issue."

43
Brian B. Boutwell et. al, "Aggregate-Level Lead Exposure, Gun Violence, Homicide, and Rape," *PLOS ONE* 12, no. 11 (2017): e0187953, https://doi.org/10.1371/journal.pone.0187953.

44
Hayon M. Choi et al., "Temperature, Crime, and Violence: A Systematic Review and Meta-Analysis," *Environmental Health Perspectives* 132, no. 10 (2024): 106001, https://doi.org/10.1289/EHP14300.

45
Institute of Medicine (US) Committee for the Study of the Future of Public Health, *The Future of Public Health* (National Academies Press, 1988).

46
Tulchinsky, "John Snow, Cholera," 77.

47
Priyanka Boghani, "They Were Sentenced as 'Superpredators.' Who Were They Really?" *PBS Frontline*, May 17, 2017, https://www.pbs.org/wgbh/frontline/article/they-were-sentenced-as-superpredators-who-were-they-really/, accessed November 30, 2024.

48
The "Ten Minute Park" is an idea I learned about from colleagues at the Trust for Public Land, an incredible organization that you can visit at www.tpl.org.

49
"Youth Incarceration in Massachusetts," *No Kids In Prison*, https://www.nokidsinprison.org/explore/massachusetts/?section=cost-interactive, accessed October 6, 2024

50
Tressa Palcheck, "Child Welfare and the Criminal System: Impact, Overlap, and Potential Solutions," *Georgetown University Law Center: Poverty and the Law Journal*, https://www.law.georgetown.edu/poverty-journal/blog/child-welfare-and-the-criminal-system-impact-overlap-potential-solutions/#:~:text=-Children%20in%20foster%20care%20are,related%20to%20poverty.%5B28%5D, accessed March 21, 2021.

51
N.T. Wright, *Surprised by Hope: Rethinking Heaven, the Resurrection, and the Mission of the Church* (HarperOne, 2008), 98.

52
Juliet Davis, "Epidemics, Planning and the City: A Special Issue of Planning Perspectives," *Planning Perspectives* 37, no. 1 (2022): 1–8.

Juvenile prisoner in her "chicken cage," juvenile carceral center, Clermont de l'Oise, 1930, photograph, ENAP – CRHCP, notice: I72740. Courtesy of Michel Basdevant.

TIME

TIME TIME

TIME III TIME

TIME TIME

TIME

TIME TIME

TIME

TIME III TIME

TIME

TIME TIME

TIME

TIME TIME

TIME III TIME

TIME TIME

TIME

⁂

Een Jabriel

THE MARK OF TIME

Avoidance – avoidance of visits or decorations that could help me keep track of time

Anticipation – the anticipation of a release date almost seemed to make it less obtainable

Detachment – ignoring emotional need for visitation or letters

Engross – finding things and issues to occupy myself with enables me to forget and not keep track

As I reflect on my experience with carceral architecture, I must acknowledge several components that either contributed to minimizing the stress of my formal circumstance or exacerbated the stress of that circumstance. Those who have been subjected to incarceration would call this knowledge knowing how to "jail." In other words, we needed to "learn the ropes." People that do not know how to jail can go through so many different challenges that can make their time spent far more difficult. They could end up in trouble with Administration, they could end up in trouble with the correctional officers, they could end up in trouble with gang members. They could even end up in a situation where their mental health diminishes as they begin to engross themselves in the reality of their confinement. Stress inside runs rampant but there are many ways to cope if you are aware and resourceful enough to learn. One of the first things to learn is which groups you will be housed with. Certain groups have certain expectations and/or requirements so it will always be beneficial to learn who you will be living amongst. Another example is understanding what kind of officer will oversee your living quarters. Despite all officers being sworn in and trained the exact same way, you'll soon learn that they do not operate the same. Some officers allow things that other officers do not allow.

One thing you need to know is which officers allow cell visits. A cell visit is just allowing residents into cells that they are not regularly assigned to. The residents may play chess, cards, work out, or just socialize. Officially, cell visits are banned because it minimizes the chance of theft and many other inappropriate activities that could take place. Some officers might allow for a higher volume on the television as well as a higher level of socializing in the dayroom where the television is located. While most facilities are very similar, a correctional officer can make or break one's entire perception of jail or prison. Prior to actually being inside of a facility, I assumed most officers were hard-nosed ex-military veterans that were afraid to be patrol officers. Once I had spent some time inside, I began to notice that each officer had their own way of doing things. I've even eaten prison food with an officer on more than one occasion. I know you're thinking "why on earth would an officer eat prison food." Technically the facility allowed for actual chicken quarters to be our Sunday dinner. The cooks would take the chicken and make some very delicious meals. A curious officer heard all the fuss about the food and asked to try it. He liked it and even started helping people pay for the additional ingredients to go with the meal. Of course, he would likely get reprimanded for doing this. But rest assured he had one of the cleanest and quietest units in the facility. Almost never a fight during his shift. If there was an altercation the involved parties would be heavily encouraged to wait until the officers' shift was over, otherwise the issue might escalate.

Now another one of your primary concerns is finding out where you will end up sleeping every night. A big factor in this would be what level of security you are classified into. Minimum security facilities typically contain large dormitories with multiple bunk beds throughout. In one sense this is good because there is no locking of a cell that takes place, so the monotony of going in and out of a cell doesn't have as much of a psychological effect on the residents. In another aspect, it's a bad place because now you are no longer able to lock yourself in your room to sleep, nor are you able to secure your belongings. Either can be beneficial or detrimental. Living in an open dorm with complete strangers isn't your typical request, but one may prefer this over being inside of a 7 by 10-foot cell with a complete stranger. Maximum security facilities are all cells. The number of residents within the cell may vary from one to two but it is highly unlikely that there will be any type of dormitory in these maximum facilities. The facility itself can have multiple units within it, and those units consist of living quarters that divide residents up according to many factors. Gang affiliation is usually the primary focus. While some members sneak through the cracks and end up being placed in the wrong location, this system prevents a lot of violence within the facility. While you have to accept and acknowledge that you are incarcerated and will continue to be for the foreseeable future, you must find a level of comfort in where you sleep. Fear of going to sleep because of what might happen to you is a real circumstance that one wants to avoid as much as possible, which is why the dormitory might not be preferred by everyone. For me, I specifically requested to be in cells for the first three years of my stay. Once I was relocated to another facility, I was more comfortable with living in the open dorm.

Once living quarters are established you will likely start participating in the activities offered at the time. That can be work, school, recreation or even mealtime depending on the time of day you arrive at the facility. At this point, you start to become more mindful of the time of day because it is attached to those activities. One revelation I had was that time management matters inside of a correctional facility. Prior to my incarceration, I was under the assumption that I would be bored out of my mind until it was time for me to be released. I had no concept of how to maneuver and handle the facility, both mentally as well as emotionally, when I first arrived. Now although you are inside and are mandated to participate in particular activities, specifically work, you still need to find ways to occupy your time. Typically, that time is filled with exercise, reading, artwork, training, drug counseling, education and also activities that are not technically allowed inside the facility. Gang activities, drug usage, etc. While I did not necessarily participate in these negative activities myself, I still bore witness to their effects. My focus was on fitness and school mostly. That focus was partly due to the vanity benefits associated with the anticipated results of obtaining an appealing aesthetic, but there was also a component of safety that was attached to being physically fit. A physically imposing stature is often correlated to one's ability to handle physical confrontation. Fighting may be a necessary evil at some point in time, but intimidation can be used in cases that prevent the fight from even transpiring in the first place. If you are some skinny, non-intimidating looking guy your chances to intimidate someone are slim to none. That mere physical presence, simply looking physically capable of defending oneself, can prevent many confrontations that could occur. This pursuit could include lifting weights or sticking to calisthenics. Some facilities have banned free weights so push-ups, pull-ups, dips and burpees are the most utilized exercises. Some may create makeshift dumbbells by adding water to trash bags and using a towel to create a handle. These can be considered contraband and land you in lockup depending on which officer discovers it.

One sincere attempt I made in really focusing on my fitness was my plan to start keeping track of the macros I consumed each day. Although a few of the measurements were rough estimates due to my inability to have access to food nutritional facts, I could still write my data within 5 grams of the actual accurate amounts noted. At that time my primary focus was the consumption of protein. In deciding to monitor what I would consume on a daily basis I made a cardinal mistake while serving prison time, I found myself inadvertently counting every day one by one. Writing this data included writing down the dates those meals were consumed–around the eighth or ninth day I realized these were probably the slowest eight days of my entire prison stint. I began to realize that this tracking would affect my psychological perception of time. Contrary to popular belief, counting days in jail is the worst thing you can do to help the time pass. It's the equivalent of looking at a clock while you are at work. The avoidance of monitoring the time made time appear to move faster. Becoming engrossed in whatever activity you are engaging in is actually the best way to "do" time. In society outside of prison, we are pretty much forced to keep track of time. At least keeping track of days of the week and the upcoming weekend. Statements like "this week went by fast" are usually uttered following a very active and productive week. While our schedules may be booked by the hour, we are still so locked into the actual work itself we almost certainly lose track of days.

This tactic is, in my opinion, not only the best strategy but anything else may be borderline idiotic.

Another example I can share is the way in which I had to ask my mother to refrain from visiting so frequently. At the time, visits were either Saturday or Sunday each week. My mother would come one of those days almost every week for pretty much the first few months after I arrived in the state facility, sometimes bringing other family members as well. I want to make a distinction between the state facility and the county facility for two specific reasons. The county facility only allowed visits to my specific tier during the weekdays. Of course, this would make it difficult for anyone to visit because they would need to take the day off work or make some sort of arrangement to either arrive at work late or leave work early. The county jail only allowed for visits through a security glass and over the phone. What's significant about this is the reality that you will not be receiving a hug from any of your visitors. Whether it be your girlfriend, your wife, or, in my case, your mother, you pretty much accept the fact that you will not be receiving any hugs while you are inside. One benefit of the state facilities is "contact visits." Visits that actually allow guests to make physical contact with residents. These visits are often scheduled more frequently and allow for contact between a visitor and a resident, like a hug. Once I gained access to these visits me and my mother were ecstatic, and her hug was extremely cathartic for both of us. We were able to enjoy these contact visits for at least seven or eight months before I noticed that our conversations were growing stale. It was at that point I asked my mother to stop coming up so frequently. She actually seemed relieved, as it was a burden for her to drive eighty minutes each way to visit me almost every week. Consequently, I later started to notice that my months seemed to be going by much faster. Once I thought about it, I realized it was because I was no longer counting my weeks. Four weeks could pass before I would get a visit and then another six weeks could pass after that. Hence, putting me in a space where I could somewhat detach myself from the outside world and stop monitoring visitation dates. Now, instead of counting weeks, at best I was counting months and even sometimes keeping track of months based on the holidays within that month.

Now, earlier, I mentioned seeing a clock at work as an example of how keeping track of time can slow down your perception of how fast time is passing. Fortunately, at one point in time my tier/living quarters did not have a visible clock. Generally speaking, the reason you would use the clock to check the time was in case you wanted to make a phone call home. Lawyer calls were reserved for a separate time where you are required to be moved to a more secluded area in order for your legal call to remain confidential. Outside of that, most things that required you to be at a specific place at a specific time were announced over the intercom. If work was required, you could expect to hear the call over the intercom. Of course, you were expected to be up and dressed already but there were no alarm clocks, just patterns and routines. This same expectation also applied to recreation, family visits, work, and any medical visits that you were scheduled for. Shift changes were the easiest means of keeping track of the time of the day. Shift change is always prefaced with a mandatory head count which requires a brief lock-in or bed check. Bed check requires that you sit on your assigned bed while the officer actively takes count.

Ironically, I initially stayed on a tier in the county jail that *did* have a clock but because of the design of the tier I was not able to see it from my cell. That particular tier was built in the shape of an "H" with a shower on one side of the H and a security booth on the other side of the H with three or four cells making up each end of the H.

The middle of the H is where the phone, microwave, and correctional officers' desk is placed along with some seats and a table. This tier was specifically a "lock up" unit that housed residents who had gotten in trouble for breaking facility rules. I had been placed there after a fight in the general population. This tier ranged from different levels of consequence ranging from ten days lock up to 364 days Administrative Segregation, also known as "Ad Seg". Ad Seg typically allows one to exit their cell for an hour every day. This hour can be used to prepare food, shower, make phone calls, and even socialize to some extent. Recreation should be an option as well but, at this particular time, the facility was not allowing this unit any recreational activity. This was mostly due to so much gang activity throughout the facility and the administration hoping to limit as much movement as possible. Our cells had a capacity of three people but one could find himself in the cell alone if no one was assigned to his cell. This was my case for around nine months. I was in the cell alone and began adapting to this confinement during my first year inside. These cells had a window that was about 48 by 8 inches through which you could see the sky and a small part of the outside staff parking lot. The cell was secured by a heavy door with a 32 by 24-inch window and in the lower middle part of the door was a slot for food, maybe 15 by 5 inches. After nine months I was eventually moved to a larger cell that included the same door and window. The view from the window was completely different but still had very limited visibility, nonetheless.

In closing, one of the key strategies I discovered and encouraged others to adopt was to try and become as engrossed in as many activities as possible. Losing track of time is the best decision I could have made inside. While there was no way to be completely oblivious to time, there were ways to get close. Fortunately for me I did not have a life sentence, and I am able to share this experience from the comfort of my own home.

Drawings by Kelvin Ross.

NEVER GIVE UP!
CHECKS & BALANCES
PICANTE BEEF RAMEN
SAN QUENTIN NEWS
RCA
ADIDAS
BIG BOX

⁂

Juan Moreno Haines

STORYTELLING FROM BOTH SIDES OF THE PRISON WALLS: WHAT IT LOOKS LIKE LIVING IN SAN QUENTIN

Natural light seeps through large dingy windows of a prison housing unit and makes its way into the cell I am assigned to. The milky-white windows are welded shut. All the cell doors are locked. I am one of the caged persons living here.

I open my eyes to the relentless cooing of a nest full of baby pigeons begging for food. Momma bird's nest sits in a darkened recess of an extremely large ventilation unit attached to the ceiling. It does not work. In the seventeen years that I've been housed here, fresh air ventilated through the housing unit has been absent. Three giant portable fans are the only thing that circulates the air in the enclosed, poorly ventilated, housing unit.

The bird shit scattered everywhere reminds me of Jackson Pollock.

I stare at seven vertical steel bars—that's the cell door. Hinged to the cell door are six more vertical steel bars that have a tray slot, which was how we were fed during the COVID-19 lockdown. As the virus swept through San Quentin, twenty-eight incarcerated people died as well as a beloved correctional sergeant.

I rise up to stretch my arms in front of me. Then, I sit cross-legged with a straight back on an upper bunk. I begin meditating. I'm paying attention to my breath, while scanning my body, from head to toe. Afterwards, I feel less anxious and less nervous than you might expect after twenty-eight years of incarceration.

Inside the cell, a small fan pushes the air around, but the stuffiness stays. I am always congested, and yet I don't feel sixty-seven years old.

I reach for bottled water from a 6-cubic-foot locker bolted to the wall. I pour enough water for two cups into a hot pot that has a designed setting not to boil. I take a teaspoon of Folgers instant coffee and dump it in a small plastic cup.

I check the time. It's about 06:30.

My cellmate is up and brushing his teeth. He gargles and spits into a stainless-steel toilet. The light is as dingy as our lives, so I turn on a fluorescent light on its lowest setting of three, so that he can better see himself in a small handheld mirror.

I begin sipping the hot coffee.

"All genders in the building," is announced over the unit's P.A. system. San Quentin is designated a "male prison," but also houses folks who identify as female or transgender and there are female and transgender corrections officials. The gender announcement is made to give notice to the residents that a female and/or transgender corrections official has entered the housing unit.

The correctional officer goes on to say workers may be released from their cells along with folks who have to be transported to outside hospitals for medical treatment and those who are returning to their communities—all are to be let out of their cells prior to the regular release for breakfast.

My cellmate has finished his morning routine and lays on the lower bunk. He's fully dressed and ready to go.

I climb down from the left side of the top bunk. The right side is bolted to the wall. It's a steel slab, two-and-a-half feet wide by six-and-a-half feet long. The slab is held up by four 30-inch steel posts on the corners of the bottom bunk.

The cell is about four feet wide and about nine feet long. It stands eleven feet high. The floor area is roughly the size of a parking space. The width is so narrow that when I fully stretch my arms, crucifix like, my palms easily touch the walls. I'm 5 foot, 3 inches. My cellmate and I cannot stand on the floor at the same time unless he's at the front and I'm in the back. We are in cell 586. It's one of the 414 in North Block. They're stacked five tiers high. The cells were originally designed for single-person occupancy, but in the prison-building years of the prison-industrial complex, more beds were placed in each cell to maximize incarceration capacity, in spite of the negative effect that packing human beings in tight quarters has on physical and mental health. It reminds me of slave ship architecture.

Half the cells are on the front side of the housing unit, half are on the back.

On the front side of the ground floor is a correctional officer's station, two large sinks, and a supply room. Next to the correctional officer's station are twelve telephone booths for folks that have not been issued a tablet or just for convenience. Next to the phone booths are five kiosks for tablet video visitation where residents mount their tablet on a holder attached to the wall. There's one kiosk for folks who qualify under the Americans with Disability Act. Right after the kiosks is an upward graded concrete walkway that leads to three pill windows, where many incarcerated folks pick up their medications. On the top side of the housing unit, opposite the correctional officer's station, are two shower stations consisting of twelve showers each. The showers are divided by race. On the back side of the housing unit is a barber station, a dayroom with two large 65-inch TVs (one stays on Spanish language stations), and administrative offices for counselors, sergeants, and lieutenants. On the bottom end of the housing unit is a long bench, used by folks waiting for appointments or waiting to go outside through large metal double doors.

This is the San Quentin Rehabilitation Center.

There's a constant tightness coming from the lack of adequate space, the result of too many people being crammed into a space not designed to hold this capacity.

Δ

Incarcerated folks are released for breakfast, from the first tier to the fifth tier, then on the next days, it's from fifth to first.

"Chow release, five down," a correctional officer says over the P.A. system.

I live on the fifth tier, so I begin to make my way down. At the end of each tier are long rounded release bars, secured by large locks that correctional officers pull to open the cell doors. As I make it past the fifth-tier correctional officer, I can see the Richmond–San Rafael Bridge through the dingy windows. The rush of tiny cars and boats tugging along the bluish bay looks inviting.

I begin the descent down four sets of metallic stairs to get to the ground floor.

I walk past the pill line. Just before I make it out of the housing unit, there is a long bench on the back wall. I step out of the housing unit through a large metal door and stand in a line about half the length of a football field.

The line moves fast, but people take cuts to talk to people they know, while others just take cuts.

The murmurs are complaints.

Inside the chow hall are 142 stainless steel tables each with four round seats welded to them.

I get to a small window about waist height and a tray of eggs and beans slides out from an unseen server. I make it to table 122, where for the last seventeen years I've eaten my meals.

When I don't eat cold cereal I give away the 1 percent, low-fat milk.

A pigeon bops toward the table. I shoo it away. I see someone, quickly, get up from his meal. He has a disgusted look on his face as he storms out of the chow hall. "A bird shitted in his food," I hear someone chuckle.

Several pigeons are hopping back and forth on the rafters above. Eaters nervously look up, paying attention to the birds. The numerous formal grievances about pigeons in the chow hall continue to go unheeded.

I walk out of the chow hall to see East Block, where those sentenced to death once were housed. Condemned folks, considered privileged, were housed in North-Seg, which is on top of North Block. Governor Gavin Newsom dismantled the death chamber and transferred all condemned folks to other prisons.

Today, 791 cells across Carson, East Block and North-Seg are unoccupied, while the general population is crammed, doubled-up, in parking-lot sized cells.

Thus, there are cells available to ease overcrowding, but prison officials are not using them. They say the housing units cannot be staffed due to a lack of funding, which makes me feel like I'm part of a system that cares little about human suffering.

2024 Incarcerated Population (between 3400 and 3600):
Cells
East Block 466
North Block 414
West Block
Alpine 257
Badger 257
Carson 257
Donner 257
Medical 51
Restrictive 98
Dormitory beds 510
End

⁂

Spencer J. Weinreich

A PHILOSOPHICAL ENQUIRY INTO THE ORIGIN OF OUR WRONG IDEAS OF SOLITARY CONFINEMENT

I began to write a history of solitary confinement in the autumn of 2019, only months before an unheralded pathogen altered the course of human events. In the years since, I have lost count of the friends, relations, colleagues, taxi drivers, interviewers, and assorted others who, upon learning what I work on, bring up lockdown. "Will you include COVID?" "I guess we all experienced solitary confinement in 2020, didn't we?" "I never understood why solitary confinement was so bad until the pandemic."

By now I am practiced at a wry laugh and a deflection; one cannot always be ranting. But there is something obscene in the comparison. If you were not in prison, perhaps your lockdown was lonely, perhaps desperately so. But you had windows you could open. You had parks you could walk in. You had a sky you could see. You had streaming services and delivery apps and all that the internet could bring you. You do not know solitary confinement. You cannot. They are not the same thing. As D. Harris-El wrote in April 2020, from the depths of a solitary cell, "You have not even had a taste of what I've been forced to eat every day year in and year out."[1]

What does it mean that such a misprision is possible? What does it tell us, that we can mistake one thing for the other? What have we misunderstood? I have come to the conclusion that there is a category error in our conception of solitary confinement. We err in thinking about solitary confinement in terms of deprivation or absence, in assuming that it is reducible to solitude. The result is an unconscionably thin sense of what solitary confinement is and what it does.

The long history of the prison offers an alternative, through which we can learn how to see nothing, and to recognize the solitude of the cell as a presence, rather than an absence. To this end, I attempt a kind of alchemy which brings together the phantasmagoric writings of John Perrot–a Quaker held in solitary confinement in seventeenth-century Rome–and the aesthetic theories of Edmund Burke, to argue that solitary confinement is exposure to a dark form of the sublime. I end by revisiting the consequences of the category error with which I began, which impedes a real reckoning with the horror of solitary confinement.

The Somethingness of Nothingness

In the second act of Gian Carlo Menotti's opera *The Medium*, the protagonist, Madame Flora, finds herself alone, not quite sober, and afraid. As snatches of a grim lullaby echo around her, she demands, "Who is there?" "Nothing," she answers herself, "but then if there is nothing to be afraid of, why am I afraid of this nothingness?"[2] There is, I suggest, a nothingness in the empty cell to be afraid of. John Perrot found the cell to be teeming. The cell in question measured 9 by 14 feet, if the calculations of constant pacing were to be trusted, and formed a part of Santa Maria della Pietà, the lunatic asylum of early modern Rome. Perrot had come to Rome in the summer of 1658, hoping to make a Quaker of the Pope.[3] Astoundingly, Perrot simply walked into St. Peter's Basilica, approached a confessor, and asked to meet the Pope. Days later, the Quaker was arrested. After a few months in the inquisitorial dungeons, Perrot was moved to the madhouse, his captors not quite sure what sort of creature they had caught.[4] According to one diplomat stationed in Rome, from the first Perrot and his comrade, John Luffe, had been "utter[ing] the greatest heresies, and countless inanities, showing themselves more crazy than clever."[5]

So began a three-year ordeal. Even for non-heretical inmates, Santa Maria della Pietà enforced a "strict segregation and separation" from the world outside.[6] At first, Perrot related, he had been

> *chained by the Neck to the wall,* in which *Chain* I had the exact liberty of *standing upstreight,* of *sitting,* or of *lying down;* but after *three nights* had passed, it was ordered that the *Chain* was to be taken from off my *Neck,* and another *Chain* lock'd on my *Leg,* which was about *six foot long,* which gave me liberty to walk the length of *three steps* from the *Wall* whereunto it was *fastened,* which abode upon me for the full time of *fourteen weeks.*[7]

He was tortured physically and psychologically: "*tryed with Wine, proved with Women, tempted with Riches* and *Honour,* and *all the Pleasures that ever my heart could desire*," then "*threatned* even *day* after *day,* and *night* after *night;* sometimes with *Tortures,* and sometimes with *Death;* by *Gallows,* by *Fire,* and sometimes *subtilly* by *Poyson*."[8]

What maddened Perrot most, however, was that he was left alone. Yet in his account of his sufferings, he describes solitary confinement in a cascade of unsolitary metaphors:

> When I was cast into Prison, … when I was separated like *Joseph* from all my Brethren, and oppressed in a strange Land; when I was left like a poor *silly Dove* without a mate; … When I was thus and

> unspeakably more proved by flatteries, threats and tortures, to turn from the Lord my God unto a Graven Image; when the hunters night and day hunted me like a forsaken Partridge in the barren Grounds, and like an alone Quail in the stubble fields; when I was as a *Wren* in a bush of Thornes, and the Eagles watched to teare me; when Wolves howled to prey upon me by night, and Lions most terribly roared to destroy me day after day; when the Seas raged on every side, and floods of the deeps heaped themselves like immoveable Mountains upon my back; when the wrath of Hell gaped as a gulf to swallow me in her belly of envy; when nets of Iron were spread about my habitation, and snares of steel set compassing my dwelling; when Serpents creeped over my body, and frogs danced on my face, when Scorpions ran over my head, and Dragons spat fire in my face, when the Spirits of infernal places encamped about me, and sirrounded [*sic*] me with their dreadful flames … .

The cell grows crowded with allegorical torments and dangers: Perrot is crushed by mountains, wrestles with the angel of God, and "cast[s] the Rivers of my bleedings on his Altar."[9] In his other prison pamphlets, Perrot reprised these images repeatedly:

> I have been *driven* in the Deeps with *Whales,* and *hunted* in the Earth by *Foxes, Wolves* and *Lions,* and been subtilly *wept* and *lamented* for by *cruel Crokadiles;* yea, *Cockatrices* have spit venom in my face, and *Serpents* have followed hard after me, to find out my footsteps, and *Dragons* spued out floods to overwhelm me.[10]

To some extent, this is surely an artifact of style. The early Quakers could be extravagant in their use of language, and for someone of Perrot's biblical nous, tribulation of whatever kind was naturally conveyed by metaphors of dragons and hunters and foxes.[11] Moreover, Perrot was heir to a long Christian tradition of the prison as a space of spiritual power, from Christ's imprisonment to Paul's to that of the martyrs.[12] But the influence of these cultural overlays on the experience of solitude is very much the point. Solitary confinement was devised by a tradition in which solitude was anything but emptiness. It was, to the contrary, a space in which to be alone with God. In the fourth century, Saint Paul of Tammah described the work of the hermit in his cell as "walking alone with God at your side."[13] In the nineteenth century, a prison reformer chose the same phrase, "alone with God," to describe solitary confinement in the new penitentiaries.[14] Perrot himself claimed that in prison he had spoken with God, "as a man doth speak with his friend." The narrow cell in Santa Maria della Pietà contained "*deep places*," where the Lord revealed "*many wonders*, yea, and shewed me things *too wonderful* for me."[15]

Kenneth L. Carroll, noting the incoherence of some of Perrot's writing about his ordeal, asks, "How much had Perrot's mind been affected by the two years of imprisonment and torture in this 'Prison of Madmen' in Rome?"[16] A great deal, I should think—but that fact does not empty his words of meaning. To the contrary, their strangeness reflects the strangeness of the experience. If Perrot's prison writings can read as madness, perhaps they are a faithful account of a maddening situation. Nigel Smith argues that the Quaker developed in prison "a unique language for his sufferings," through "the allegorising of Scripture and the interiorising of verbal symbols." A series of stylistic experiments during his travels reached their mature form in the crucible of solitary confinement.[17]

I grant the layers of allegory and allusion, and I grant the disturbing effects of solitary confinement. But

I still contend that Perrot told the truth: he bears witness to something real about solitary confinement. If his language is figurative or fantastic, let us take seriously the nature of those figures and the shapes of those fantasies. The sheer busyness of Perrot's prose, the number of things to-ing and fro-ing across that cell, seems to me a significant piece of data.

Other survivors have reported much the same thing, that the solitude of the cell is not a nothingness but a something—a vast, powerful, and dangerous presence (often comprising innumerable presences). After years of isolation in New Jersey, Judith Vazquez recalls,

> it seemed as though I was standing right at the edge of a cliff. The floor had somehow cracked open and for a moment or so I was not at the jail or in the cell. I was on top of the edge of some ledge where when I looked down I saw an endless pit of fire and darkness. I saw people screaming, crying, and burning. In my eyes and thoughts I was looking at hell.[18]

Or, as Perrot expressed it, "the wrath of Hell gaped as a gulf to swallow me in her belly of envy."[19] Put another way, I wonder whether the "Sea of sorrows" and "immence Ocean of miseries" in which Perrot nearly drowned[20] might be the same body of water as the "grey, limitless ocean" that Sarah Shourd confronted in solitude in an Iranian prison four centuries later.[21]

The Carceral Sublime

What is it that lurks within the cell? What is this vast and boundless thing that is to be found within the narrowest of spaces? Jack Henry Abbott wrote that surrealist art was the best representation of the waking dreamworld that is solitary confinement; generations later, the incarcerated artist Ernest Jerome DeFrance rendered the oppressive, crowded solitude of isolation in a series of haunting ballpoint-pen drawings. Monstrous, ghostly faces flicker out of a heavy darkness, swirling with teeth and arms and holes.[22] Another work of art from the depths of the prison, Ronnie White's *Dreamtime* likewise depicts the prisoner in solitary surrounded by demons, ghosts, and monsters, to evoke what the artist described as "the dead air filled with hatred."[23] If solitary confinement is a space in which reality itself warps, we must learn to attend to the faces that prisoners see and the voices they hear—in a world of madness, the hallucinatory becomes a form of realism.

Edmund Burke described encounters with a vastness that swallows up reason itself under the rubric of the sublime. In the sublime, we confront infinity, that which breaks all human measure. Burke contends that the most potent instances of the sublime *astonish*: "astonishment is that state of the soul, in which all its motions are suspended, with some degree of horror." Prisoners in solitary confinement frequently speak of being overwhelmed by the infinitude of time that stretches out before them, to say nothing of the profound dislocation of their sense of space. Paradoxically—but perhaps solitary confinement resolves the paradox—Burke identified the sublime with the infinite, but also acknowledged that small things, like a poisonous serpent, could invoke the sublime because of the fear they inspire.[24]

In elaborating his theory of the sublime, Burke had something to say about solitude. In the eleventh chapter of *A Philosophical Enquiry into the Origin of Our Ideas of the Sublime and Beautiful* (1757), he notes that society as such is not necessarily pleasurable, "but absolute and entire *solitude*, that is, the total and perpetual exclusion from all society, is as great a positive pain as can almost be conceived." He continues, "an entire life of solitude contradicts the purposes of our being, since death itself is scarcely an idea of more terror."[25] And terror, for Burke, was always "the ruling principle of the sublime."[26]

Aptly enough, Burke was to play a minor role in the history of solitary confinement. He was a confidant and collaborator of William Eden, one of the architects of the Penitentiary Act of 1779, which launched a global movement of prison reform that emphasized solitude. Burke had his doubts about the penitentiary, but agreed that it was "an happy exchange, if there be no other, for the Butchery which we call justice."[27] More influentially, the ideological forefather of the penitentiary in the United States, Benjamin Rush, drew upon Burke's theory of the sublime in articulating his vision of how the violence of punishment, not least the violence of solitude, could redeem. The historian Jonathan Nash even coins the term "penitentiary sublime" to characterize the aesthetic theories undergirding nineteenth-century punishment.[28]

Burke's characterization of the sublime may help to explain how seldom prisoners feel that the reality of solitary confinement can be put into words. According to the philosopher, the sublime paralyzes the mind, which becomes "so entirely filled with its object, that it cannot entertain any other, nor by consequence reason on that object which employs it." In solitude, there is literally nothing else to think about but solitude. The result is that the sublime "anticipates our reasonings," rather than being produced by them, "and hurries us on by an irresistible force."[29] Perrot expressed a similar thought in a pamphlet addressed to fellow prisoners everywhere: upon the "*solitary paths*" of tribulation, the ecstasy of union with the divine "swallowes up words and thoughts."[30]

To be sure, Burke's aestheticized sublime—one thinks of the raging ocean or a towering mountain—does not fit the weaponized ugliness of the modern prison cell, nor does his faith that the experience was, or could be, ennobling.[31] But the sublime does reframe solitary confinement as a matter of presence, not absence—of something done or inflicted, rather than something taken away. Immanuel Kant, the other great theorist of the sublime, mused that "[s]olitude is yet inhabited by dreamy shadows and the deathly silence of graves."[32]

The Evil of Banality

The reader may feel I have been breaking a butterfly upon the wheel. If lockdown taught people to abhor solitary confinement, even if shallowly understood, surely that is to be encouraged? In May 2020, the incarcerated writer Dortell Williams penned an essay expressing the hope that the experience of the pandemic might mean that "lockdown and empathy can intersect."[33] I might even allow that the lockdowns did give a measure of insight into solitary confinement, as a demonstration that the human is a social animal. That the fleeting communion of the checkout line or the subway platform is just as necessary for our equilibrium as sustained, soulful connections with those we love best. Yet I remain convinced that the category error is not an innocent one.

By way of illustration, former Secretary of Defense Donald Rumsfeld made—or made use of—a similar category error. At the bottom of one of the infamous "torture memos" sanctioning the use of "counter-resistance techniques," including standing in stress positions for up to four hours, Rumsfeld scrawled, "However, I stand for 8–10 hours a day. Why is standing limited to 4 hours?"[34] Here are two acts—Rumsfeld, in all his pomp, and the half-starved, half-naked detainee spreadeagled against a wall—with nothing in common save for the vertical posture of the body. Yet the same verb serves for both. And so, it becomes thinkable that the two acts are somehow comparable, somehow the same. The bloodlessness of a word becomes a weapon.

Whether Donald Rumsfeld made the category error in good faith or not I cannot say. But his annotation clarifies the stakes of misunderstanding solitary confinement. The medievalist Gabriel de Carvalho Godoy Castanho coins the invaluable term "demographic isolation" (*isolement démographique*) for the mere fact of being alone, of having no one else around.[35] This, like standing, is something we know. And because we are all sometimes by ourselves, we think we understand what it means to be solitary.[36] The solitudes of a momentarily empty room, such as the one in which I write these lines, or the one in which you are perhaps reading them, are not always pleasant, but they are not torture. I believe that solitary confinement is camouflaged by these ordinary solitudes. There is nothing violent in the kind of solitude we encounter every day, just as there was nothing violent in the kind of standing Donald Rumsfeld did—and so it becomes harder to conceive that there might be other kinds.

Solitude is only the beginning of what solitary confinement does to a person. For one thing, solitary confinement is often accompanied by physical violence, sensory deprivation, sleep deprivation, inadequate food and medical care, poor sanitation, and innumerable other forms of violence. It may even inflict upon the prisoner a cellmate—in this instance hell becomes other people in claustrophobic, inescapable proximity.[37] Sometimes the cell seethes with actual, physical others, in the shape of insects or rodents, potently rendered in James Connors's drawing *Cockroach Insanity*.[38] But for another, as I have argued, solitary confinement exposes prisoners to a fearful sublimity, a nothingness to be afraid of.

The survivors themselves point the way. I close with a revelatory metaphor from a prisoner in Washington State, given the pseudonym "Stephen Tillich" by the anthropologist Lorna A. Rhodes. Asked about life in maximum security, he described what Rhodes termed "a sense of ominous strangeness whose meaning hovers just out of reach." It seemed to Tillich

> there is some type of chemical in the air like a gas ... You can smell it. I have a feeling in my chest ... I don't know what it is, but they have these yellow, these bluish tanks ... and I don't know whether they are putting chemicals in the air or not.[39]

The emptiest cell is still filled with gases. Solitary confinement is a gas, suffocating the prisoner in *something*—something invisible, intangible, and perhaps indefinable, but something all too real.

1
D. Harris-El, "Cabin Fever?" (April 3, 2020), American Prison Writing Archive.

2
Gian Carlo Menotti, *The Medium: Tragedy in Two Acts* (G. Schirmer, 1997), 217.

3
Nigel Smith, "Exporting Enthusiasm: John Perrot and the Quaker Epic," in *Literature and the English Civil War*, ed. Thomas Healy and Jonathan Sawday (Cambridge University Press, 1990), 248–64, here 250–52; Stefano Villani, *Tremolanti e papisti: Missioni quacchere nell'Italia del Seicento* (Edizioni di Storia e Letteratura, 1996), 26, 36; Kenneth L. Carroll, *John Perrot Early Quaker Schismatic* (Friends' Historical Society, 1971), 22.

4
John Perrot, *Battering Rams against Rome; or, The Battel of John the Follower of the Lamb, Fought with the Pope and His Priests, Whilst He Was a Prisoner in the Inquisition-Prison of Rome* (Printed for Robert Wilson, 1661), 98–123; Villani, *Tremolanti e papisti*, 54–57; Carroll, *John Perrot*, 22.

5
"dicono grandissime Heresie, et moltissime pazzie mostrandosi piutosto pazzi che furbi." Quoted in Villani, *Tremolanti e papisti*, 56.

6
"una severa segregazione e separazione." Vinzia Fiorino, "Il manicomio di Roma Santa Maria della Pietà: il profilo istituzionale e sociale (1548–1919)," *Mélanges de l'école française de Rome. Italie et Méditerranée* 116, no. 2 (2004): 831–81, here 839.

7
Perrot, *Battering Rams against Rome*, 128. Italics in the original.

8
Perrot, *Battering Rams against Rome*, 127–30, quotation at 130.

9
John Perrot and Charles Bayley, *A narative [sic] of some of the sufferings of J.P. in the city of Rome* (Printed for Thomas Simmons, 1661), 3–5, quotation at 5.

10
John Perrot, *To the Suffering Seed of Royalty, Wheresoever Tribulated upon the Face of the Whole Earth the Salutation of Your Brother under the Oppressive Yoak of Bonds, in Rome-Prison of Madmen* (Printed for Robert Wilson, 1661), 7.

11
See Jackson I. Cope, "Seventeenth-Century Quaker Style," *PMLA* 71, no. 4 (September 1956): 725–54.

12
Anthony Bale, "God's Cell: Christ as Prisoner and Pilgrimage to the Prison of Christ," *Speculum* 91, no. 1 (January 2016): 1–35, here 1; Thierry Ginestous, *Généalogie de la solitude en Occident*, 2 vols. (Harmattan, 2011), 1:41.

13
Paul of Tamma, "Saint Paul of Tamma on the Monastic Cell (de Cella)," ed. Tim Vivian, trans. Birger A. Pearson, *Hallel: A Review of Monastic Spirituality and Liturgy* 23, no. 2 (1998): 86–107, here 102; Darlene L. Brooks Hedstrom, "The Geography of the Monastic Cell in Early Egyptian Monastic Literature," *Church History* 78, no. 4 (December 2009): 756–91, here 775.

14
Quoted in Philip Priestley, *Victorian Prison Lives: English Prison Biography 1830–1914* (Methuen, 1985), 27.

15
Perrot and Bayley, *Narative*, 8; Perrot, *To the Suffering Seed of Royalty*, 6–7. Italics in the original.

16
Carroll, *John Perrot*, 40.

17
Smith, "Exporting Enthusiasm," 252.

18
Judith Vazquez, "On the Verge of Hell," in *Hell Is a Very Small Place: Voices from Solitary Confinement*, ed. Jean Casella, James Ridgeway, and Sarah Shourd (The New Press, 2016), 55–60, here 58.

19
Perrot and Bayley, *Narative*, 3–4.

20
Perrot and Bayley, *Narative*, 5.

21
Sarah Shourd, "A Play About Solitary Confinement," *HuffPost*, June 25, 2013, https://www.huffpost.com/entry/a-play-solitary-confinement_b_3499882, accessed January 6, 2025. See also Daniel S. Throop, "The Island Effect: Social Marooning in Corrections as Extra-Judicial Punishment," American Prison Writing Archive, November 5, 2019, 8.

22
Jack Henry Abbott, *In the Belly of the Beast: Letters from Prison* (Random House, 1981), 49. See Pete Brook, "A Prisoner's Near-Opaque Pen Drawings That Mirror the Horrors of Solitary Confinement," *Prison Photography*, November 7, 2015, https://prisonphotography.org/2015/11/07/a-prisoners-near-opaque-pen-drawings-that-mirror-the-horrors-of-solitary-confinement/, accessed January 6, 2025.

23
Phyllis Kornfeld, *Cellblock Visions: Prison Art in America* (Princeton University Press, 1997), 52.

24
Edmund Burke, *A Philosophical Enquiry into the Sublime and Beautiful and Other Pre-Revolutionary Writings*, ed. David Womersley (Penguin Books, 2004), 230–31, 243, quotation at 230. See also Immanuel Kant, *Observations on the Feeling of the Beautiful and Sublime and Other Writings*, ed. Patrick Frierson and Paul Guyer (Cambridge University Press, 2011), 16–18.

25
Burke, *Philosophical Enquiry*, 220.

26
Burke, *Philosophical Enquiry*, 230–31.

27
Edmund Burke, *The Correspondence of Edmund Burke*, ed. Thomas W. Copeland, 10 vols. (University of Chicago Press, 1958), here 3:252.

28
Jonathan Nash, "An Incarcerated Republic: Prisoners, Reformers, and the Penitentiary in the United States, 1790–1860," (Ph.D. diss., University at Albany, SUNY, 2011), 41–42, quotation at 42. See also Mitchell Oliver, "Carceral Sublime 2020," *p-e-r-f-o-r-m-a-n-c-e* 6 (2022).

29
Burke, *Philosophical Enquiry*, 230.

30
John Perrot, *A Voice from the Close or Inner Prison unto All the Upright in Heart, Whether They Are Bond or Free* (Printed for the author, 1662), 17.

31
E.g., Steven Cresap, "Sublime Politics: On the Uses of an Aesthetics of Terror," *Clio* 19, no. 2 (Winter 1990): 111–25.

32
Kant, *Observations on the Feeling of the Beautiful*, 78.

33
See Dortell Williams, "The Power of Words: How Lockdown and Empathy Can Intersect," May 27, 2020, American Prison Writing Archive.

34
See NSA archives, https://nsarchive2.gwu.edu/NSAEBB/NSAEBB127/02.12.02.pdf, accessed 21 November, 2024.

35
Gabriel de Carvalho Godoy Castanho, "Dans la solitude des autres: pour une histoire sociale et politique du concept de *solitudo* au Moyen Âge," *Bulletin du centre d'études médiévales d'Auxerre* 20, no. 2 (2016): 1–18, here 8.

36
See also William Blake, "A Sentence Worse than Death," in *Hell Is a Very Small Place: Voices from Solitary Confinement*, ed. Jean Casella, James Ridgeway, and Sarah Shourd (The New Press, 2016), 27.

37
Taylor Pendergrass and Mateo Hoke, eds., *Six by Ten: Stories from Solitarity* (Haymarket Books, 2018), 11.

38
See Kornfeld, *Cellblock Visions*, 21.

39
Lorna A. Rhodes, *Total Confinement: Madness and Reason in the Maximum Security Prison* (University of California Press, 2004), 112.

⁂

Dolfinette Martin, Syrita Steib, Anastasia Pelias, and Miriam Taylor Fair

CURATORIAL STRATEGIES WITH A LASTING IMPACT: THE *PER(SISTER)* EXHIBITION

Syrita Steib and Dolfinette Martin, social justice advocates, talk about using their experience of being formerly incarcerated in the preparation of the *Per(Sister)* exhibition with contributing artist Anastasia Pelias and Miriam Taylor Fair, the curator of special projects at Tulane University. The exhibition, which began at New Orleans's Newcomb Art Museum in 2019, showcased the stories of thirty formerly and currently incarcerated women in Louisiana and highlighted issues such as the impact of incarceration on mothers, the health toll on women, and the challenges of re-entry. It won the Louisiana Endowment for the Humanities Museum of the Year Award and premiered its traveling tour at the Ford Foundation Gallery in New York City.

Miriam Taylor Fair

(MF) The exhibition shared the stories of thirty formerly incarcerated and currently incarcerated women in Louisiana, shining a light on the myriad issues facing this community as identified and expressed by the women themselves, as well as stories of individual and collective resilience and perseverance. The women's stories came to life through a pairing of a "persister," as the women came to call themselves, and an artist who took inspiration from a persister's interview to create new artwork–ranging across voice recordings, photographic portraits, illustrations, sculptures, paintings, mixed media, pieces, songs and performances. The exhibition sought to find common ground and pathways for society to empathetically move forward together. To kick off our conversation today, and with a view to the theme of confinement, I was hoping y'all could share a bit about how the exhibition came to be, considering that Tulane University is a predominantly white institution with a hard history in New Orleans, and in itself a space that can feel quite confined and exclusive.

Syrita Steib

(SS) It was a trying situation initially, because we were rightfully distrustful of Tulane University as a whole, because of the history that it had in the community. It took about three years for us to get to a point where we were all able to say we could move forward in collaboration and begin to work together. It took us about three years to get to a place where the community was on board, the University was on board, the [Newcomb Art] Museum was on board, and then the advocates in the community were on board. We were going through a period at the time in 2017, where there was this focus on Louisiana having more incarcerated people *per capita* than anywhere else in the world. How could we reduce incarceration and change that conversation? For me, it was problematic that a lot of times when people were talking about addressing mass incarceration in Louisiana, and in the country as a whole, it was as if women didn't go to prison. It was as if no one was aware that the incarceration rate of women had risen 800 percent over the last forty years. We weren't talking about that. That wasn't a part of the conversation. And for me, it was like, okay, so where do I fit in this? I'm formerly incarcerated. I served almost ten years in prison. I've gotten out, I've done things to change. You know all of this. I know what the process looks like, but where am I represented in all of this talk around mass incarceration and around how we incarcerate people in this country?

(MF) How women are impacted by the system—or overlooked or misunderstood or just not talked about at all—ended up influencing the themes of the exhibition. Newcomb Art Museum has four main galleries, and each gallery was divided around four themes of the root causes of female incarceration: the impact of incarcerating mothers, the physical and behavioral health toll on women, and the challenges and opportunities of re-entry. Can you talk about what you wanted to make sure wasn't getting overlooked?

(SS) You know, I always talk about how systems are created all the same. They're all similar. Sometimes you would think that there is one architect across the country who designed hospitals, schools, and prisons, because they all are similar, and they all resemble one another. Structures are not inclusive. They are not going to think automatically about gender or about color. But I didn't think that art was like that, right? But, also, some questions are: whose art is valued? Whose art is held up? I wanted to make sure that this exhibit was created as much as possible outside of those constructs. And I think the initial thing was that we focused on something that was non-traditional. If we are going to ask people to come in and to talk about their stories and about who they are and to relive the worst experiences of their life, how are we protecting and compensating them for those things

Exhibition installation images of *Per(Sister): Incarcerated Women of Louisiana* at the Newcomb Art Museum of Tulane University in 2019. Photograph by Jeffery Johnston, courtesy of the museum.

Entrance to the Newcomb Art Museum featuring the temporary installation *A Solitary Garden for Incarcerated Moms* by artist jackie sumell, created for the 2019 exhibition *Per(Sister): Incarcerated Women of Louisiana*. Photograph by Jeffery Johnston, courtesy of the museum.

that they are participating in? So, for me, it was very important that we were being equitable in this whole process.

Dolfinette Martin

(DF) And those were some contentious conversations. It's like when I was first released from incarceration and came home ten years ago: I wanted it to become clear that there's a reason why women end up in those types of places; and not to water it down, to sugarcoat it or to put it out there in the Museum's voice, but in our voice. Our story is told by us in its raw, uncut form, because prison is a completely different world to out here. And you know, a lot of times, society has this notion that what goes on inside of a prison is tied to rehabilitation. But oftentimes when we go to a jail or a prison, it wasn't because of the sentence. It was because of the trauma, the unresolved trauma, that led us to that place.

(MF) To give some more background, when you walked into the exhibition space, you would hear the stories of women in their own words and their own voices in the way that they speak, accompanied by a brochure. And then the third component of that was that their stories were given to artists as a way to turn these stories of resilience, stories of persistence, these stories of trauma, into a new artwork. And so, to bring Anastasia into this conversation and to relate to the theme of confinement—whether that's within our architecture, our urban landscape, our institutions, or even within our own bodies—could you speak about your process as an artist, telling Syrita's story and taking inspiration from it? I imagine that for you, confinement comes up within the limitations of a canvas or the tools of a particular medium, and also within the structures of a museum.

Anastasia Pelias

(AP) Music is a really big part of my studio practice. We started talking about music for some reason and I asked Syrita, when she came to my studio, about what she had listened to when she was in prison, and how she listened to music. How did you listen to music? It was your Sony Walkman radio, right? And then you told me about the musicians, all female singers and songwriters. And I kept thinking about what that must have been like for you to be in there listening, I mean, listening to those lyrics about love and loss, when you were confined to the space and did not know when you were going to get to experience those sentiments outside of that space. The way that I made this painting was by listening to the interviews and Syrita's sweet voice talking about some really terrible experiences.

(SS) I chose Anastasia as my artist strictly on the basis of her energy. Her presence was immediately drawn to mine. But I think for me, that was the best part about being paired with your artist. It was really dependent upon the women picking who they wanted to work with rather than somebody approaching you as their subject, which a lot of times can almost feel voyeuristic. And it kind of took that away to say, hey, I want to work with you to do this.

(MF) To that point, we had thirty women, thirty artists. We had given all the women a kind packet of artists to look through and then asked them to list their top three, because we figured there was going to be a little bit of overlap. Every single woman chose a different artist, and so everybody got their top choice, which was completely unique and unexpected and just really made it incredible. And speaking of that, could you tell us, Dolfinette, about your experience working with the artist Carl Joe and the piece that was inspired by you?

(DM) I looked through the whole catalog three times and still didn't know, because I knew there was a lot of trauma that I was going to have to share. And, you know, my artist was going to have to be able to hear some things that weren't so pretty. My trauma is deeply rooted in Black men. And I had to tell my artist, an African American man, about my pain and he created beauty, right? I knew that I had chosen the right person. With the piece he took my pain—this side of the piece where I'm upside down, that's how my life was, just completely upside down. There's glass around me, broken pieces of glass, and there's pictures around the ladies that's in the pictures. I don't know the ladies inside of those frames, but I am one of these women, right? And you see there's numbers, which represent time over the years. And there's this clock in the middle. What was so amazing for both Syrita and me on the night of the opening was that, passing by this piece, I could see that he took his time and put everything he had into making this piece come alive for me. My life was upside down: I was at the bottom, broken. For a long time, I was hopeless. But as time passed, I made it to where I am now. I was able to see, to breathe, and hope. Like Syrita, I go into prisons and we bring back hope, because when we were in prison, I never saw one of the ladies come back who had made it right on the outside. They always came back as prisoners, and I didn't think that you could leave prison and make it, because

Anastasia Pelias, *Star (for Syrita)*, 2018, oil and oil stick on canvas. Courtesy of the Newcomb Art Museum of Tulane University.

I never saw anybody coming back saying, I made it. So we go back regularly to show the ladies that there's hope.

(MF) To give a broader understanding of the exhibition, which was free and open to the public, it contained thirty pieces and an exterior piece by artist jackie sumell, which was the recreation of solitary confinement. Around it was a garden—women who were mothers and who were currently incarcerated chose the flowers. This was an interactive piece: people could take seeds home, plant them, take pictures, send the pictures back to the Museum, and then postcards were sent to the facility to send the idea of hope. This is just one element contributing to the pedagogical mission of the Museum and the exhibition. We did not want this to retrigger or re-traumatize any person who came in. The *Per(Sisters)* brought up this specific point to the Museum, by saying there needs to be a space that feels safe. Could you talk about the sensory room and the need for that room?

(SS) I think it was important to have the room and to also have contact with a mental health specialist, because we can never really predict what can be triggering. Some people may have had an experience that they hadn't thought about in a while, and it brings up emotions. So it was really important for us to have a safe space. It was a roped-off area with curtains, and it had little things in there that a person could pick up—a toy, a distraction—but it was also a space for kids, right? Because the other piece of that is that if you're incarcerating more people *per capita* than anywhere else in the world, this has an effect on the children. If 80 percent of the women who are incarcerated are parents, then we also need to provide a space for the children who are going through this exhibit where they can feel safe. So that was something that was really, really important to us, especially when we knew some things were going to be very...

(DM) Provoking for people.

(MF) Yeah, it was intentionally interactive with all senses. So, there was something to smell, to taste, to touch, to hear, all of it. One of the big aspects of the *Per(Sister)* exhibition was relationship building. Could each of you talk about the relationships that were formed during and after the exhibition, moving beyond the idea of confinement?

(AP) The exhibition was a life-changing experience for the artists. Do you know that it changed us?

(SS) I know that we've gained lifelong relationships and friendships from being a part of this exhibit, but, I mean, we also spent a lot of time together, and I think we shared things. I just think it's also a testament to uncovering something that is really important and to all of us being fortunate enough to occupy the same space at the same time and bring these issues to light. And it has its own life now. It's traveling. It's moving. It's busting open those stereotypes of confinement.

(DM) Showing emotions cleanses the soul. And that doesn't really happen inside of a prison. There's absolutely no crying. It's almost prohibited: if you have a family member die, the chaplain is going to go to the head of security and they're going to call you up over this loudspeaker and say "report to the chapel." Everyone in the prison knows if you're being summoned to the chapel, death has come to your doorstep. Imagine going to get this news, and you're expected not to fall apart, because you may have to be sedated, and if you're sedated, then you can absolutely scratch going to the funeral. That's what's expected of us inside of prison. And so for me, I'm grateful that I can still tap into my emotions, because for twelve years—I went to prison four times—I left five children each time. So imagine me having to control my emotions inside of the prison. But with Carl, for the first time in my life, I sat with a man and told him some of my deepest secrets and pains, and I was okay doing that. I had never, ever shared all of me with someone. And so, of course, we're bonded for life.

(MF) Thank you all again. I want to open it up to audience questions.

Question 1

Thank you to the entire panel. As someone who's trying to foreground the female experience within carceral spaces, and also being a child of a formerly incarcerated parent, this is very powerful. There are two things I'm thinking of. It's almost a whole other conversation about who owns these stories. But then I'm sort of thinking about, how do we take it digital to allow the voices to move even further beyond time and space?

(SS) The exhibition has been traveling, the other great thing is that it is digital. Online, you can access interviews, see how it was set up, different paintings... but to your point, how do you remain invested in making sure that people can access the opportunity that you've given them? We made

Carl Joe Williams, *Whispers to God, Being Here When Women Need Me to Be Here!* Courtesy of the Newcomb Art Museum of Tulane University, gift of the artist.

Rontherin Ratliff, *All Black & Blue, Bruises of a Queen's Crown*. Courtesy of the Newcomb Art Museum of Tulane University.

sure that the public was involved and invited. We had multiple events. We had transportation that would bring people in and take them out. We're definitely making sure that it stays alive as it relates to us.

Question 2

Being involved with the exhibition, I remember that one of the judges in the juvenile justice system in New Orleans was requiring their staff to come to the Museum, and Syrita led a tour. They were all incredibly impacted. Could you share what was the best and worst thing about that?

(SS) The best thing for me is just being able to watch how women who have had the worst things imaginable happen to them in their lives see themselves in perpetuity on walls and turn their experiences into something so beautiful. And for some of the women, that was their first time in a museum in their whole life, and then they're in a museum looking at something that was created about their life. The most difficult thing was finding the right time balance in the preparation of the exhibition. You're doing something because you feel like it needs to be done. But when this is not your job, the demands on your time to participate are extremely hard. So, how does that translate into compensation for your time?

Question 3

Thank you. This is such an inspiring project because it involves collaboration with multiple universities and art museums. How do you see this collaboration as a model for both universities and art museums to be more engaged in some of these issues?

(SS) Yeah, thank you for bringing this up. There is this assumption that because you went to prison, you're somehow uneducated, or you went to prison because of your lack of education or intelligence. I cannot tell you, the million of times I have shown up somewhere to speak and the compliment I get is, oh you're so articulate. But why would I not have a great command of the English language? Because it's not just the fact that I'm a woman or I'm Black, it's because I've been incarcerated. And there is this preconceived notion that if you've been incarcerated, somehow you are at a lesser intelligence level. And I think that when we go and have these communications with universities, it's important to call out possible preconceptions.

⁂

Falk Bretschneider, Isabelle Heullant-Donat, and Élisabeth Lusset

TRANSFORMING AN ABBEY INTO A PRISON: CLAIRVAUX AND THE WEB DOCUMENTARY *LE CLOÎTRE ET LA PRISON*

Since when can we legitimately speak of "carceral architecture" in the true sense of the term? For a long time, research appeared to have provided a definitive answer to this question. In the wake of Michel Foucault's work and his analysis of the "panopticon" as a matrix of disciplinary techniques in bourgeois society, attention primarily focused on the nineteenth century and the invention of the "machine prison."[1] The modern penitentiary was equally the result of new socio-therapeutic approaches and the advancement of engineering, which not only produced bridges, railway stations, and exhibition palaces from stone, glass, and steel, but also prisons. The Pentonville Prison in London, which opened in 1842, became a model that was replicated in many European cities such as Berlin, Paris, and St. Petersburg in the following years.[2] It was founded upon a technically sophisticated and precisely organized automation of the penal system that left nothing to chance, at least in theory. The radial architecture, the cells arranged in galleries and soundproofed, the individual yards, the face masks, or the isolation chairs for religious services and school lessons guaranteed perfect surveillance and control, which seemingly did not miss a single movement of the prisoners.[3]

However, such model prisons were exceedingly expensive and therefore remained the exception. Even

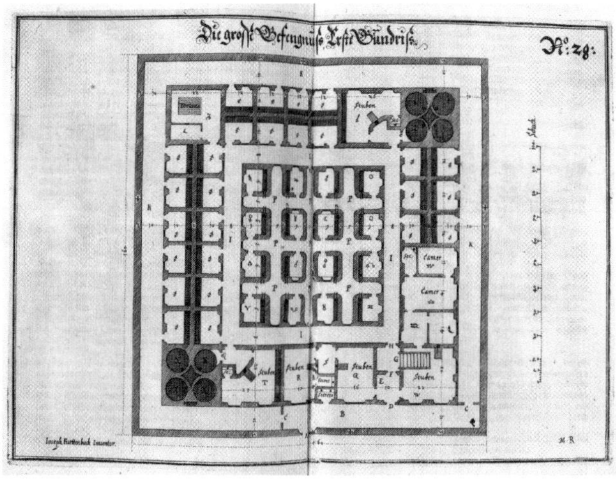

"The great prison." Engraving taken from Joseph Furttenbach's *Architectura Universalis* (J.S. Medern, 1635), pl 28 between p. 74 and 75.

in the nineteenth century, most prisons in Europe were still housed in buildings that had originally been constructed for entirely different purposes: castles, fortresses, royal palaces, or monasteries. But why was this the case? For a long time, researchers assumed that such buildings were simply repurposed because they had lost their original function: castles had become inconvenient for their inhabitants, fortresses no longer held military value, palaces no longer met the demands of aristocratic splendor, and monasteries had been abolished during the Reformation or the French Revolution. While this is certainly true, architects were already discussing the principles according to which a good prison should be built in the early modern period.[4] In his *Architectura Universalis*, published in Ulm in 1635, the German Joseph Furttenbach drew up plans for both a large and a small prison, designed not only to interrogate, torture, and detain offenders until execution, but also to hold debtors and prisoners of honor. Two elements of his design stand out in particular: firstly, Furttenbach envisaged confining most prisoners in individual cells, and secondly, these cells were arranged in a manner strongly reminiscent of the cloisters of a monastery.

This example suggests the unique historical relationship between monasteries and prisons. We would like to explore this further, focusing specifically on the architectural aspects. Firstly, we will examine the spatial transformations of confinement from the late Middle Ages to the early nineteenth century. Secondly, we will delve into the case of Clairvaux, a Cistercian abbey located 250 kilometers southeast of Paris, detailing the development of spatial structures as it transitioned from an abbey to a prison. Finally, we will analyze the web documentary *Le cloître et la prison*, assessing how this format effectively engages an audience beyond the specialized field of incarceration history.

Spaces of Confinement

Notable instances of ancient confinement spaces include Socrates's prison in Athens and the Carcere Mamertino in Rome's Forum, where the apostles Peter and Paul were imprisoned before their martyrdom. However, these two cases do not illustrate prisons in the modern sense: Socrates and the apostles were not serving sentences in jails. Rather, these "prisons" were simple dungeons in which suspects or convicts were held until their trial or execution, often resulting in banishment or capital punishment.[5] Such remand prisons can also be found in the late Middle Ages. For security reasons, the towers of the city fortifications were particularly popular,[6] but most town halls also had underground prisons, such as the infamous *Lochgefängnisse* in Nuremberg, where one can still visit today the torture chamber, the forge, and the prison kitchen. Most manor houses or administrative buildings, including castles, fortresses, and city palaces, also had cells for imprisoning the accused. A special form of detention was molded by debtors' prisons, such as the Grand Châtelet in Paris, where debtors were imprisoned at the expense of their creditors until a solution to their financial problems was found, or they served a substitute prison sentence because they were unable to pay a fine.[7] Finally, there were numerous "state prisons" in which potentates imprisoned their political opponents.

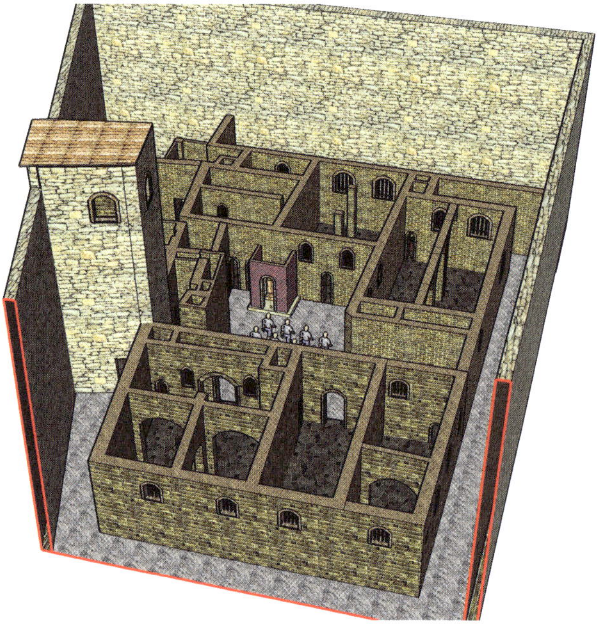

Le Stinche in Florence, 3D reconstruction of the interior, seen from the west. Rendering by Guy Geltner and Yuval Samuelov.

The transition from such "makeshift prisons"[8] to purpose-built prisons can be traced back to northern Italy. In Venice, consecutive doges continuously expanded the number of prisons within the ducal palace from the nineteenth century onwards. This included the dreaded Piombi prison, which consisted of six rooms directly under the palace's roof covered in lead. In the sixteenth century, Venice had a new building built on the other side of the canal with numerous cells.[9] At this time, there were also numerous prisons in the other city-states of the peninsula. The most famous was certainly Le Stinche in Florence, a complex that opened in 1297 and was in use until the nineteenth century, when it was demolished to make way for today's Teatro Verdi. Most of the prisoners were imprisoned for debts, while others were incarcerated for illegal possession of weapons or gambling. Additionally, there were enslaved individuals and children who were sent for correction (*pro ammendare*).[10] The Florentine prison is impressive not only because of its long history, but also because—unlike the municipal prisons in Siena or Bologna, for example—it was housed in a new building with numerous rooms for sleeping, eating, and working. Seventeen people were employed to supervise and care for the prisoners, including an accountant, a clergyman, and a doctor, in addition to the guards. This made Le Stinche not only probably the largest and most important municipal prison of the late Middle Ages, but also the first real penal institution in Europe.

However, another development was to be decisive for the emergence of the modern prison. In the face of massive social and economic problems, new institutions were established throughout Europe in the sixteenth and seventeenth centuries to combat poverty, begging, and crime through forced labor and religious exercises. In 1553, such an institution was first established in the former Bridewell Palace near London, followed by the Rasphuis for men (1596) and the Spinhuis for women (1597) in Amsterdam.[11] Both institutions were housed in former monasteries, which was a common practice at the time. Johann Heinrich Zedler wrote in his *Universal-Lexicon* in 1750: "The form of the monastery is probably best suited to the construction of such houses and it is particularly important to ensure that a church is built right next to it".[12] Medieval monastery architecture thus provided the model for the spatial design of the new prison-workhouses throughout Europe. These institutions imitated the monastic "enclosure," adopting the wall as a means of room closure and dividing the interior into functional areas for sleeping, eating, working, and praying. This continuation of monastic principles can be traced right through to the dining rooms, where meals were served at long tables separated by gender—as in the Waldheim prison-workhouse, founded in 1716 in Saxony. Religious writings were read aloud from pulpits or standing desks during the meal. The monastic table fellowship was thus re-established, placing the preservation of body and soul through food and prayer in a community-building context.

"The men's room, where the poor, orphans and prisoners are fed." Detail from "Eigentliche Abbil-dung aller Gebräuche Des Chur-Sächs. allgemeinen Zucht-, Wayßen- und Armen-Hauses zu Waldheim," 1726. Dresden, Sächsische Landes- und Universitäts-bibliothek/ Deutsche Fotothek SLUB/KS B3139.

Clairvaux: from Abbey to Prison

This conversion of former monasteries continued into the nineteenth century, including in France. During the French Revolution, Church properties were nationalized in 1789, and religious orders were dissolved in 1790. Many buildings were demolished and used as quarries. Others were converted into military depots or stud farms. And some became prisons, such as the abbeys of

Mont-Saint-Michel in Normandy, Fontevraud in the Loire Valley, and Clairvaux in Champagne. Clairvaux, whose foundation was laid in 1115 by Bernard of Clairvaux and a few monks, subsequently had numerous daughter foundations throughout Europe.[13] The abbey buildings dating back to the twelfth century were demolished around the middle of the eighteenth century (only the medieval lay brothers' house remains today) and replaced by new buildings in the Neoclassical style, of which the large cloister is particularly noteworthy. A new refectory was added to this. In 1791, the last monks of the abbey were expelled and Clairvaux was sold as *bien national* (national property) in 1792, to an architect from Bar-sur-Aube (a small town located 14 kilometers from Clairvaux), who set up a paper factory and glassworks there, with the furnaces located in the church. After the abbey was sold again in 1799, the remaining furnishing was scattered. Finally, in 1808, the French State acquired the complex and, by Napoleon's decree, converted Clairvaux into a central prison (*maison centrale*) with three sections for beggars, reformatory prisoners, and convicted criminals. Between 1812 and 1815, the monastery church was demolished so that its stones could be used as building material.[14]

In contrast to Mont-Saint-Michel, which ceased to be used as a place of detention as early as 1863, and to Fontevraud, which served as a prison until 1963, Clairvaux remained a penal institution until October 2023; the last prisoners, who have lived in a modern cell building since 1971, left the site in May 2023. At Clairvaux, the traces of the abbey's transformation into a prison remain highly visible. Since 1979, L'Association Renaissance de l'Abbaye de Clairvaux has been preserving and promoting Clairvaux's dual monastic and penal history, particularly by organizing site visits and tours of the historical buildings.[15] For example, you can visit the monks' former refectory, which was converted into a chapel for the

Views of the refectory at Clairvaux. On the left, the restored eastern part with eighteenth-century decoration; on the right, the western part with traces of the former tribunes of the prisoners' chapel. Photograph by Thomas Salva.

prisoners in 1814. Restoration work in 2015 reestablished the room in its original state. However, the altar is still in place, and traces of the galleries from which the prisoners watched the service can be seen on the walls in the western section. The numerous changes are also visible in the cloister: here, the monks' former living quarters have been converted into communal sleeping cells. This type of accommodation, which encouraged promiscuity and violence, was heavily criticized by prison reformers during the nineteenth century and led to the so-called "system controversy" about solitary confinement.[16] At Clairvaux, the layout of the buildings and the lack of financial resources led the prison administration to adopt makeshift solutions. To implement the cellular regime from the end of the nineteenth century, prisoners were locked up at night in *cages à poules* (hen cages): these individual wire-mesh cells were lined up in a large room. The prison guard could close them all at once using a lever located at the end.

View of the *cages à poules* at Clairvaux. Photograph by Thomas Salva.

Other parts of the former monastery complex, such as the infirmary, retained their function from the monastic era even during the prison period. This underscores that the transformation of an abbey into a prison is a complex interplay of continuities and ruptures.

This also applies to the mighty wall that surrounds the complex and which, despite numerous repairs and elevations, has essentially fulfilled the same function of separating the inside from the outside for centuries. Above all, however, the history of these conversions demonstrates how much the prison spaces themselves are subject to constant change, whether to meet new requirements or to prevent misuse by the prisoners. In Clairvaux, for example, a women's prison was established in the former lay brothers' house in 1817, necessitating numerous structural measures in other buildings to prevent any contact between incarcerated men and women. Workshops were set up on the site of the former monastery church, as there was not enough space in the existing buildings. At the same time, the organization of everyday life (work, meals, rest periods) and the requirements for hygiene (sewage system, washroom, laundry) and security (bars, walls, surveillance facilities) led to a constant stream of new construction sites.

The Web Documentary *Le cloître et la prison*

Available online since 2018 (http://cloitreprison.fr), the web documentary *Le cloître et la prison* is an innovative and multimedia format that combines text, image, video, and audio playback.[17] Based on the example of Clairvaux, it examines a hypothesis formulated in the 1970s by Erving Goffman, Michel Foucault, and others, which suggests that monasteries served as spatial models for punitive confinement institutions.[18] Beyond the availability of monastic buildings following the French Revolution, abbeys were transformed into prisons due to a kinship between these two institutions. While pursuing objectives that were conceived or experienced as radically different, monasteries and prisons implemented partly similar mechanisms and methods (rules and regulations, enclosure, timetables or spatial distribution of individuals), which facilitated the transition from one use to the other.[19]

After a brief introductory video on the history of Clairvaux, the homepage opens with an aerial view of the abbey-prison, in which the church—destroyed at the beginning of the nineteenth century—is inserted as a drawing. The web documentary proposes a virtual tour of Clairvaux, taking in nine locations: the surrounding wall, the gate, the lay brothers' building, the refectory, the church, the dormitory, the great cloister, the disciplinary quarters, and the infirmary. These nine locations have been identified as historically emblematic of the spaces of voluntary and punitive confinement.

Homepage of the web documentary *Le cloître et la prison*. Courtesy of Lumento.

To interconnect the specific history of Clairvaux, the narrative's focal point, and the broader history of confinement spaces, each of the nine locations has been assigned a theme that users can explore from four or five distinct perspectives. For instance, the location "1. Wall" is associated with the theme "Protecting–Enclosing". After viewing an introductory video on the wall of Clairvaux, users are directed to four entries that delve into the construction of the enclosure, its significance in various contexts of voluntary or imposed seclusion, and the material devices employed to implement it.

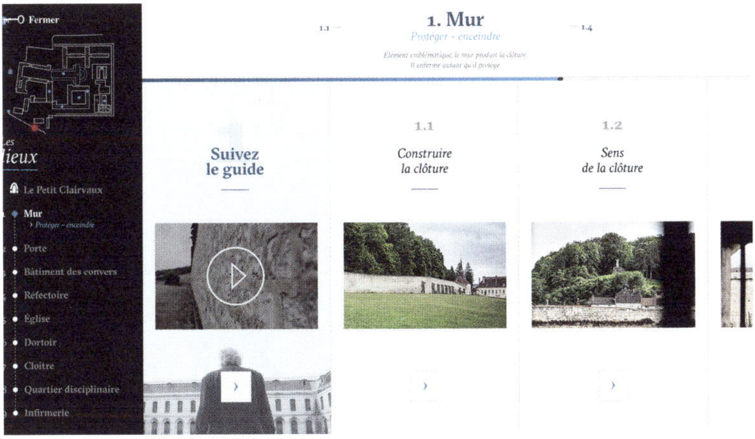

Location "Protéger-enceindre" of the web documentary *Le cloître et la prison*. Courtesy of Lumento.

Each entry integrated decryption text, images, and multimedia elements that enrich the overall message. The web documentary comprises a total of forty-three entries and over 300 textual, visual, and audiovisual documents, including interviews with historians. From Clairvaux, which remains on the left of the screen in the form of a photograph, the user is introduced to dozens of European places of retreat or punishment.

The site's design was developed by Lumento, a creative narrative lab.[20] To make it easier for the user to understand the materiality of the Clairvaux site and to give the web documentary an immersive aspect, Thomas Salva and Olivier Lambert carried out several photographic, film, and sound campaigns at Clairvaux, documenting areas previously inaccessible to visitors. Photographs and videos capture the furnishings—such as the *cages à poules*, the screen of the prison cinema, and objects made by the prisoners in the workshops—as well as the traces of their daily life (e.g., graffiti or magazine pages stuck to the cells).[21] The web documentary also presents a substantial number of archival documents, which were collected through partnerships with various institutions. Most of the documents on Clairvaux come from the Archives départementales de l'Aube (Troyes). For the web documentary, the National Archives (Paris) have restored and digitized a selection of documents from the F16 series devoted to prisons—a treasure trove for understanding how the French heritage of abbey-prisons has been repeatedly redesigned.

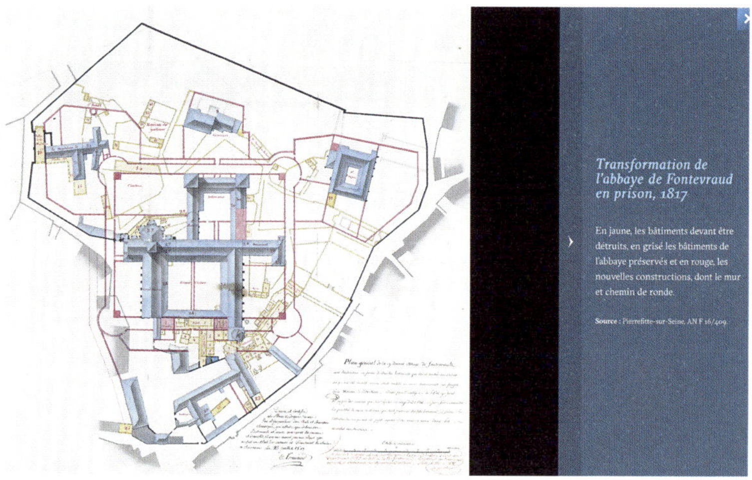

Plan of works to be carried out during the conversion of Fontevraud Abbey into a prison, 1817 (AN, F16/409). Web documentary *Le cloître et la prison*. Courtesy of Lumento.

In addition, the Henri Manuel collection, held at the Centre de Ressources sur l'Histoire des Crimes et des Peines (Centre for Resources on the History of Crimes and Punishments) at the École Nationale de d'Administration Pénitentiaire (National School of Prison Administration) proved invaluable. Between 1929 and 1931, Henri Manuel's studio carried out a series of photographic reports in prisons at the request of the Ministry of Justice. Unlike many other photographers, who captured lifeless places, Henri Manuel had both prisoners and institutional staff pose for him, with some of the shots being staged.[22] Finally, the web documentary integrates numerous iconographic representations of the prison, including sketchbooks, prints, and postcards from the first third of the twentieth century.

The web documentary concludes with the question of the future of Clairvaux. Wouldn't it be the ideal place, among other things, to house the collections of the short-lived Musée national des prisons (1995–2010), which was once located in the Fontainebleau prison?[23] Be that as it may, the French government must decide the future of the site's 32 hectares and recently announced its intention to oversee a heritage, economic, tourism and cultural conversion project at Clairvaux, which will be conducted in collaboration with private partners.[24] Beyond *dark tourism* and the necessary defense and rehabilitation of prison architecture, there is a scientific and political challenge in preserving Clairvaux and the unique traces of its dual history.[25]

1
Michel Foucault, *Surveiller et punir, Naissance de la prison* (Gallimard, 1974).

2
Joshua Jebb, *Report of the Surveyor-General of Prisons on the construction, ventilation, and details of Pentonville Prison* (W. Clowes and Sons for H.M. Stationery Office, 1844); Alan Brodie, Jane Croom, and James O. Davies, eds., *English Prisons: An Architectural History* (English Heritage, 2002), 84–119.

3
Thomas Nutz, *Strafanstalt als Besserungsmaschine. Reformdiskurs und Gefängniswissenschaft 1775–1848* (Oldenbourg, 2001), 174–207.

4
Norman Johnston, *Forms of Constraint: A History of Prison Architecture* (University of Illinois Press, 2000), 28–41.

5
Jens-Uwe Krause, *Gefängnisse im Römischen Reich* (Steiner, 1996); Julia Hillner, *Prison, Punishment and Penance in Late Antiquity* (Cambridge University Press, 2015).

6
Gerd Schwerhoff, *Köln im Kreuzverhör. Kriminalität, Herrschaft und Gesellschaft in einer frühneuzeitlichen Stadt* (Bouvier, 1991), 95–104; Martine Charageat, Élisabeth Lusset, and Mathieu Vivas, eds., *Les espaces carcéraux au Moyen Âge* (Ausonius éditions, 2021), https://una-editions.fr/les-espaces-carceraux-au-moyen-age/.

7
Julie Claustre, *Dans les geôles du roi. La prison pour dette à Paris à la fin du Moyen Âge* (Publications de la Sorbonne, 2007).

8
Johnston, *Forms of Constraint*, 5–16.

9
Johnston, *Forms of Constraint*, 32.

10
John K. Brackett, *Criminal justice and crime in late Renaissance Florence, 1537–1609* (Cambridge University Press, 1992), 44–56; Guy Geltner, *The Medieval Prison: A Social History* (Princeton University Press, 2008).

11
Pieter Spierenburg, *The Prison Experience: Disciplinary Institutions and Their Inmates in Early Modern Europe* (Amsterdam University Press/Amsterdam Academic Archive, 2007), 12–38.

12
Johann Heinrich Zedler, *Grosses Vollständiges Universal-Lexikon*, Leipzig and Halle, vol. 63, 1750, col. 1003.

13
Arnaud Baudin and Alexis Grélois, eds., *Le temps long de Clairvaux: nouvelles recherches, nouvelles perspectives (XIIe-XXIe siècle)* (Somogy, 2017).

14
Dominique Fey and Lydie Herbelot, *Clairvaux. Vies emmurées au XIXe siècle* (The Book Edition, 2013), 11–36.

15
See Association Renaissance de l'Abbaye de Clairvaux, https://www.abbayedeclairvaux.com, accessed January 6, 2024.

16
Nutz, *Strafanstalt als Besserungsmaschine*, 165–174.

17
Julie Claustre and Élisabeth Lusset, “Concevoir un web-documentaire historique. Retour sur l’expérience du web-documentaire ‘Le cloître et la prison,’” *Memini* 26 (2020), https://journals.openedition.org/memini/1723, accessed January 6, 2025; Isabelle Heullant-Donat and Élisabeth Lusset, “Les enjeux patrimoniaux d’une abbaye-prison en reconversion: le cas de Clairvaux,” *In Situ. Revue des patrimoines* 48 (2022) https://journals.openedition.org/insitu/36020, accessed January 6, 2025.

18
Erving Goffman, *Asylums: Essays on the Social Situation of Mental Patients and Other Inmates* (Anchor Books, 1961), 5; Foucault, *Surveiller et punir*, 168 or 175; Hubert Treiber and Heinz/Steinert, *Die Fabrikation des zuverlässigen Menschen. Über die “Wahlverwandtschaft” von Kloster- und Fabrikdisziplin* (Westfälisches Dampfboot, 2005).

19
Isabelle Heullant-Donat, Julie Claustre, and Élisabeth Lusset, *Enfermements. Le cloître et la prison (VIe-XVIIIe siècle)* (Publications de la Sorbonne, 2011).

20
Tour guide: Jean-François Leroux; photography: Thomas Salva; video: Olivier Lambert and Thomas Salva; design: Denis Trichet/Irregulart; web development: Alexandre Croizard/Lanfoster.

21
Laure Bulmé, “Les graffitis de la maison centrale de Clairvaux,” *Musée Criminocorpus* (2014) https://criminocorpus.org/fr/ref/25/17636/, accessed January 6, 2025.

22
Françoise Denoyelle, “Le studio Henri Manuel et le ministère de la Justice: une commande non élucidée,” *Revue d’histoire de l’enfance “irrégulière”* 4 (2002): 127–143.

23
Catherine Prade, “L’impossible musée? 1989–2005, le musée national des Prisons,” *Criminocorpus* (2012) http://journals.openedition.org/criminocorpus/1774, accessed January 6, 2025.

24
Élisabeth Lusset, “Un patrimoine en reconversion: l’abbaye-prison de Clairvaux,” in *Le patrimoine, objet d’études interdisciplinaires à l’université Paris 1 Panthéon-Sorbonne*, ed. Aurélie Condevaux, Alain Duplouy, Maria Gravari-Barbas (Alma DL, forthcoming).

25
Sonya Faure, “Les prisons font aussi partie de notre patrimoine,” *Libération*, 18 September 2014; Gwenola Ricordeau and Fanny Bugnon, “Introduction,” *Système pénal et patrimonialisation: entre lieux de mémoire et tourisme carceral = Déviance et Société* 42 (2018): 605–618; Philipp Artières, *La prison en héritage? Pour une patrimonialisation critique du pénitentiaire* (Éditions de la Sorbonne, 2024).

Prisoners' meals in the corridor, Montpellier central prison. circa 1930, photograph.
Courtesy of Henri Manuel / Fonds Manuel / ENAP – CRHCP, M-07-011.

CARE

CARE

IV CARE

CARE

CARE

CARE

CARE

CARE IV

CARE

CARE

CARE

CARE

IV CARE

CARE

CARE

⁂

Joel Negron

CARE

Imagine an animal trapped in a cage. Malnourished, abused, abandoned, and suffering. Imagine the trauma inflicted upon the animal. Imagine it sick and, because of a lack of care, being eaten from the inside by something that could've been cured. Hair or feathers no longer attached to its body, skin spotted, bones clearly visible. Now imagine the animal dying, slowly deteriorating. This image would cause heartbreak for most human beings and make us take action. How dare someone do harm to such a fragile soul? To humanity, every soul is precious. What kind of a monster could do this? Now imagine this same image, except replace the animal with a human being, trapped in a prison cell.

Society has made this kind of image fathomable when considering incarcerated persons. It has been trained to believe that most, if not all, persons who are in prisons are worse than animals and deserving of such treatment. But then what happens to every soul being precious? In a carceral setting, many things occur that take away from the individual's humanity. One of those things is the failure of care, in more ways than one. The carceral space is not set up to give concern to the care of incarcerated persons. There are medical units and staff, but the measure of care is in many ways less than in an overcrowded animal shelter. To call it inadequate is not enough. My experience concerning care in prison taught me a good lesson, that morality and integrity are not required for doctors when working for a department of corrections (DOC). DOC medical staff are not there to help their patients, but to save the state and insurance provider money. But who cares?

Self-care is often a better option. There is a fear of relying on the incompetence of someone else's care for you. As such, many incarcerated persons turn to self-care. Physical activities are always a point of self-care. Hence, why we see so many men with great physiques. But a good external appearance is not indicative of what is happening internally. Care for incarcerated persons is important. Most eventually return to society and no one wants to return in worse shape than they went in. But not enough people care. So, when I think about care in prison, without self-care it is non-existent.

⁂

Andrea Armstrong

FOOD-BORNE PUNISHMENT

"This is jail… . You don't get to choose your mommy and your daddy, and your aunt Lily doesn't get to make your meals. I'm your aunt and your grandpa. I'm the one that gets your meals prepared, makes sure it gets done."

—Butler County, OH Sheriff Richard Jones[1]

Carceral spaces create their own rules.[2] As our jails, prisons, youth detention centers, and immigration detention centers are typically closed to the media and the public, they operate with little oversight or public accountability. They are also often unregulated;[3] even accreditation by professional organizations, such as the American Correctional Association or the National Commission on Correctional Health Care, is voluntary and generally not required.[4] The only "check" on the exercise of a warden's power is the U.S. Constitution, which prohibits "punishment"[5] for people detained pre-trial and forbids "cruel and unusual"[6] punishments for people serving convictions. Courts also generally defer to the decisions of prison administrators and have held in a series of cases that people in custody have fewer constitutional rights than free people.[7]

This lack of transparency and accountability enables Sheriff Jones of Butler County, Ohio to punish people in his custody with a meal called the "warden burger." "The burger is made of tomato paste, flour, dry milk, oats, beans, ground turkey, cabbage, carrots, potatoes, onion, celery, and 'a pinch of salt,'"[8] all ground up and cooked together, according to a local journalist. The "warden burger" is not unique to Butler County Jail—a version of the burger, more commonly known as "nutraloaf," is served in carceral spaces across the United States.

Variations on the nutraloaf are endless. A prison can take yesterday's leftovers, "grinding [them] up ... into a dense mass that's reheated" or making "loaves from scratch out of shredded and mashed vegetables, beans and starches."[9] In Minnesota, the recipe called for "blended bread, potatoes, non-dairy cheese, beans, fruits, and vegetables baked into a loaf."[10] Incarcerated people describe the experience as akin to eating "cardboard,"[11] but administrators—including Sheriff Jones—say the real punishment is the monotony of eating the same meal over and over, for days at a time.[12]

Serving nutraloaf is just the most obvious version of food-borne punishment for incarcerated people. Food is a key determinant of a person's overall health[13] and people in custody are fully dependent on whatever food the facility serves. One of the many freedoms a person loses upon incarceration is the ability to choose (and prepare) food for themselves. While U.S. courts have ruled that food, or more accurately caloric and nutritional value, cannot be used to punish for incarcerated people, it is nevertheless one of many carceral tools that foster the dehumanization of incarcerated people.

Carceral spaces control almost every aspect of food behind bars. Administrators set the budget for the purchase of food supplies and select the vendors; they develop and/or approve the menu of meals to be served; the food is usually prepared behind bars, most often by incarcerated workers, and served via prison-owned plates and cutlery; and meals are eaten in a place chosen by the administrator, namely a person's 6-by-9-foot cell or perhaps a cafeteria or dayroom. Administrators are responsible for the cleanliness of the food preparation area and the training of the people preparing the food. Carceral administrators also control access to supplemental food sources through selecting vendors, setting prices, and facilitating financial transactions. They additionally control access to food through their disciplinary policies, which may forbid purchases when a person is in solitary confinement, limit the amount or type of food to be purchased and/or stored in a person's cell, and prohibit sharing of food. Lastly, carceral environments control the access, content, and quality of any necessary healthcare services.[14] Incarcerated people are not free to arrange for their own healthcare and are thus fully reliant on the services provided by their facility.[15]

This chapter explores how food both underpins and compounds punishment in two different systemic domains within incarceration, including healthcare and labor. Second, this chapter critiques the existing fragmented legal architecture regulating carceral food, which is a patchwork of municipal, state, and federal law and court opinions. Finally, this chapter reimagines the potential of food and explores how food-borne punishment undermines other carceral and institutional goals.

Domains of Food-borne Punishment

The use of food to punish and control people in custody is not new. Before the Civil War, a local newspaper notes that the New Orleans jail not only meted out whippings to "refractory slaves" but also "in extreme cases the rebellious [B]lacks were kept immured in the dark cells on a diet of bread and water until reduced to the proper degree of submission."[16] In fact, it is only recently that U.S. courts have held that "evolving standards of

Two person cell in the New Orleans House of Detention jail, closed in 2012.
Photograph by Andrea Armstrong, 2020.

decency" prohibit the use of "bread and water" diets for people in custody.[17]

Food-borne punishment, however, extends far beyond the explicit use of food as a disciplinary measure, like serving nutraloaf or a warden's burger. A year-long investigation in Arizona documented filthy kitchen conditions, including pest infestations, expired food, and broken equipment in all state-operated prisons.[18] Despite repeated "critical violations," all of the prison kitchens were deemed "satisfactory" and allowed to continue food operations.[19] A study with responses from forty-one states included accounts of "weevils in grits, rocks in turnip greens, maggots in meat, a rat tail buried in one day's entree, and oatmeal ladled up with human hair, pieces of metal, or cockroaches."[20] Incarcerated people tasked with working in kitchens have shared their experiences serving "chicken and beef marked [as] 'not for human consumption.'"[21]

As a result, incarcerated people may experience short- and long-term repercussions for their physical health due to carceral food. The type and quality of food can impose additional punishments on incarcerated people. They can also be punished for attempts to mitigate the harsh food environment. The only approved form of mitigation is purchasing (usually unhealthy) supplemental food at elevated prices from the prison commissary, increasing coercive pressure to engage in exploitative work that pays pennies per hour. However, a person's ability to work can be compromised by their health, which is fully dependent on the quality of the food and healthcare provided by the prison. These domains of healthcare and labor create independent and additional punishment. Moreover, within the context of incarceration, healthcare and labor also reinforce one another, compounding the punishment experienced.

Health

Incarcerated people face further punishments from carceral food through its negative impacts on their short- and long-term health. In the short term, an incarcerated person is six times more likely to experience food poisoning than a free person.[22] The most common contributing factor for a food-borne disease outbreak in carceral environments is food remaining at room temperature.[23] A 2017 study documented the impact of 200 foodborne outbreaks in correctional institutions from 1998 to 2014, resulting in 20,625 illnesses, 204 hospitalizations, and five deaths.[24]

A person's diet—i.e., the food he or she consumes—is also a key determinant of that person's long-term health.[25] Nutrient needs also change over a person's lifespan.[26] Thus, the appropriate nutritional content for a young incarcerated adult will be different than for an elderly incarcerated person. Regardless of age, a healthy diet should be nutrient-dense, with minimal added sugars, sodium or saturated fat.[27] The federal *Dietary Guidelines for Americans 2020–2025* identifies "[v]egetables, fruits, whole grains, seafood, eggs, beans, peas, and lentils, unsalted nuts and seeds, fat-free and low-fat dairy products, and lean meats and poultry" as examples of nutrient-dense food when properly prepared.[28]

These general propositions for healthy diets have added significance in the carceral context. For example, national data indicates that approximately 40 percent of people in state prisons currently have a chronic condition.[29] For people in both state and federal prisons, the most common chronic condition is hypertension,[30] which is a "preventable risk factor for cardiovascular disease and stroke."[31] Incarceration is associated with a higher likelihood of heart disease[32] and accelerated aging.[33] Thus preventative strategies, such as reduced sodium intake and other dietary modifications,[34] are especially important in the carceral context.

At the same time, a national study by Impact Justice found that 62 percent of respondents rarely—if ever—had access to fresh fruit or vegetables.[35] Similarly, meals in Pennsylvania prisons have "twice the recommended amount of starchy vegetables and refined carbohydrates and half the fruit and vegetable servings recommended," according to analysis by the Pennsylvania Prison Society.[36] Hence, prison food—through facilitating and exacerbating chronic medical conditions—may be contributing to shorter life expectancies for people who have been incarcerated.[37]

More generally, incarcerated people report being hungry. The Pennsylvania Prison Society documented how, based on federal dietary guidelines, prison menus fail to consistently provide sufficient calories for a moderately active incarcerated man.[38] Eighty percent of survey respondents in the same study reported being hungry between prison-issued meals.[39] Carceral mealtimes can also create periods of twelve hours or more in which food is simply not available for incarcerated people. For example, a jail in Georgia served only two meals a day, with a gap of between ten to fourteen hours a day between each meal.[40] At least one court has described continuing hunger—the constant physical pain from a lack of adequate food—as a form of corporal punishment.[41]

Forced Labor

The poor food environment ultimately contributes to coercive carceral work environments. People convicted of a crime can be forced to work while incarcerated, an exception to the prohibition of slavery and involuntary servitude under the 13th Amendment to the U.S. Constitution.[42] People in jail pre-trial, as well as people held civilly for immigration detention, may also be forced to work in some limited circumstances.[43] They may face increased pressure to "volunteer" for work in exchange for additional food or other privileges.[44] Food scarcity can also lead to other forms of exploitation and harassment where prison staff seek "favors" in return for half-eaten food or a slice of pizza.[45]

The lack of adequate and nutritious food creates additional coercion within the context of forced incarcerated labor. Incarcerated labor can be dangerous, as it is unprotected by standard labor safety laws. Incarcerated workers may not be provided with essential safety equipment[46] or training[47] to safely complete the assigned tasks. Federal laws regulating workplaces do not generally apply to working conditions in state prisons, as incarcerated workers are not considered "employees."[48] Incarcerated workers also do not have a right to strike or even to sign a petition for safer workplaces.[49] Further, a majority of states explicitly allow the use of forced incarcerated labor in disaster recovery efforts, environments that are often unpredictable and may be particularly dangerous.[50]

Prisons nationwide have shifted the cost of adequate food from the facility budget to the incarcerated individual. Incarcerated people overwhelmingly purchase food items from prison commissaries to mitigate hunger.[51] In Pennsylvania, the daily cost of meals per person has plummeted from $8.96 in 1991 (adjusted for inflation) to a paltry $2.61 in 2018,[52] with smaller and less nutritious meals as a result. At the same time, commissary prices for food purchased by incarcerated people have steeply increased.[53] In at least one case, a private food contractor appeared to profit from serving substandard meals, since it also managed the jail's commissary services selling supplemental food.[54] Commissary prices are often higher than general market prices,[55] increasing the financial cost of ensuring adequate food.

At the same time, incentive wages for forced prison work in 2017 averaged 86 cents per hour for standard prison jobs.[56] In Louisiana, a person can earn 2 cents an hour working in the field. To purchase a single cup of ramen from the prison commissary for 70 cents requires working thirty-five hours. The real-world equivalent price at the federal minimum wage of $7.25 per hour for that same cup of ramen would be $253.75.

The only legal way for incarcerated people to address carceral food scarcity is through the prison commissary. Yet, prison commissaries may actually aggravate the lack of a nutritious diet (despite addressing short-term hunger), reinforcing the punishment of unhealthy prison meals. Prison commissaries typically sell highly processed foods, such as snacks like honey buns or packaged meals like instant ramen or macaroni and cheese.[57] These foods are often higher in sodium,[58] compounding the challenges of eating healthily within the carceral environment. Only rarely will a prison commissary sell fresh fruits or vegetables, which then necessitates access to a refrigerator to extend the life of the produce.[59]

The lack of protection against food-borne punishment can actually undermine institutional order. Both short-term and long-term health impacts create unnecessary life-altering emergencies, straining resources and staff. Lack of adequate food can disrupt a person's attention on the job, for instance, creating increased risk of injury in already unsafe forced work environments. It also undermines general adherence to the rules of the institution. For example, 70 percent of survey respondents in the Impact Justice study reported breaking the rules to obtain more or healthier food.[60] Scarcity of food increases incentives for theft from the kitchen or from other incarcerated people—both of which would be considered a violation of facility rules.[61] In this way, food-borne punishment is not an isolated experience, but rather a recurring hardship that exacerbates negative outcomes for incarcerated people.

Legal Architecture Governing Food-borne Punishment

Carceral spaces—both literally and legally—are fenced off fiefdoms omitted or excluded from standard rules and laws.[62] The primary mechanism for addressing the harmful conditions of confinement, including food, is litigation alleging violations of the U.S. Constitution.[63] However, these claims rarely succeed because of the deference courts extend to carceral decisions.

Courts have generally placed only two limitations on the potential use of food as punishment. First, carceral spaces cannot deprive people of food[64] and must provide adequate nutrition for people in custody (including caloric intake).[65] What constitutes "adequate nutrition," however, is often not defined. A recent report by a prison monitoring agency, the Correctional Association of New York, highlighted how state rules require meals to be nutritionally adequate, but simultaneously "[do] not set minimum standards for caloric intake, or reference national nutritional standards, like the federal Dietary Guidelines for Americans."[66]

Moreover, this narrow limitation still allows prison and jail decision makers broad discretion on the content and delivery of food to a captive population. Adequate nutrition does not necessarily mean that a meal must be appetizing. Thus, in most cases, courts have held that nutraloaf—because it contains adequate nutritional elements—is not a "cruel and unusual" punishment.[67] Similarly, as "coffee is not a necessity of life," courts have found that deprivation of coffee is not a constitutional violation.[68] Courts have likewise deferred to prison decisions on access to meals. For example, a court affirmed a prison's decision to stop serving hot meals for nine consecutive days, serving only cold sandwiches during an extended lockdown.[69] Courts have also upheld "reasonable conditions" on the receipt of food, such as requiring the prisoner to clean his cell or to stand or kneel in the middle of their cell to receive a meal.[70] Lower courts, meanwhile, have decided that the Constitution doesn't guarantee a person's access to the prison commissary to purchase supplemental food.[71]

The second limitation protecting incarcerated people's access to food is related to that person's medical or religious needs. Prisons and jails must provide meals that are consistent with an incarcerated person's medical condition.[72] Medical needs could include a low-sodium diet based on a diagnosed medical condition such as hypertension, or a nut-free meal if the person has a significant allergy to peanuts, for example. For religious needs, courts have held that prisons and jails must accommodate a person's request for a special diet when it is based on a sincerely held religious belief.[73] However, this doesn't mean that the prison must supply the meal that is requested. Instead, prison administrators can still choose the way they accommodate the religious belief. For example, prisons are not required to provide incarcerated Muslims with meals that contain Halal-certified meats but instead may choose to provide a vegetarian meal (which does not violate the Halal requirements).[74] However, prisons may not shirk their responsibility to provide religiously compliant meals by making those meals available for purchase from the prison commissary.[75]

This meager constitutional protection guaranteeing calories and medical or religious compatibility—instead of protecting against food as punishment—leads to predictable consequences. A federal court found that serving a maggot-infested meal, after which emergency medical treatment was required for the incarcerated plaintiff, did not violate the U.S. Constitution.[76] Another court upheld a prison policy that required people to kneel and face the wall with their hands behind their backs to receive their meal.[77] In addition, claims about the long-term health impacts of carceral food are difficult to prove as a matter of causation and constitutional law. To win a claim of "cruel and unusual" punishment, an incarcerated plaintiff must show a sufficiently serious injury or deprivation and provide evidence that a prison official was "deliberately indifferent" to their health, i.e., showed a conscious disregard of a substantial risk.[78]

Carceral food policies are also not consistent with generally applicable food safety rules and policies. For example, in federal prisons, the *Food Service Manual*, which details the policies and procedures for prison food operations, does not require sick leave for incarcerated kitchen workers.[79] This conflicts with food safety best practices articulated by the Centers for Disease Control.[80] Moreover, the enforcement of generally applicable federal and state regulations on food safety is lacking in carceral spaces.[81] In some cases, as in South Carolina, a satisfactory health inspection rating stands in stark contrast to videos showing maggot-infested food.[82] Thus, incarcerated people ultimately have little protection—constitutional or regulatory—against food-borne punishment.

Reimagining Food

Food is a central part of our shared humanity, reflecting our values, culture, and history.[83] It is essential to sustaining life, but also to a sense of personhood. What would it look like to explicitly recognize and disrupt the myriad and compounding ways that food becomes punishment in carceral spaces? An initial step would be to enact laws that recognize that food should not be intentionally used as punishment. In Washington, for example, the administrative code provides that disciplinary sanctions shall not include "lowering the quantity or nutritional value of food."[84] Similarly, Nebraska state law prohibits disciplinary restrictions on an incarcerated person's diet.[85]

To truly sever food from its potential as a form of punishment, we need to rethink incarceration and carceral spaces entirely. We could increase the independence and ability of people in prisons and jails to prepare food for themselves and others. This means access to food preparation spaces and tools; access to vendors for healthy food; and education about nutrition and food safety. Though this may sound impossible, men in one Pennsylvania prison currently share access with others to a communal kitchen as part of a broader pilot project to improve prison safety and wellbeing.[86]

Carceral spaces could also explicitly include incarcerated individuals on planning committees for facility food service, including menu review, evaluations, and inspections. As recipients of the food, incarcerated people are best positioned to offer meaningful feedback on food operations in a prison or jail. They might advise on commissary selections and vendors or offer creative and participatory approaches. The hospice program at Louisiana State Penitentiary is but one of many examples of programs developed by incarcerated people that reaffirmed, rather than demeaned, their shared humanity.[87]

Prisons and jails also lack consistent transparency and meaningful oversight. One mechanism to increase both transparency and oversight would be to explicitly empower state agencies to administer their respective mandates inside of carceral spaces. Carceral agencies are not trained experts in food nutrition or dietary guidelines, but health departments are. Instead of forcing carceral spaces to assume duties and knowledge of other fields, local and state health departments could (and should) take primary responsibility for standards and for evaluating food operations in carceral spaces. States and municipalities could require that periodic health, sanitation, and safety inspections be conducted by non-carceral agencies, instead of being performed in-house. Like some public schools, prisons and jails could also be required to publicly share their monthly menus, food service budgets, and contracts with food service providers.

To detain a person behind bars requires an order from a judge. Those orders never include the types of food-related punishments and consequences detailed in this chapter. And for good reason. For people detained pre-trial, there has not yet been a determination of their guilt or innocence, so punishment of any sort would be wrong. If convicted, the punishment imposed is measured in time away from a person's family and community, not in the increased probability of chronic disease, pounds gained or lost, degrees of labor coercion, or even death. These extra-judicial punishments through food occur in secret, hidden by law, and enabled by our failures to hold prisons accountable. Ending food-borne punishment requires recognizing the humanity of people behind bars through disrupting and re-envisioning both the literal and legal architecture of carceral spaces.

1
Courtney King, "Butler County sheriff defends serving the 'warden burger' to inmates," Fox 19 News, WXIX, June 14, 2023, https://www.fox19.com/2023/06/15/butler-county-sheriff-defends-serving-special-burger-inmates-this-is-jail/, accessed January 6, 2025.

2
Many thanks to Lily McLemore for her invaluable research assistance. The author also thanks Alejandro Medina, Andru Okun, and Caroline Raymond for their assistance in the drafting of this chapter, as well as Victoria Bergbauer and Basile Baudez for their support and leadership in the Carceral Architecture project at Princeton University.

3
Aaron Littman, "Free-World Law Behind Bars," *The Yale Law Journal* 131, no. 5 (March 2022): 1390.

4
Sharon Dolovich, “State Punishment and Private Prisons,” *Duke Law Journal* 55, no. 3 (December 2005): 437–546 (discussing the ACA accreditation process); Ira P. Robbins, “Managed Health Care in Prisons as Cruel and Unusual Punishment,” *Northwestern Journal of Criminal Law and Criminology* 90, no. 1 (1999): 204 (discussing NCCHC accreditation).

5
Bell v. Wolfish, 441 U.S. 520, 534 (1979) (applying the Due Process Clause of the Fifth Am.).

6
U.S. Const. amend. VIII.

7
Turner v. Safley, 482 U.S. 78 (1987) (establishing deferential test for prison rules); Hudson v. Palmer, 468 U.S. 517 (limiting application of the Fourth Amendment prohibition on unreasonable searches and seizures in prisons) (1984); Beard v. Banks, 548 U.S. 521, 527 (2006) (limiting applicability of First Amendment to government censoring reading material in prisons for people in solitary confinement).

8
King, “Butler County sheriff defends serving the ‘warden burger’ to inmates.”

9
Eliza Barclay, “Food as Punishment: Giving U.S. Inmates ‘The Loaf’ Persists, Morning Edition,” NPR, January 2, 2014, https://www.npr.org/sections/thesalt/2014/01/02/256605441/punishing-inmates-with-the-loaf-persists-in-the-u-s, accessed January 6, 2025.

10
Jackie Cuellar, “Note: Gruel and Unusual: Prison Punishment Diets and the Eighth Amendment,” *Minnesota Law Review* 107 (November 21, 2022): 475–476 (describing a complaint filed in federal court challenging the death of Terrill Thomas, who lost 34 pounds and ultimately died of dehydration in a Milwaukee County jail.)

11
Cuellar, “Note: Gruel and Unusual.”

12
Cuellar, “Note: Gruel and Unusual”; see also King, “Butler County sheriff defends serving the ‘warden burger’ to inmates.”

13
U.S. Department of Agriculture and U.S. Department of Health and Human Services, “Dietary Guidelines for Americans, 2020–2025,” 9th Edition, December 2020, https://www.dietaryguidelines.gov/sites/default/files/2020-12/Dietary_Guidelines_for_Americans_2020-2025.pdf (hereinafter Dietary Guidelines), accessed January 6, 2025.

14
“Adequacy of Healthcare Provided in Louisiana State Prisons, Study Brief: House Concurrent Resolution 91 (2020),” May 2021.

15
“Adequacy of Healthcare Provided in Louisiana State Prisons, Study Brief”; Brown v. Plata, 563 U.S. 493, 510 (2011) (noting “[p]risoners are dependent on the State for food, clothing, and necessary medical care” in affirming lower court findings and remedial orders to improve healthcare in California state prisons).

16
Daily Picayune, “From the Old Prison to the New Jail,” January 18, 1895.

17
Compare Novak v. Beto, 453 F.2d 661, 670 (5th Cir. 1971) (upholding Texas prison policy of bread and water diet for people in solitary confinement with a full meal every three days) with Cunningham v. Jones, 567 F.2d 653, 657 (6th Cir. 1977) (holding a diet of bread and water violates “evolving standards of decency” and is therefore unconstitutional under the Eighth Amendment).

18
Jimmy Jenkins, "Blood, Cockroaches And 'Gigantic' Rats: Inspection Reports Reveal Filthy Conditions In Arizona Prison Kitchens," KJZZ, May 16, 2021, https://www.kjzz.org/2021-05-17/content-1683207-blood-cockroaches-and-gigantic-rats-inspection-reports-reveal-filthy-conditions, accessed January 6, 2025.

19
Jenkins, "Blood, Cockroaches And 'Gigantic' Rats."

20
Leslie Soble, Kathryn Stroud, and Marika Weinstein, "Eating Behind Bars: Ending the Hidden Punishment of Food in Prison," Impact Justice, 2020, 24 (hereinafter Impact Justice) https://impactjustice.org/wp-content/uploads/IJ-Eating-Behind-Bars.pdf, accessed January 6, 2025.

21
Soble, "Eating Behind Bars," 25.

22
Mariel A. Marlow, et al., "Foodborne Disease Outbreaks in Correctional Institutions: United States, 1998–2014," *American Journal of Public Health* 107, no. 7 (2017): 1150.

23
Marlow, "Foodborne Disease Outbreaks in Correctional Institutions: United States," 1150.

24
Marlow, "Foodborne Disease Outbreaks in Correctional Institutions: United States," 1150.

25
U.S. Department of Agriculture, "Dietary Guidelines," 3.

26
U.S. Department of Agriculture, "Dietary Guidelines," 6.

27
U.S. Department of Agriculture, "Dietary Guidelines," 95.

28
Ibid.

29
Laura M. Maruschak and Jennifer Bronson, "Medical Problems Reported by Prisoners," U.S. Department of Justice, *Bureau of Justice Statistics*, June 2021, 5, Table 3, https://bjs.ojp.gov/sites/g/files/xyckuh236/files/media/document/mprpspi16st.pdf, accessed January 6, 2025.

30
Maruschak, "Medical Problems Reported by Prisoners," 5, Table 3.

31
U.S. Department of Agriculture, "Dietary Guidelines," 102.

32
Michael Massoglia and William Alex Pridemore, "Incarceration and Health," *Annual Review of Sociology* 41 (August 2015): 295.

33
Mark T. Berg, Ethan M. Rogers, Kendall Riley, et al., "Incarceration Exposure and Epigenetic Aging in Neighborhood Context," *Social Science & Medicine* 310 (2022), https://www.sciencedirect.com/science/article/abs/pii/S0277953622005792, accessed January 6, 2025.

34
U.S. Department of Agriculture, "Dietary Guidelines," 102.

35
Soble, Stroud, and Weinstein, "Eating Behind Bars."

36
Hungry and Malnourished in Prison: Food Service in the Pennsylvania Department of Corrections, 11 (Pennsylvania Prison Society, 2024).

37
See, for e.g., Evelyn Patterson, "The Dose–Response of Time Served in Prison on Mortality: New York State, 1989–2003," *American Journal of Public Health* 103, no. 3 (March 2013): 523 (estimating a two-year decline in life expectancy for each year of incarceration).

38
Hungry and Malnourished, 8.

39
Hungry and Malnourished, 9.

40
Alysia Santo and Lisa Iabon, "What's in a Prison Meal?", The Marshall Project, July 15, 2015, https://www.themarshallproject.org/2015/07/07/what-s-in-a-prison-meal, accessed January 6, 2025; see also Steve Visser, "Gordon County Inmates Underfed, Human Rights Group Alleges," *Atlanta Journal-Constitution,* October 29, 2014.

41
Cooper v. Sheriff, Lubbock Cnty., Tex., 929 F.2d 1078, 1083 (5th Cir. 1991).

42
U.S. Const. amend. XIII ("Neither slavery nor involuntary servitude, except as a punishment for crime whereof the party shall have been duly convicted, shall exist within the United States, or any place subject to their jurisdiction").

43
Andrea Armstrong, "Unconvicted Incarcerated Labor," *Harvard Civil Rights-Liberties Law Review* 57 (2022).

44
See, for e.g., Ford v. Nassau Cnty. Exec., 41 F. Supp. 2d 392, 395 (E.D.N.Y. 1999).

45
See Carla J. Simmons, "Food Insecurity in Prison Makes People Like Me Vulnerable to Labor Exploitation, Truth Out," January 17, 2024, https://truthout.org/articles/food-insecurity-in-prison-makes-people-like-me-vulnerable-to-labor-exploitation/, accessed January 6, 2025; see also Lauren Lee White, "The California Jail where Women say Guards and Medics Preyed on them," *The Guardian*, May 2, 2019, https://www.theguardian.com/lifeandstyle/2019/may/02/california-prison-women-say-they-are-preyed-on-by-guards-and-staff, accessed January 6, 2025.

46
See, for e.g., Stephens v. Johnson, 83 F.3d 198, 200–01 (8th Cir. 1996) (holding that failure to provide "safety equipment such as hard hats, protective eyewear, back braces, and steel-toed boots" did not violate the U.S. Constitution.).

47
See, for e.g., Buckley v. Barbour Cnty., 624 F. Supp. 2d 1335, 1341 (M.D. Ala. 2008) (incarcerated plaintiff claimed failure to train him in use of equipment to clear trees led to him becoming a paraplegic).

48
OSHA Instruction FAP-01-00-002 (Department of Labor, April 1995), https://www.osha.gov/enforcement/directives/fap-01-00-002, accessed January 6, 2025. (When federally incarcerated workers "perform work similar to that outside of prisons," then the labor protections "should apply.")

49
See, for e.g., Jones v. North Carolina Prisoners' Lab. Union, Inc., 433 U.S. 119 (1977) (upholding prison punishments for circulating a petition).

50
Jordan Carlee Purdum, "Inmate Populations in a Disaster: A Labor Force, a Vulnerable Population, and a Hazard," 37 (master's thesis, LSU, December 2016) 37 (currently on file with author).

51
Purdum, "Inmate Populations in a Disaster," 4; Steven Raher, *A Deeper Look at Prison Commissaries* (Prison Policy Initiative May 2018), https://www.prisonpolicy.org/reports/commissary.html, accessed January 6, 2025.

52
Hungry and Malnourished, 4.

53
Hungry and Malnourished, 4.

54
Kaitlin Durbin, "Cuyahoga County jail's new commissary provider raises prices as sister company's meal services decline," Cleveland, June 4, 2023, https://www.cleveland.com/news/2023/06/cuyahoga-county-jails-new-commissary-provider-raises-prices-as-sister-companys-meal-services-decline.html, accessed January 6, 2025; more generally, see Michael McKirgan,

"Under-Regulation in the State Prison Food System: Consequences and a Proposal for Change," *Journal of Food Law and Policy* 9, no. 2 (2013): 275, 278–281 (discussing issues stemming from state contracts with Aramark, a private food contractor).

55
Alexandra Arriaga, "Why Inflation Price Hikes Are Even Worse Behind Bars," The Marshall Project, May 2, 2023, https://www.themarshallproject.org/2023/05/02/why-inflation-price-hikes-are-even-worse-behind-bars (detailing analysis of commissary price lists from twenty-six different states), accessed January 6, 2025.

56
Wendy Sawyer, "How Much do Incarcerated People Earn in Each State?", Prison Policy Initiative, April 10, 2017, https://www.prisonpolicy.org/blog/2017/04/10/wages/, accessed January 6, 2025.

57
Soble, "Eating Behind Bars," 61.

58
Soble, "Eating Behind Bars," 10–11.

59
Michael Capers, "How the Prison Food System Denies People Healthy Choices," The Appeal, July 5, 2022, https://theappeal.org/prison-food-system-health/, accessed January 6, 2025.

60
Soble, "Eating Behind Bars," 33.

61
Simmons, "Food Insecurity in Prison Makes People Like Me Vulnerable to Labor Exploitation."

62
See, for e.g., Andrea Armstrong, "No Prisoner Left Behind: Enhancing Transparency of Penal Institutions," *Stanford Law and Policy Review* 25 (2014): 435; see also Littman, "Free-World Law Behind Bars," 1385.

63
For people serving convictions, plaintiffs allege violations of the Eighth Amendment of the U.S. Constitution, which prohibits "cruel and unusual" punishments. For people civilly detained or detained pre-trial, plaintiffs allege violation of the Due Process Clauses of either the Fifth Amendment (federal actor) or Fourteenth Amendment (state actor) of the U.S. Constitution. See Margo Schlanger, "The Constitutional Law of Incarceration, Reconfigured," *Cornell Law Review* 103 (January 2018): 357 (discussing doctrinal differences and changes following the U.S. Supreme Court's decision in Kingsley v. Hendrickson).

64
See Brown v. Plata, 563 U.S. 493, 510–11 (2011) (analogizing providing adequate healthcare to providing food and other forms of sustenance where deprivation can produce "physical torture" that would violate the Constitution); see also Reed v. McBride, 178 F. 3d 849, 853 (7th Cir. 1999) (deprivation may violate the Constitution depending on the "amount and duration" of deprivation).

65
See, for e.g., Johnson v. Gummerson, 198 F.3d 233 (2d Cir. 1999) (Restricted diet, consisting of a "food loaf" for seven days, was not an Eighth Amendment violation without an allegation that the restricted diet was nutritionally inadequate or otherwise posed a threat to plaintiff-appellant's physical wellbeing).

66
Food and Nutrition in New York State Correctional Facilities, 10 (Correctional Association of New York, 2024), https://static1.squarespace.com/static/62f1552c1dd65741c53bbcf8/t/674519bd594da52685b924a7/1732581833039/CANY_Food+and+Nutrition+in+NY_Nov2024.pdf, accessed January 6, 2025.

67
See, for e.g., Johnson v. Gummerson, 198 F.3d 233 (2d Cir. 1999), but see Prude v. Clarke, 675 F.3d 732 (7th Cir. 2012) ("[d] eliberate withholding of nutritious food or substitution of tainted or otherwise sickening food, with the effect of causing substantial weight loss, vomiting, stomach pains, and maybe an anal fissure ... or other severe hardship, would violate the Eighth Amendment").

68
Day v. Samuels, no. CIV.A. 07-4131 NLH, 2007 WL 2990670, at *4 (D.N.J. October 5, 2007).

69
Rust v. Grammer, 858 F.2d 411, 414 (8th Cir. 1988).

70
See, for e.g., Freeman v. Berge, 441 F.3d 543 (7th Cir. 2006); Talib v. Gilley, 138 F.3d 211 (5th Cir. 1998).

71
See, for e.g., Tokar v. Armontrout, 97 F.3d 1078, 1083 (8th Cir. 1996) (noting "we note that we know of no constitutional right of access to a prison gift or snack shop").

72
See, for e.g., Taylor v. Anderson, 868 F.Supp. 1024 (N.D. Ill. 1994) (allowing civil rights litigation to proceed alleging failure to provide a medically compliant meal for his diabetes condition).

73
See, for e.g., Dehart v. Horn, 227 F.3d 47 (3rd Cir. 2000). This constitutional right is further supported by federally enacted law, the Religious Land Use and Institutionalized Persons Act. 42 U.S.C. §§ 2000cc-1 et seq. (2006).

74
Williams v. Morton, 343 F.3d 212 (3rd Cir. 2006).

75
Pendleton v. Jividen, 96 F.4th 652 (4th Cir. 2024) (holding under Religious Land Use and Institutionalized Persons Act, or RLUIPA, the government cannot force an incarcerated person to choose between a government-provided benefit and the individual's religious convictions).

76
Islam v. Jackson, 782 F. Supp. 1111, 1115 (E.D. Va. 1992).

77
Talib v. Gilley, 138 F.3d 211, 215 (5th Cir. 1998) (abrogated on other grounds by Garrett v. Lumpkin, 96 F.4th 896, 901 (5th Cir. 2024).

78
Wilson v. Seiter, 501 U.S. 294, 298 (1991); Farmer v. Brennan, *511* U.S. 825, 839 (1994).

79
Amanda Chan and Anna Nathanson, "Not for Human Consumption: Prison Food's Absent Regulatory Regime," *William & Mary Bill of Rights Journal* 29, no. 4 (May 2021): 1009, 1028.

80
Chan, "Not for Human Consumption," 1028.

81
Littman, "Free-World Law Behind Bars," 1400–1.

82
Soble, "Eating Behind Bars," 94.

83
See Andrea Freeman, *Ruin their Crops to the Ground: The Politics of Food in the United States, from the Trail of Tears to School Lunch* (Metropolitan Books, 2024).

84
Wa. Admin Code 137-28-370, accessed January 6, 2025.

85
Neb. Rev. St. § 83–4,114 (1).

86
Scandinavian Prison Project, https://www.scandinavianprison-project.com, accessed December 7, 2024. This inclusion isn't intended to fetishize Scandinavian prisons; a prison is still a prison, which is also a site of involuntary and continuous control over another person's body.

87
Katherine Cloyes, Susan J. Rosenkranz, Katherine P. Supiano, et al., "Caring to Learn and Learning to Care," *Journal of Correctional Health Care*, 2017, https://pmc.ncbi.nlm.nih.gov/articles/PMC5484572/, accessed January 6, 2025.

Elizabeth Austin, Tommaso Bardelli, Sam Johnson, Tammy Ortiz, and Ess Pokornowski

"A SANCTUARY FROM THE JAIL": COUNTERING CARCERAL LOGICS IN PRISON EDUCATIONAL SPACES[1]

On September 13, 1994, President Bill Clinton signed into law the Violent Crime Control and Law Enforcement Act, commonly known as the 1994 Crime Bill. The most far-reaching piece of criminal justice legislation Congress ever passed, the bill incentivized states to pass harsher sentencing laws and build more prisons.[2] Among a slate of punitive and "tough on crime" measures, the Bill also eliminated access to federal Pell Grant funding for incarcerated students. The effect on higher education in prison was swift. In the early 1990s, there were an estimated 772 college programs operating in 1,287 correctional facilities, but by 1997 only eight such programs remained.[3] As both federal and state financial aid funding dried up, the few programs that survived did so primarily by relying on private donation and philanthropy.

Despite overwhelming evidence about the benefits of attending college in prison for incarcerated people, their communities, and society as a whole, it took Congress almost thirty years to fully reverse the policy.[4] After extending federal financial aid to approximately 40,000 incarcerated students under the Second Chance Pell Experiment starting in 2015, Pell Grant funding was reinstated for all eligible incarcerated people on July 1, 2023. According to the Department of Education's estimates, 800,000 people could now be eligible to receive federal financial aid and tuition assistance to attend college in prison.[5]

The reinstatement of Pell Grant funding has also initiated a sector-wide re-examination of how higher education in prison is provided and how its impact and success are measured. Revised regulations note that academic services inside must be "comparable" to those provided outside prison walls, but it is left up to the oversight entities (primarily departments of correction) to decide what exactly "comparable" might mean. This begs a simple question with no simple answers: what might equitable education look like inside a prison? Research has already begun to interrogate what equity might look like in terms of instructional delivery and practices, and technological access and use.[6] Drawing on qualitative interviews with formerly incarcerated students and prison education program staff, as well as site visits conducted in six correctional facilities, this chapter follows a third line of inquiry: how do spatial, architectural, and design features impact the experience of studying and learning inside prison, and what does equity mean in this context?

While a growing body of research explores barriers such as lack of access to technology and conflicts with correctional staff, little is known about the educational effects of the built environment in prisons. Yet, the physical infrastructure of the prison impacts every aspect of higher education in carceral settings. As one of our participants said: "Every conversation we have with corrections starts with space." Negotiating availability and competition over classroom space, however, is just the beginning. Once classroom space is secured, students, and instructors still need to navigate an infrastructure—from physical facilities to furniture and equipment—that is not designed with learning and education in mind.

Some of the challenges incarcerated students experience are not different in nature from the ones faced by their peers in the most dilapidated corners of the American public education system.[7] Students and instructors involved in prison education programs told us about malfunctioning HVAC units, rusty water leaking from a ceiling, and poor ventilation inside their classrooms. After teaching for decades in public high-schools and community colleges across New York State, a faculty member told us the conditions he witnessed in his first prison classroom at Groveland Correctional Facility didn't feel shocking to him: "it just felt like another college classroom."

Aging infrastructure and outdated equipment aside, however, carceral settings have little in common with even the most underfunded and neglected higher education facilities on the outside.[8] The design and aesthetics of the prison, Yvonne Jewkes notes, are deeply infused by an "architecture of harm."[9] "Hard architecture"–from thick bars and bare concrete walls to hard-surface floors and metal furniture–Jewkes explains, is meant to enhance security but also to dehumanize the incarcerated, destroying their self-esteem and influencing the ways in which staff think of, and behave toward, people in their custody. Similarly, Karen Morin argues that the layout and architectural design of carceral spaces, and the modes of social control that go along with them, result in higher levels of stress, fear, and violence.[10]

This built environment poses unique challenges to both students and instructors. First, these spaces feature a laundry list of design and environmental elements that are proven to negatively impact learning, including overcrowded classrooms, persistent and loud noise, poor lighting and temperature control, and issues with air quality and circulation. Put simply: the environmental conditions prevalent in correctional settings often do not align with, and at times directly contradict, learning and educational best practices.[11] As importantly, the punitive and dehumanizing nature of the carceral built environment clashes with the primary purpose of higher education: not only providing knowledge and building skills, but nurturing independent and critical thinkers, able to question established assumptions and dogmas.

This chapter explores how students and their instructors experience prison educational spaces. We show how factors such as classroom layout and uncomfortable furniture impact the ability of incarcerated students to focus and assimilate new information. Beyond that, we argue, the prison's built environment undermines their identity as college students. Despite these limitations, many of our participants still saw their classrooms, libraries, and other educational settings as spaces where punitive and debilitative regimes of control gave way, at least partially and temporarily, to rehabilitative and de-carceral experiences. Building on these findings, the last part of the chapter advances actionable strategies to integrate educational best practices in the (re)design of these spaces. Ultimately, we propose that architects and designers working in the correctional education field should not only foster better learning experiences for incarcerated students but must aim to shift the balance from punishment toward rehabilitation in carceral settings.

Data and Methods

This chapter is based on twenty-five semi-structured interviews we conducted between February and November 2023 with formerly incarcerated people who attended college-in-prison classes, faculty and staff members involved in prison education programs, and department of corrections officials. It also draws on focus groups and ethnographic observations conducted by two of the authors (Tammy and Sam) while visiting educational spaces in six different facilities across Maine, Kansas, and North Carolina, during the summer and fall of 2024.

All interviews were conducted remotely, lasted between forty-five and sixty minutes, and were audio recorded. Formerly incarcerated students were paid $50 as compensation for their time, and as a token of appreciation for sharing their experiences and insights with us. All audio recordings from in-depth interviews and focus groups were transcribed and analyzed using qualitative thematic analysis procedures, in which coding and sub-coding categories are derived iteratively from the data.

Studying and Learning in Carceral Spaces

All of our interviewees emphasized the importance of educational spaces in their experiences as students or faculty inside prison. Students described the impact that the classrooms' size and design, the quality of artificial lighting, and the presence or absence of study spaces such as libraries and computer labs, among other factors, had on their ability to focus and learn while incarcerated. Faculty and staff's observations largely mirrored those of their students. They offered their perspectives on the impact many of these same factors had on their pedagogical style and efficacy, while also describing the often-complex negotiations they had to make with the department of corrections for space allocation and access. The following sections document their experiences, starting with the barriers they faced even getting to their classrooms and other study spaces, and concluding with proposals inspired by our participants' aspirations and thoughts on how to improve educational spaces inside the prison.

In addition to documenting how spatial factors hindered their ability to teach and learn inside the prison, many participants also pointed out the meanings that these spaces conveyed to them. The uncomfortable and mismatched furniture, or the lack of decoration and poor acoustics of most prison classrooms, for instance, were not just an inconvenience: they said something about how the prison system saw them. At every turn, the brutal—or, at times, just dull—design of educational spaces reminded them of their status as inmates, rather than students.

Getting to Class

When asked about their experiences with educational spaces in prison, most of the students we interviewed started by telling us about their journeys to the classroom. We learned that the way incarcerated students experienced educational spaces didn't just depend on factors such as classroom size and furniture, the quality of acoustics, or the presence of windows and natural light—it was also shaped by the barriers they faced in attempting to access these spaces. After all, even the best designed class is not worth much if you cannot get there.

Some of the barriers students faced had to do with the classroom location, or with other physical features of the prison. In some cases, classrooms were not accessible for people who had a disability, were elderly, or just had a hard time covering long distances by foot due to injury, resulting in students dropping off or deciding not to attend college.[12] Bryan[13], for instance, who served his sentence in Ohio, recounted having to walk almost twenty minutes through several dorms and yards, and with no cover from weather, to attend classes at Marion Technical College in his facility. When classrooms were located on a different floor from people's living quarters, people told us, elevators were rarely available. Because of that, Ramesh, who earned two associate degrees while incarcerated for almost twenty years in Texas, said that there was an unspoken rule in one of the facilities where he attended college: if you were a wheelchair user or walked with crutches, you were not going to be eligible for college.

At Greene Correctional Facility, a medium-security prison in New York's Hudson Valley, people who want to attend college face a different kind of accessibility problem, a staff member at the University of Rochester's Education Justice Initiative explained to us:

> The college program at Greene is on exactly the wrong side of the jail, the north side. Greene is intentionally divided into a south side and a north side… The north side is much more heavily policed. The rapid response units are located there, and it's known to be a place where, especially out of view of the cameras, assaults both peer-on-peer and officer-on-prisoner are much higher. So, people who live on the south side fear the north side, and many don't attend college because they don't want to go down there.

In addition to inaccessible and even dangerous locations and various architectural barriers, our interviewees also spoke of the myriad rules and regulations that restricted their ability to move inside the prison, often making their journey to class akin to an obstacle course. Bryan, for instance, reported that classes in his facility ended up being canceled quite frequently, at least once a week, due to lockdowns or security issues resulting in the closing down of one or the other section of the prison.

Even when lockdowns and other restrictions were not in place, some students had to go through multiple security checkpoints just to reach the educational wing in their prisons. At each one of them, a missing paper, or simply an unsympathetic correctional officer, could derail the entire journey, making them late, or even missing a class. Jason, who studied psychology and African American literature while incarcerated in New York, recounted what it was like having to jump through all those hoops, and manage fraught relationships with officers just to get to class:

> Some days, after having those experiences, you just get to class and you are done... . Some days I would just get pissed off and could not assimilate anything. And sometimes, just to avoid those same issues, we would try to [leave class] early, not to face some of those challenges.

For faculty, that meant accepting the fact that students would often trickle in at different times, or systematically miss parts of the lecture. Some experienced instructors told us how they adapted their pedagogy to those kinds of constraints, avoiding covering important material in the first half an hour of class time.

Despite the barriers most students faced on their way to class, a few still described those walks as a liberatory journey. Andrea, for instance, who was fourteen years old when he was first incarcerated in California, and earned both his GED and associate degree while in prison, recounted the liberatory feeling he experienced while walking to the classroom:

> Just going out there with our books and toward the classroom and thinking that we were actually college students. We were in a special place apart from the prison. It helped me, and I know other people [felt the same], it made us feel like we left the prison.

Feeling Like a Student

Once people finally reached their classrooms, they found physical spaces that, at least in most cases, had not been designed and configured with education in mind. As one faculty member said, "security is their priority, and if they have to eliminate education for security, they will do that." This securitarian mindset, coupled with the systematic lack of resources for educational programming in most prison systems, made for classroom spaces that are poorly equipped—and occasionally utterly inadequate—for teaching and learning.

Lack of space and small classroom sizes, uncomfortable furniture and seating arrangements, and environmental factors, such as excessive heat or poor lighting, were some of the features most often mentioned by our participants when describing their college classrooms inside prison. Some prison education programs had to share space with other educational programming, making for a cramped and chaotic environment. Bryan, for instance, said that the higher ed program at his Ohio facility was holding classes in the computer lab, even though they could not actually use the computers, because that was the only space that had been assigned to the program. At the beginning of the semester the same room would also double up as library and storage for college textbooks, so students would keep coming in and out during the session to pick up coursework material. In the facility where he was housed in Nebraska, Bruce said, the prison education program—offered by the Metropolitan Community College of Omaha—had to hold multiple classes in a single open space, with only a bookshelf dividing the two "classrooms."

Many interviewees, both students and faculty, mentioned seating and furniture arrangements as another obstacle to learning and focusing inside the classroom. One student said that furniture inside his classroom felt "random." One instructor with the Cornell Prison Education Program, reported having a similar reaction, and elaborated further:

> The chairs were all different heights, they were all different kinds of desks. It really was just like people threw a bunch of classroom supplies together into a room and then whatever you got was what you got.

In addition, classrooms typically featured fixed tables or desks and detachable chairs. Movable furniture, which could be rearranged to facilitate different teaching styles, like group setups for seminars, was rarer. Even when in use, some facilities had policies against such flexible arrangements, due to security concerns, which ended up overriding educational needs for different pedagogical and learning styles.

Environmental factors such as poor lighting, either too dim or too bright, the absence of windows, and malfunctioning temperature regulation systems were also often mentioned by both students and faculty we interviewed. Ramesh, for instance, described what it was like to take classes in the Texas summer, whenever the A/C system was out of service, which happened quite often:

> It was miserable. You had fans around the room, but when the temperature was in the upper 90s (°F), you're sitting there sweating and having a hard time to write.

Poor acoustics were also commonly brought up by our participants as another obstacle they had to contend with in their prison classrooms. Common prison architectural features, such as high ceilings or tiled concrete walls, caused sound reverberation and made for echoey classrooms. That noise was often exacerbated by malfunctioning or old HVAC systems, another staple of prison life. A Cornell faculty member, for instance, recounted having a hard time hearing his students when he taught at Five Points, in Upstate New York:

> We had this gigantic fan in the classroom that was in full blast, it was like the most rickety fan imaginable, and we really had to shout. Not literally shout, but really had to speak up in order to hear each other. Got drowned out quite a bit. We couldn't watch movies because the TV wouldn't go up loud enough to trump the sound of the fan. I remember that being a frustrating experience.

All of this—the lack of space, the haphazard classroom setups, the malfunctioning HVAC and poor acoustics—inevitably hinders students' learning experiences. Several faculty members, for instance, noticed that the badly designed chairs and desks commonly found in prison classrooms didn't just make students less comfortable, but directly impacted their ability to focus and absorb information over long periods of time. Similarly, when classrooms were too hot, students reported feeling exhausted, lacking energy and motivation to learn.

Beyond hindering learning, subpar and poorly equipped educational spaces sent a clear message to incarcerated students, undervaluing their educational experience and constantly reminding them of their identity as "inmates." Yet, as many of our participants explained to us, leaving that identity behind, and learning to see oneself as a student first was a crucial part of pursuing higher education. Educational spaces—including their design, organization, and small details such as wall decor—can support that difficult process of personal transformation, or they can reinforce carceral logics of dehumanization and oppression. Bryan, for instance, still remembered the difference that it made for him when Marion Technical College was assigned more spacious and better maintained classrooms: "[in those new spaces] I felt more like a participant, rather than an inmate." Similarly, some interviewees told us about how even minor details, like a college banner or an educational poster on the classroom walls, impacted their sense of the space. A faculty member for Columbia-Greene Community College, for instance, told us that even just adding some sticky notes with students' self-reflections on the classroom wall had completely changed the "feeling" of the space at the facility where the program operated in Upstate New York:

> I teach a first-year course, and it begins with an activity of reflection where people share their aspirations, their goals, their reasons for entering the college program. And so, these anonymous sticky notes with people's goals and aspirations are there on the wall outside the computer lab. And so many will say that the building has begun to feel like a campus building and a sanctuary from the jail in that respect.

Sometimes, what made a space feel like a "sanctuary" inside the prison—a space, like one of our participants put it, where one could finally "breathe" and "the walls came down"—was even more elusive. When comparing Attica and Groveland, two of the facilities in Upstate New York where the University of Rochester Education Justice Initiative offers college classes, a staff member couldn't really put his finger on what set Groveland apart, but the feeling was undeniable. Probably, he reasoned, "the fabric" of Groveland and the unique histories and cultures of the two facilities made Groveland a more welcoming place for higher education:

> Groveland was built out of a former Shaker colony that later was redesigned by the firm of Frederick Law Olmsted into a state epileptic asylum. It's a rather strange campus. We often tell first-time visitors that if you squint really hard it kind of looks like a Midwestern liberal arts college, with its old Victorian and Queen Anne-style buildings, lush rolling hillsides, flowers. It's a surreal space. The education building itself is a rather beautiful building. Inside it's been sort of stripped of all its charm, but the upper floor, the classrooms are actually quite good, with huge sort of picture windows, a sometimes-operational HVAC system. Attica is quite different. The rooms feel kind of cramped, they have no charm whatsoever, very bleak kind of institutional spaces with barred windows that look onto nothing… . Attica is a really sort of gruff and imposing place, seems like everyone there is performing a role. And so, traversing these spaces is a really cold experience. No one says hi, you walk through giant bays of COs who are all super muscular and could just crush me like an ant. I really feel like I am invading their space there. At Groveland, I feel more just like a program person who is showing up and is there to help make the facility more livable.

While institutional history and culture are impervious to change, in the next section we present actionable strategies for redesigning prison educational spaces. Our goal is to address the needs and aspirations voiced by the students and faculty we interviewed–to create spaces that foster educational outcomes and contribute to loosening, rather than extending, the grip of carceral logics on the lives of incarcerated learners.

Reimagining Educational Spaces

In our interviews with college-in-prison faculty and students, we asked participants about their views on what would make for an ideal educational space within prisons. This part of the chapter draws on their insights to advance actionable recommendations that aim to improve these spaces in U.S. prisons.

When talking about the challenges they faced, our participants highlighted both discrete improvements they would like to see, as well as broader aspirations for more humane educational spaces, fostering students' dignity and autonomy. As one student said, "[educational] spaces should make prison walls come down." The following sections invite designers to address both aspects of the experiences of incarcerated students—striving to create not just more effective learning environments, but "sanctuaries" where students can escape from carceral and punitive logics.

Designing within Constraints

When asked to imagine an ideal classroom inside the prison, many of our participants started by talking about environmental factors such as good lighting and optimal acoustics. They were right: a growing body of research on educational spaces in both K-12 and higher education contexts reveals that environmental factors can play a critical role in shaping students' outcomes and success.[14] In this section, we look at how class layout could be reimagined to optimize acoustics and allow proper sightlines, with the end goal of improving students' focus and engagement.

Drawing on existing research into educational spaces on the outside, the first two illustrations (p. 281) present a variety of layouts for small and medium-size classes that have been proven to work for both teachers

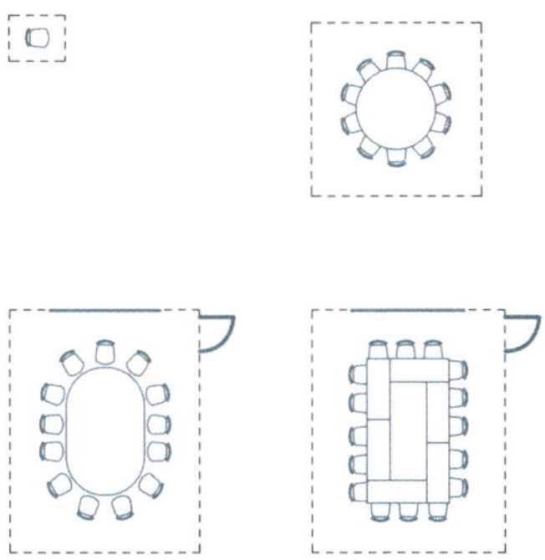

Standard layouts, small classes.

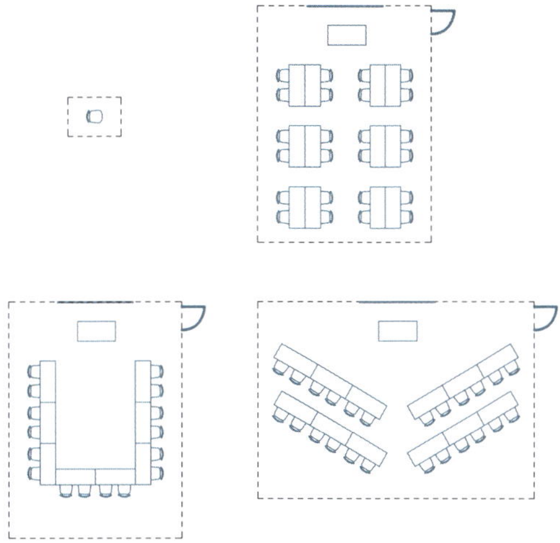

Standard layouts, medium classes.

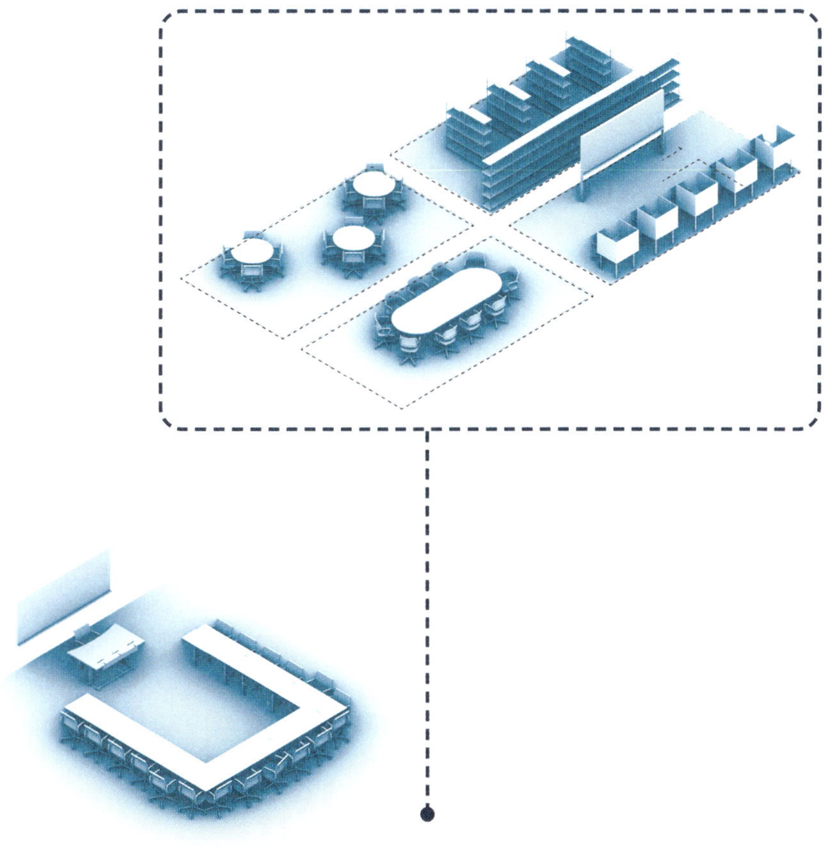

Application of standard layouts in non-typical spaces.
All illustrations by Elizabeth Austin, Tommaso Bardelli, Sam Johnson, Tammy Ortiz, and Ess Pokornowski, Ithaka S+R, Enneab Lab.

and students. In some cases, designers or even prison education program staff could simply use these models to propose more functional furniture arrangements inside existing classrooms. However, based on our interviews—as well as site visits conducted in Maine, Kansas, and North Carolina—we know that those layouts and dimensions are often not available within the existing infrastructure. The next illustration shows how these standards could be achieved under non-ideal conditions. Existing spaces, which are often not dimensionally consistent with these standards, can still be subdivided into ideal modules. This can be done, for instance, by converting part of the space into support uses, such as for storage or group breakout tables.

Creating New Learning Spaces

Nearly all our interviewees told us that their programs didn't simply need better educational spaces, they needed more of them. Faculty reported how their programs couldn't offer certain courses, or enroll more students, due to the lack of available classrooms. Students often complained about overcrowded classrooms, the almost complete absence of study spaces inside the prison, and how that affected their ability to learn. "It was hard for me to focus"—one student told us, talking about having to do all his studying in the dayroom—"with people arguing, screaming over the TV, and talking to their wives on the phone all around me." With hundreds of thousands of new incarcerated people becoming eligible to receive federal financial aid to attend college under the new Pell Grants regulations, the competition over scarce educational space is likely to further intensify.

As designers, this poses a thorny challenge: how to address this chronic shortage without further expanding the carceral infrastructure? When thinking about creating new educational spaces, we argue, designers should first look to carve out additional space inside existing prison structures, starting with housing units. The benefits of targeting these units as sites for conversion are numerous, from providing more seamless access to educational spaces for residents, to reducing staffing demands associated with prison education programs—an issue mentioned by several interviewees as another hurdle in scheduling classes and accessing spaces.

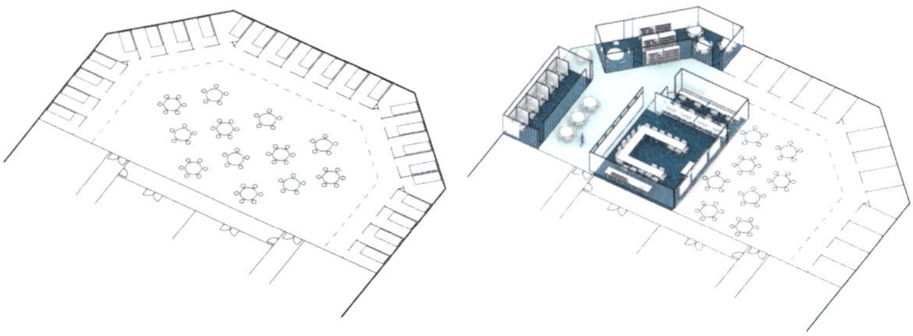

Left: Housing unit layout. Right: From housing to educational space.

Illustrations by Elizabeth Austin, Tommaso Bardelli, Sam Johnson, Tammy Ortiz, and Ess Pokornowski, Ithaka S+R, Enneab Lab.

Our conceptual plan, represented here, proposes the inclusion of both classroom and study spaces for groups and individuals inside an existing housing unit. Modifications such as the one presented here could be phased in as more space becomes available, with the eventual aim of converting an entire structure into educational space. Figure 5 shows some examples of how that could be achieved, by rethinking communal areas and converting unused cells into individual and group reading spaces.

Under some circumstances, however, this sort of spatial conversion might not be an option or may be insufficient to meet educational needs. If, for example, a college wishes to offer a major, such as life sciences or engineering, where the technical demands on the space would prove too great to implement within existing spaces, a new structure which meets mechanical requirements might be necessary. In these cases, proper safeguards need to be put in place to ensure the new educational spaces will not be repurposed in the future, inadvertently feeding the carceral infrastructure. Temporary structures like the one depicted here—which houses the college-in-prison program at Lansing Correctional Facility, in Kansas—help to mitigate that risk, especially if the educational program retains ownership of the new structure and can remove it if the program is discontinued.

Temporary structure for college-in-prison program at Lansing Correctional Facility, KS. Photograph by Sam Johnson, 2024.

Conclusion

At their best, educational spaces—including classrooms, libraries, and other learning spaces—play a pivotal role in amplifying the positive impact of attending higher education while incarcerated, from improving mental health to fostering better outcomes post-release. Effectively designed spaces integrate and adapt to the unique circumstances of the prison, supporting the implementation of best practices and learning habits that have been proven to work in educational spaces on the outside. As this chapter demonstrates, these positive educational and learning effects are mediated by the feelings and meanings that these spaces elicit in their primary users, namely incarcerated students.

In reimagining these spaces, thus, designers have a responsibility to not only address their technical shortcomings but to ensure they do not reproduce modes of carceral control, surveillance, and hierarchy. In the words of one of our participants, educational spaces should feel like "sanctuaries" inside the prison, spaces where autonomy and dignity are encouraged, rather than stifled. In this way, education-first spaces can signal a shift away from punitive ideologies and rebalance the tension between punishment and rehabilitation inside carceral facilities.

1
This study was made possible with funding from Ascendium Education Group, whom we thank for their support. Most importantly, a big thank you to the higher education in prison instructors, administrators, and students who spoke with us—your voices and experience make this work possible. We hope this chapter will be as useful to them as to the wider higher education in prison community. Thanks also to our collaborators on the project at Ennead Lab, Amy Mielke and Tinglan Guo.

2
Udi Ofer, "How the 1994 crime bill fed the mass incarceration crisis," *ACLU: News & Commentary*, June 4, 2019, https://www.aclu.org/news/smart-justice/how-1994-crime-bill-fed-mass-incarceration-crisis, accessed January 6, 2025.

3
Nathaniel J. Pallone, "Abolition of Pell Grants for higher education of prisoners: Examining antecedents and consequences," *Journal of Offender Rehabilitation* 39, no. 2 (2004): 73–85.

4
See Alexandra Gibbons and Rashawn Ray, "The societal benefits of postsecondary prison education," *The Brookings Institute*, 20 August 2021.

5
"U.S. Department of Education to launch application process to expand federal Pell Grant access for individuals who are confined or incarcerated," *Department of Education: Press Release*, June 30, 2023. https://www.ed.gov/about/news/press-release/us-department-of-education-to-launch-application-process-to-expand-federal-pell-grant-access-for-individuals-who-are-confined-or-incarcerated, accessed January 6, 2025.

6
Ithaka S+R has a robust body of work on these issues. For more see: Meagan Wilson, Rayane Alamuddin, and Danielle M. Cooper, "Unbarring access: A landscape review of postsecondary education in prison and its pedagogical supports," *Ithaka S+R: Research Report*. Last modified May 30, 2019, https://doi.org/10.18665/sr.311499, accessed January 6, 2025; Kurtis Tanaka and Danielle Cooper, "Advancing technological equity for incarcerated college students: Examining the opportunities and risks," *Ithaka S+R: Research Report*. Last modified May 7, 2020. https://doi.org/10.18665/sr.313202, accessed January 6, 2025; Ess Pokornowski and Kurtis Tanaka, "Between two systems: navigating censorship and self-censorship in higher education in prisons," *Ithaka S+R: Research Report*. Last modified April 3, 2024. https://doi.org/10.18665/sr.320526, accessed January 6, 2025;

Ess Pokornowski, “Technology in higher education in prison programs: A report on survey findings,” *Ithaka S+R: Research Report*, September 7, 2023, https://sr.ithaka.org/publications/technology-in-higher-education-in-prison-programs/, accessed January 6, 2025.

7
Victoria Jackson and Nicholas Johnson, “America’s School Infrastructure Needs a Major Investment of Federal Funds to Advance an Equitable Recovery,” *Center on Budget and Policy Priorities*, May 17, 2021, https://www.cbpp.org/research/state-budget-and-tax/americas-school-infrastructure-needs-a-major-investment-of-federal, accessed January 6, 2025.

8
That is not to say carceral logics play no role in the design of our educational infrastructure, especially K-12 grades. See: J. Schept, T. Wall, and A. Brisman, “Building, staffing, and insulating: An architecture of criminological complicity in the school-to-prison pipeline,” *Social Justice* 41, no. 4 (2014): 138.

9
Yvonne Jewkes, “Just design: Healthy prisons and the architecture of hope,” *Journal of Criminology* 51, no. 3 (2018).

10
Karen M. Morin, “The Late-Modern American Jail: Epistemologies of Space and Violence,” *The Geographical Journal* 182, no. 1 (2016): 38–48.

11
A large literature has documented the impact of spatial and environmental factors on both K-12 and post-secondary education outside of prison. See: Mary C. Hill and Kathryn K. Epps, “The Impact of Physical Classroom Environment on Student Satisfaction and Student Evaluation of Teaching in the University Environment,” *Academy of Educational Leadership Journal* 14, no. 4 (2010): 65; Nurul Jannah Amirul, C. N. Ahmad, A. F. Yahya, M. F. N. L. Abdullah, N. M. Noh, and M. Adnan, “The Physical Classroom Learning Environment,” *Proceedings of the International Higher Education Teaching and Learning Conference* 2, no. 1 (2013): 1–9.

12
On the prevalence of disabilities in the U.S. prison population see Jennifer Bronson, Laura M. Maruschak, and Marcus Berzofsky. “Disabilities Among Prison and Jail Inmates, 2011–12.” U.S. Department of Justice, Office of Justice Programs, Bureau of Justice Statistics. Special Report. December 2015. https://bjs.ojp.gov/content/pub/pdf/dpji1112.pdf, accessed January 6, 2025. Individuals in prison, the report found, were nearly three times more likely and those in jails were nearly four times more likely to report having a disability than the general population. Further, more than half of those incarcerated in jails and prisons who reported having a disability also reported a co-occurring chronic condition.

13
All names have been changed in order to protect the privacy and safety of our research participants.

14
See, for instance: G. Marchand, N. Nardi, D. Reynolds, and S. Pamoukov, “The impact of the classroom built environment on student perceptions and learning,” *Journal of Environmental Psychology* 40 (December 2014): 187–197.

⁂

Victoria Bergbauer

CARE IN THE COUNTRYSIDE: REHABILITATING CHILDREN IN THE NINETEENTH CENTURY

Questions of care and space are connected. A development in the incarceration of children illustrates the entanglement between these two entities. In the middle of the nineteenth century, correctional facilities arose in the countryside across Europe. Children and adolescents were moved from prisons, located in the city, to these spaces of rural confinement. State officials, institutional administrators, and religious representatives promised that rural employment in prison was going to effectively prepare boys and girls for a life in freedom. The countryside was represented as a tool for achieving care and permanent rehabilitation. The removal of children from cities was articulated as a decision that was concerned with adolescents' futures. Put differently, it was a concept that materialized across borders: it was in the interest of their rehabilitation that "bad children" were removed from "bad cities," enabling them to be reintegrated through engagement with the surrounding landscape.

This development took shape through the transfer of already-existing institutions and the creation of new facilities. The following three spaces of confinement—Redhill for boys (Surrey, England), Val d'Yèvre for boys (Cher, France), and Asyl zu Kaiserswerth for girls (Düsseldorf, Germany)—provide a glimpse of this growing carceral project. From a reading of the location, design, and architecture of these establishments emerges a shared logic. Relocation to the countryside was made out to be an effective opportunity for correcting children both during *and* after their incarceration.

Redhill, England, 1848

The English institution of Redhill was originally founded in 1788 as The Philanthropic Society. Located in St. George's Fields (Southwark) in the south of London, the Society would receive the children of incarcerated parents, as well as children who themselves had been tried and incarcerated from 1793 onward.[1] By the middle of the century, those in charge of the institution changed their views about its correctional program.

Newspaper cutting. *The Illustrated London News*, Redhill, Surrey History Center, Woking, 2271/43/2, 1848. Public domain.

In 1848, at this point still located in the City of London, the administration decided on the purchase of rural land. Shortly thereafter, the project was finalized, and the construction of "a farm of 133 acres taken at Redstone in immediate vicinity of Redhill" began in the county of Surrey.[2] Instead of being enclosed by a city, nature was to frame the rehabilitation of the young boys sent to the Philanthropic Society, which, after its relocation, became known as Redhill. The transfer raised immediate interest in the press. *The Architect and Building*

Operative reported enthusiastically that architect William B. Moffatt was selected for the construction of four connected houses, all "designed in the old English farmhouse style, substantial and good in their proportion, but not ornate in character."[3]

Val d'Yèvre, France, 1844

A similar development took root in France, where rural institutions for imprisoned boys grew across the nation. Materializing the French Law of 1850, which encouraged the privatization of prisons for children and adolescents, such spaces were meant to grant a lasting correction through their removed location and to rehabilitate rather than solely punish individuals through the mobilization of rural life.[4]

Photograph. Colonie de Val d'Yèvre, Departmental Archives, Cher, 4F/11, date unknown. Public domain.

One such attempt at rehabilitation through the countryside was present at the Colonie de Val d'Yèvre, located 150 miles south of Paris in the Cher department. In 1844, Charles Lucas, Inspector General of Prisons, purchased parts of marshes from the Compagnie Générale de Desséchement. The facility, as Lucas termed it, started out as "a real camp of inmates, thrown into the countryside with no other measure than that of a discipline that had to be established ... just like its buildings, little by little, day by day."[5] It was the untouched ground in itself that laid the foundation for Lucas's project: the marshland became an integral part in the correction of the boys, who were forced to engage in fieldwork during their imprisonment there. The institution was less preoccupied with the need for drawing up firm separations between the place of confinement and the surrounding environments. Rather, the administration of Val d'Yèvre located its disciplinary program in the space per se, which was situated at a 7-kilometer distance from the next town, Bourges, and enabled rural employment.

Kaiserswerth, Germany, 1833

A similar conception of the countryside could motivate the relocation of girls, as emerges from the Protestant institution, Asyl zu Kaiserswerth. In 1833, pastor Theodor Fliedner opened the facility near Düsseldorf (Germany) for girls and women, who had been either released or transferred from imprisonment. Work, accommodation, as well as moral and religious guidance were meant to provide the necessary care to prevent recidivism and to help these individuals (re)find their place in society. In his calls for donations for an extension of his Asyl, Fliedner continued to stress the importance of the facility's space in this endeavor. To "the Christian friends of the institution," he considered the removed location, as well as elements like larger living and working rooms, separated sleeping cells, stables, sheds, and pigsties as effective instruments for a lasting correction.[6]

As the statutes stated, all girls were trained in tasks like knitting, sewing, cleaning, cooking, gardening, and caring for two cows.[7] Fliedner's reference to a cowshed makes the ties between space and care especially visible. Its presence, according to the institution's founder, could assure the employment of girls in rural tasks and, thus, qualify them for a safe future in the countryside. While the orientation of the cells toward the courtyard would avoid potentially dangerous contact between the confined population and their environment, the idea that their re-entry into the outside world could be secured through rural tasks had a twofold purpose. The implementation of spatial tools, like isolation or the construction of stables and sheds, was hailed as creating infrastructures of care that would endure throughout the period of incarceration and beyond.

Painting, *Das Gartenhäuschen*, Wilhelm Degode, 1917. Courtesy of Fliedner-Kulturstiftung Kaiserswerth.

***

As the programs of English Redhill, French Val d'Yèvre, and German Kaiserswerth make clear, a shared goal of mobilizing space impacted the experiences of incarcerated children and adolescents. We should not see the creation of such spaces as unequivocal proof of rehabilitation in the countryside. Their creation demonstrates, rather, how developments in political, economic, religious or moral thinking were tied to conceptions of space. The transfer and establishment of juvenile imprisonment in the countryside also shows an intensifying fear of cities at that time, which historians have illuminated from various perspectives.[8]

What is more, their presence across European borders illustrates how the spatial context and the architectural organization became correctional mechanisms in their own right. Albeit differing in their individual makeup, Redhill, Val d'Yèvre, and Kaiserswerth each evoke a carceral system that developed through a rethinking of both care and space. State and administrative representatives correlated the countryside—namely the incorporation of fields, marshes, open lands, and sheds into their carceral experience—with the provision of lasting care for incarcerated children.

But the countryside did not necessarily represent the ideal context for rehabilitation, as rural institutions continued to confront obstacles.[9] Local populations were fearful that the labor of imprisoned boys and girls could create market competition. And requests, sent by urban families, that their children be returned to them after their release, put pressure on these facilities in their end goal of total removal from cities. Indeed, would it be lawful to prepare the rehabilitation of individuals by ignoring their social origin and trying to force their permanent residence in the countryside? Were states and institutions within their power to arrange for such a permanent relocation of adolescents, who had often reached maturity by the time of their release? Would it be moral and legal to consider cities or an urban background as reasons for criminal behavior, and thus exile individuals to the countryside?

At first glance, these instantiations of juvenile imprisonment in nineteenth-century England, France, and the German territories appear like elements of a far-removed past. But the questions and ideas that animated, modified, terminated, and prolonged the correctional projects of Redhill, Val d'Yèvre, Kaiserswerth 200 years ago remain relevant today. Their analysis demonstrates the importance of considering space and architecture in the context of incarceration and its aftermath. Space is never a neutral category; it is manipulated for individual means and correctional goals. When looking at the possibilities of care in the countryside, we see how rehabilitation is never an unequivocal process. The ideas that undergirded how children and adolescents were incarcerated are not limited to the nineteenth century. Redhill, Val d'Yèvre, and Kaiserswerth act as reminders of the nature of rehabilitation as a constant negotiation of architecture(s), which is propelled forward by both the denial and the promise of freedom. Just as the possibilities of care have often been articulated in spatial terms, place has also shaped the execution of care. From the marshlands of Val d'Yèvre to the farm site of Redhill to the sheds at Kaiserswerth to our present day: thinking about care necessarily means thinking about space.

1
Surrey History Center, Woking, 2271/38/1, Deed and Plan at St. George's, 1793.

2
Surrey History Center, Woking, 2271/38/1, Deed and Plan at St. George's, 1793.

3
Surrey History Center, Woking, 2271/43/1, Excerpt: *The Architect and Building Operative*, 1848.

4
One famous example of this development is the creation of the colony of Mettray (near Tours, Indre-et-Loire).

5
Departmental Archives, Cher, 1Y/156, Charles Lucas, 1847.

6
Archiv der Fliedner Kulturstiftung, Kaiserswerth, 3/1/3/15, Theodor Fliedner, *Unterstützungsgesuch*; Theodor Fliedner, *Vertrag zwischen den Direktoren Asyls einerseits und dem Maurermeister, Herrn Pater Overheid zu Rate, andererseits*, 1840.

7
Archiv der Fliedner Kulturstiftung, Kaiserswerth, 02/12, *Statuten*, article 2.

8
See for example: Brian Ladd, *Urban Planning and Civic Order in Germany, 1860–1914* (Harvard University Press, 1990); Kristin Poling, *Germany's Urban Frontiers: Nature and History on the Edge of the Nineteenth-Century City* (University of Pittsburgh Press, 2020); Louis Chevalier, *Classes laborieuses et classes dangereuses à Paris pendant la première moitié du XIXe siècle* (Librairie Plon, 1958); Andrew Israel Ross, *Public City/Public Sex: Homosexuality, Prostitution and Urban Culture in Nineteenth-Century Paris* (Temple University Press, 2019).

9
For the contested nature of rehabilitation after incarceration, see Victoria Bergbauer, "Fragments of Freedom: Incarcerated Adolescents and Their Afterlives in 19th-Century Europe," PhD dissertation, Princeton University, 2025.

⁂

Liz Trumbull

RELIGIOUS PRACTICES AT EASTERN STATE PENITENTIARY: A CASE STUDY

Philadelphia's Eastern State Penitentiary opened in 1829 as the world's first penitentiary, a prison designed to inspire penitence within the people incarcerated there. An early attempt at prison reform, Eastern State represents a massive shift in penal ideology: the belief that individual rehabilitation is possible.

The founders of Eastern State emerged from the Philadelphia Society for Alleviating the Miseries of Public Prisons, established in 1776 and now known as the Pennsylvania Prison Society. The values of the Prison Society were underpinned by Quaker beliefs held by many of its members, particularly that the goodness of human nature is present in every person, and even when that goodness is obscured, reform is still possible.[1] The Prison Society advocated for incarceration in near total isolation, removed from the negative influences of one's life and given time for personal reflection and improvement to enable a successful return to society. For reform to be expected, founders believed that religious instruction was essential. However, from its inception, Eastern State did not function the way founders intended. A structure built for solitary confinement posed substantial challenges for daily operation, including the delivery of religious instruction. During its 141 years in operation, the campus was repeatedly adapted to meet the needs of administrators and the prison population, needs which were often at odds with the existing structure—thereby forcing maladaptive physical or operational modifications that often only partially addressed the underlying issue.

Religious practices at Eastern State were routinely affected by the shortcomings of both the building and its administration. Despite these circumstances, incarcerated individuals, outside volunteers, and some prison staff continuously sought ways for religious practice and spaces of worship to evolve for the better. Worship became a form of placemaking for incarcerated people, a way in which they were able to positively influence their surrounding environment to enable moments of beauty, community, and devotion in a setting meant to deny those very experiences. Today, the history of religion at Eastern State is best told through a study of its chapel, the Alfred W. Fleisher Memorial Synagogue—likely the first synagogue in an American prison—and the chaplain's office.

The Design of Eastern State Penitentiary

The architectural task at hand was to design a new facility where people would be kept in separate confinement for their entire sentence, leaving their cells only for brief periods of outdoor exercise in a private yard, a practice that would come to be known as the Pennsylvania System. A massive technological challenge in an era without indoor plumbing, the architect of Eastern State's original 250 cells would have to provide clean air, sanitary plumbing, adequate heat, and secure access and surveillance to enable true isolation. The moral aspects of the design were equally challenging: the building commissioners believed in the power of the built environment to cultivate the Quaker notion of inner goodness in each incarcerated person, and the design was predicated on religious instruction occurring individually in each person's cell.[2]

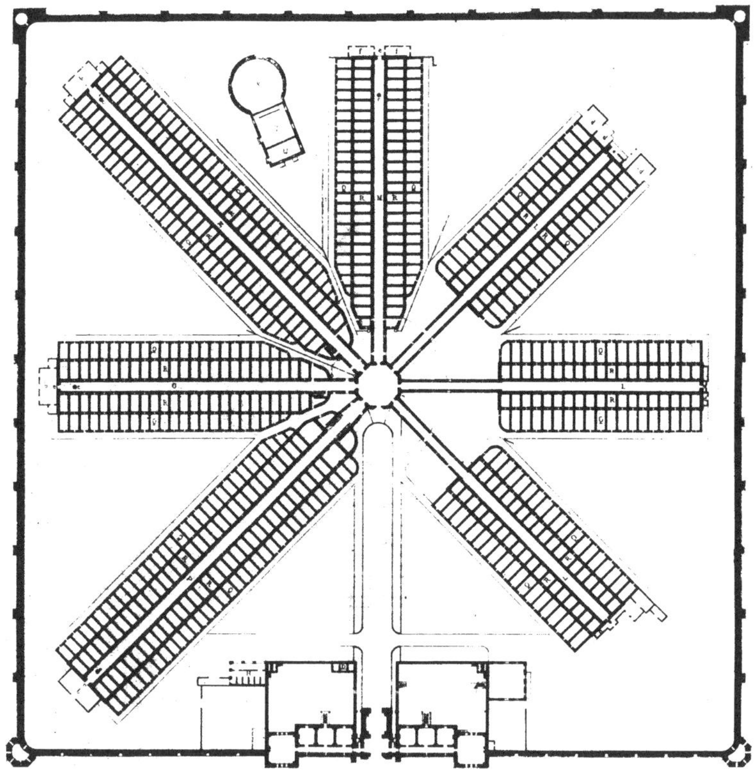

F.-A. Demetz and A. Blouet, *Rapport... sur les pénitentiers des Etats-Unis* (Paris: Imprimerie Royale, 1837), pl. 23 showing the as-built version of John Haviland's radial plan design. Public domain.

The building commission ultimately selected Philadelphia architect John Haviland's design for Eastern State Penitentiary. Haviland's proposal included an oppressive gothic façade and a 30-foot-tall, half-mile long perimeter wall surrounding seven cellblocks radiating from a central hub to enable easy surveillance, order, and control. Cellblocks were lined with large, vaulted, and sky-lit cells, accessed via the exterior exercise yard such that the interior corridor had only a small door for passing through food. At the time of its construction, the 10-acre campus that comprised Eastern State Penitentiary was the most expensive construction project in the country and became a model for the world: more than 300 prisons on six continents were influenced by Haviland's radial plan.[3]

Religion during Solitary Confinement

Despite the religious ideals underlying Eastern State's conception, policies and practices began to weaken the founding intent almost immediately. In the early 1830s, the ability to labor in one's cell and access religious texts were regarded as favors that administrators withheld as punishment.[4] By 1839, the small number of incarcerated people who could read were given a Bible and access to a library of nearly 1000 volumes, while those who could not read were left without a means of solitary religious instruction.[5] Despite the importance of religion in Eastern State's founding, administrators did not enable adequate access to religious instruction.

Though founders aimed for separate confinement, they intended for those incarcerated to interact with people they deemed a positive influence, including frequent meetings with the chaplain.[6] However, the founding legislation called for an unpaid chaplain. It was not until 1831, two years after the first incarcerated person arrived at Eastern State, that volunteer clergy began visiting the penitentiary part time.[7] The first paid moral instructor did not join the staff for another seven years, and yet, due to the physical constraints of solitary confinement, it was still impractical for him to meet with individuals more than once every two months.[8] By 1845, services held in the corridors of each block began to supplement individual religious instruction, working around the physical challenges of the building. Four to six ministers, including the penitentiary's first moral instructor Reverend Thomas Larcombe, provided nondenominational Christian services to the entire prison population on Sundays by addressing one cellblock at a time. Wooden doors were left ajar to allow individuals to hear the services, and a curtain was strung down the center of the cellblocks to limit communication.[9] These services continued throughout the nineteenth century, often facilitated by Larcombe and Quaker ministers, and less frequently by Methodist, Baptist, and other Protestant ministers.[10] The first Catholic priest participated in December of 1895.[11]

Outside of Sunday services, visits for the purpose of religious guidance were permitted and made most frequently by Catholic, Quaker, and Jewish visitors during the nineteenth century. The first documented Jewish visitor arrived in 1845—the same year that Christian services in the cellblocks began.[12] While Jewish services were not provided until the early twentieth century, religious leaders from the Jewish community regularly visited Eastern State throughout the year and on holidays, most commonly after 1884.[13]

Religious affiliations of people incarcerated at Eastern State were not consistently collected during this era, leaving only snapshots of religious life at the time. Reception records from 1854 and 1855 indicate that most people arriving at Eastern State identified as either Catholic (21 to 29 percent) or Methodist (24 to 33 percent), followed by German Lutheran (14 to 17 percent) and Presbyterian (8 to 16 percent). Christians represented 96 percent of incoming people, 4 percent were not religious, and only one person of the 252 receptions between 1854 and 1855 was Jewish.[14] Thirty years later, Catholic representation remained about the same: 300 people in a total population of approximately 1,150 (26 percent).[15] In 1889, twelve individuals identified as Jewish, growing to twenty-three by 1904—a small percentage of a relatively stagnant prison population of about 1,110 during this period.[16]

A Place for Islam

Few records provide insight into religious practice outside of Christianity or Judaism until the final decades of Eastern State's operation. The first mention of Islam was in September 1959 when Robert Payne (E-3449), a member of the Nation of Islam (NOI), was placed in isolation for assaulting five guards while in the mess hall.[17] Three days later, nearly thirty state troopers arrived at Eastern State to quell an expected demonstration related to Payne's isolation. Twenty-three incarcerated NOI members, likely the entire Muslim population at Eastern State at the time, were preemptively moved to Cellblock 15 which was used for punishment.[18]

Almost a decade later, in 1967, five Muslims incarcerated at Eastern State sued the penitentiary and the Department of Corrections, in a case known as Knuckles v. Prasse, on the premise that Islamic religious practices were not permitted in the facility—including congregate prayer meetings and access to Muslim ministers or texts.[19] In 1969, the court ruled that the Department of Corrections must allow for visits by a Muslim minister "under reasonable prison regulations for a collective worship service."[20] However, as Eastern State closed in 1970, if or where Islamic services were held is unknown. In an institution and an era with well-established Christian and Jewish practices and spaces for worship, it seems that incarcerated Muslims were not afforded similar religious freedoms.

Dissolution of the Pennsylvania System

The difficulty of providing religious instruction in a structure built for solitary confinement was but one of the many challenges administrators faced in enforcing isolation. Most pressing was the rising prison population in a static facility: by 1870, there were 671 people incarcerated at Eastern State but only 560 cells, requiring individuals to share a cell.[21] Despite many concessions made to the Pennsylvania System in the preceding decades, the policy of mass solitary confinement was not officially abandoned by state legislature until 1913.

The legal ability to congregate was quickly followed by changes to religious practice at Eastern State, enabling people to gather for services later that same year for Rosh Hashanah and in spring of 1914 for Easter.[22] In the following decades, dedicated religious spaces would be identified and continuously invested in by incarcerated people, outside volunteers, and prison administrators alike.

Founding and Evolution of the Chapel

After the dissolution of the Pennsylvania System, the first congregate Christian service was offered in the corridors of the cellblocks on Palm Sunday in 1914 when people were "for the first time in the history of the Institution allowed outside their cells for the purpose of religious worship."[23] One week later, on Easter Sunday, Catholic Mass was held on the second floor of the Industrial Building for the first time using an altar dedicated a few weeks earlier.[24] The Industrial Building was built for manufacturing in 1906 entirely by people incarcerated at Eastern State, likely from designs prepared by Morris & Vaux, a lesser-known Philadelphia architectural firm with familial ties to Richard Vaux, a long-serving inspector and supporter of Eastern State.[25]

Today, the Industrial Building consists of a two-story granite structure with a single-story addition, forming an L-shaped building. On the second floor of the main building, the decorated heavy-timber roof trusses are exposed. However, a 1917 map of Eastern State depicts a main building with two-and-a-half stories.[26] The existence of a "half story" suggests an attic space, perhaps created by running floor planks between the wood trusses. It is likely that this attic comprised the early chapel per descriptions of the space at the time: a "small, dim and depressing loft over one of the prison storage buildings" with "dusty rough boards." Warden

McKenty noted that "the loft in question is so full when 500 convicts are in it that movement is almost impossible ... It is reached by a narrow stairway, up which the prisoners have to file one at a time."[27] On a campus built for solitary confinement, there were few spaces available that could seat an audience, including the rather large Christian population. The use of the loft may have been a creative response by prison administrators while they developed a longer-term solution.

View of Industrial Building from central tower (looking northwest), circa 1960, photograph negative. Eastern State Penitentiary Archives, gift of Alan J. LeFebvre, 2012.046.024.

Two years later, a very different type of space is described: "The large store room of the Industrial Building has been fitted up as a Chapel and Assembly Room, furnishing conveniences for the rites of the various churches and audience room for entertainment and lectures."[28] If the first services were held in the attic of the Industrial Building, it seems this makeshift loft was soon abandoned and the chapel was relocated to the second floor. It was in this much larger space where rather elaborate Easter services were held in 1916 with "ornate candelabra," a "profuse array" of flowers, and attended by a record-breaking 740 people.[29] Later the same year, nearly 800 people attended Christmas Mass there.[30]

Denominational record-keeping improved in the early twentieth century. From 1925 to 1940, the Catholic population typically hovered around 40 percent, then dropped to 30 percent by 1943. During the same period, the Baptist population grew from 17 percent to 32 percent while the Methodist population grew from 10 percent to 19 percent. Christian denominations, overall, comprised about 95 percent of the total population.[31] Women were incarcerated at Eastern State from its opening until 1922 and, during the congregate era, comprised only 1 to 2 percent of the total population.[32] They did not use the chapel, but rather were incarcerated in Cellblock 2 where they had a "Sunday School room" by 1913 and their own movie theater by 1918.[33]

As intended by prison administrators, the chapel was also used as an assembly room for non-religious purposes. Lectures were held in the chapel on Friday afternoons while Saturdays were reserved for moving picture shows.[34] On Sundays, the chapel was typically used for Catholic and Episcopal services while non-sectarian services were held in the cellblocks.[35] The multi-purpose use of the chapel at this moment in history was not uncommon in western carceral settings.[36]

After many unanswered calls to construct a purpose-built structure for use as a chapel and auditorium, the last major campaign in the extant chapel occurred in 1957, executed by people incarcerated at Eastern State and designed and overseen by Frank Frei of Adolph Frei & Sons, an ecclesiastical decorator with work in more than 500 churches in Europe and America by 1935.[37] The prison newspaper described the chapel improvements, noting plasterwork made to simulate wood moldings, while other surfaces were finished with "hand wood-graining and a stipple pattern in beautiful colonial harmony." [38]

The work was completed by members of Eastern State's Building and Trades Department, a department focused on teaching incarcerated people the basics of a trade while completing maintenance work to the aging penitentiary. The crew worked alongside Frei and his staff for six months, careful not to disrupt the chapel's schedule of religious services and entertainment. Frei left an impression on the crew, who recognized him in the prison newspaper by thanking him for his kindness, time, expertise, and the materials he donated. Frei's staff "led off, as it were, the finer details of the job," teaching the Eastern State crew along the way as they fostered a sense of ownership of the work: "the boys took a real interest in this job. It is only natural that they should. They assemble here for religious worship. It is a common Chapel, but it is the INMATE'S church."[39]

In addition to construction work, individuals invested personally in the chapel by contributing their time and handiwork. In 1932, John Hullar (C-6150) donated two wrought-iron candelabras to be used on the altar.[40] On Christmas Eve in the mid-1930s, a handful of incarcerated people were permitted to stay in the chapel until 11 p.m. to decorate for Christmas Day services, an example of trust built between administrators and incarcerated people.[41] One person's contributions, however, stand out in this era: those of Theodore Fedevich (C-5451), who worked as a "high salaried toolmaker for Westinghouse Electric Company" before his incarceration.[42] Between 1935 and 1938, Fedevich produced a statue of the Crucifixion carved by hand; a carving of "the likeness of the face of our Lord," described by Father Farley as "indeed a work of art"; an altar rail for use every Sunday; a pedestal for the statue of the Blessed Virgin and, later, a throne for the same statue; and finally a portable and collapsible altar to be used in Cellblock 14.[43]

Chapel interior, looking north, circa 1968, photograph. Eastern State Penitentiary Archives, 1998.002.003.

In a campus built for isolation, the chapel's creation marks a critical moment in Eastern State's history as the first space designated solely for gathering, community, and education. The beauty imbued in the space through painted roof beams, ornate wood and plasterwork, floral arrangements and expertly crafted décor disrupts the standard aesthetic language used throughout the penitentiary, announcing the chapel as a sanctuary. Innumerable outside organizations volunteered in the chapel, working alongside and supporting the people incarcerated at Eastern State. The chapel continued to function in this way until Eastern State's closure in 1970.

Founding and Evolution of the Synagogue

Congregate Jewish services began almost immediately after the dissolution of the Pennsylvania System, notably six months earlier than the first documented Christian gathering. In early October of 1913, Rosh Hashanah was celebrated in the unoccupied Emergency Hospital.[44]

Like the Industrial Building, Morris & Vaux appear to have designed the Emergency Hospital (1907–1908) which was built to house and treat people with contagious diseases.[45] Despite the functional differences between spaces used for medicine and worship, the Emergency Hospital likely housed the improvised synagogue until at least 1917 when a new, permanent location was identified.

THE NEW EMERGENCY HOSPITAL

Eastern façade of the Emergency Hospital in 1910, where Jewish services were held from 1913 through at least 1917. *Eighty-First Annual Report of the Inspectors of the State Penitentiary for the Eastern District of Pennsylvania for the Year 1910*. Philadelphia, 1911.

In late September 1914, an article in the *Evening Ledger* highlighting Yom Kippur services provides a particularly detailed snapshot of Jewish life at Eastern State in these early days. Thirty-eight people attended the service in the Emergency Hospital with five non-Jewish incarcerated people serving as guards. Attendees chose between a prayer book printed in Hebrew and one translated into English. While no rabbi or cantor was present, one of the incarcerated attendees had been a student at a Jewish seminary prior to his incarceration and offered to run the service. Congregants were permitted to stay in this makeshift synagogue until after sunset, at which point they ate a dinner of roast beef, mashed potatoes, and bread.[46] It is unclear whether the beef provided for this service was kosher; by 1919 kosher meat was brought in from outside the institution for the High Holidays, and by Passover in 1927 kosher food was purchased by Eastern State and prepared onsite by Jewish volunteers.[47]

Though these early services seem to be facilitated by incarcerated people with the support of the warden, by 1916 the Jewish population received regular assistance from the Prison Aid Committee—a Jewish volunteer organization comprised of Philadelphia members of B'nai B'rith, the oldest Jewish service organization in the world. Volunteers coordinated and conducted services, including the High Holidays, and provided matzah for Passover. The Prison Aid Committee served as an essential support for the Jewish population, including appointing the first Jewish chaplain for Eastern State in 1918, and continued their involvement through the 1960s.[48]

The creation of the synagogue in Cellblock 7 followed widespread architectural change within the 10-acre campus, prompted by the dissolution of the Pennsylvania System. With the ability to exercise in groups outdoors, individual yards were no longer needed. Former yards were converted into much-needed workshops to expand the scope of trade work at Eastern State. Many of the walls separating the Cellblock 7 outdoor exercise yards were demolished between 1912 and 1917, followed by the installation of concrete floors and flat, reinforced concrete roofs.[49] The space that would become the synagogue was initially used as two rooms of a weaving shop, combined into a single room with two skylights between 1917 and 1924.[50] Despite little evidence of what the synagogue looked like in its early years, the scheduled uses of the synagogue are well documented. Members of the Jewish population gathered on Wednesday afternoons to share "news of the day" whereby "educational, political and scientific subjects are discussed." Religious services were held on Saturday mornings, and the Jewish chaplain met with people individually on Sundays.[51]

The first campaign to formalize the synagogue took place in 1928, likely establishing Eastern State as the first prison in the United States with a synagogue.[52] Two incarcerated people, "at their own expense, reconstructed the interior of the synagogue from plans prepared by the Hoffman-Henon Co. firm of architects."[53] Hoffman-Henon is associated with more than 160 buildings and was relatively well-known for their work on theaters and movie houses.[54] They completed a few religious structures, but it is unclear if they designed any synagogues beyond Eastern State. The firm's involvement may be explained by Israel Demchick, an architect on staff who was "an authority on synagogue design."[55] It is unknown when exactly Demchick worked for Hoffman-Henon, but it is possible he advocated for the firm to take on the project at Eastern State.[56] The color scheme for the new synagogue was facilitated through Kayser & Allman, a respected decorator and furnisher of the time that later focused exclusively on wallpaper sales.[57]

The realization of the synagogue required significant commitments from both design firms and people incarcerated at Eastern State. Congregants also had the support of many prominent Jewish Philadelphians, including Alfred Fleisher who served as the President of the Board of Trustees of Eastern State from 1924 until his death in December 1928. During his short tenure at Eastern State, he made a profound impact on the Jewish population who, in April 1929, installed a bronze plaque and "dedicated the Synagogue in his name" as a "lasting memorial of the kindness and justice [Fleisher] had always shown them."[58] The meaning and significance of the synagogue is represented by the many people who found it worth their time and effort to ensure that

Eastern State's Jewish congregation had not just a suitable space, but a beautiful space, in which to practice their faith.

Entertainer Joseph Paull dedicated decades of his life to supporting Eastern State's Jewish population and received a portrait in recognition of these efforts in 1959. Photograph courtesy of the Historical Society of Pennsylvania, Joseph Paull Photograph Collection.

In contrast to Eastern State's chapel, its synagogue seemed to fit its intended purpose from the time of its dedication in 1929. The space was never deemed inadequate or too small for the (at times) relatively large Jewish population. In 1918, there were forty Jewish people incarcerated at Eastern State, a number that grew steadily to a peak of eighty people by 1940.[59] The population then dropped from seventy-five to forty-eight between 1941 and 1942, at which point denominational data became limited.[60] However, the "Warden's Daily Journal" entries throughout the 1950s consistently note about ten people in attendance at Jewish services.[61]

It wasn't until the late 1950s that the synagogue received another update. The prompt for this improvement is unclear, but it may be as simple as falling into alignment with the chapel's renovations and having the capacity to renovate under the purview of the Building and Trades Department. Work commenced in April 1960 by the same plastering team that worked on the chapel, under the guidance of Mr. McMenamin who endeavored "to teach the inmates working under him the highly decorative art of molding with plaster." No longer working with an outside architect, the crew held multiple meetings with the Jewish congregation to solicit suggestions for decorative schemes.[62] By August 1960, the synagogue light fixtures were replaced, the room repainted and replastered, the wood paneling and seats resurfaced, the floor retiled, and a food preparation area completed with a cabinet sink installed in the rear of the room.[63] After repairing significant damage from an untimely burst steam pipe in November that same year, fifty guests attended the rededication of the Alfred W. Fleisher Memorial Synagogue in February 1962.[64]

Though relatively small, the incarcerated Jewish population at Eastern State was part of a much larger community of religious leaders and volunteers. The community worked continuously to improve not just their place of worship, but the spiritual wellbeing of those incarcerated.

The Chaplain's Office

At some point between 1939 and 1955, the office for Eastern State chaplains was relocated from halfway down the corridor of Cellblock 6, between inhabited cells, to a similarly central structure nestled between Cellblocks 1 and 9.[65] Originally built between 1881 and 1885 to house the warden's office, the interior finishes were more elaborate than much of the prison. One room contained a fireplace and was clad entirely in wood paneling, while others contained ornately molded doors and doorframes. Large skylights filled the spaces with natural light.

The chaplain's office was not used for worship, but rather as a space for chaplains to meet with and support the population of Eastern State. The office was used by, at minimum, the Protestant and Catholic chaplains, who were both on staff in 1955. With the support of prison staff, incarcerated people could visit the chaplain's office at any time, except during "lock up" hours. Chaplains offered assistance in both religious and social matters, such as "settlement of wage and pension claims, reconciliation of estranged relatives, commutation and parole assistance."[66]

Lester Smith during his incarceration with some of his work, 1955. Photograph. Eastern State Penitentiary Archives, gift of the Smith Family, 1998.002.003.

The most remarkable feature of the chaplain's office is the twenty-three murals painted by Lester Smith, a self-taught artist incarcerated at Eastern State between 1955 and 1956. Within two months of his arrival, the Catholic chaplain noticed Smith sketching on the walls of his cell and invited him to paint murals in his office. Smith, who converted to Catholicism during incarceration at a different institution, used the opportunity to paint murals depicting religious scenes from the life of Jesus Christ, Catholic icons, and remorseful prisoners.[67] Fifteen of the twenty-three murals line the skylights and correspond to the mysteries of the rosary.[68]

Smith signed the murals as Paul Martin, a name he adopted to honor his patron saints, and depicted St. Martin de Porres in one of his murals. Though not yet a saint at the time of Smith's incarceration, St. Martin de Porres was canonized in 1962 as the patron saint of the poor, the socially outcast, mixed-race people, as well as those seeking racial harmony. He was the fifth Black saint in the history of the Catholic Church. Smith believed his sentence of one to five years was lenient and credited this to his religious convictions. He was paroled after only seven-and-a-half months at Eastern State.[69]

Eastern State Today

After decades of calls to shutter the now antiquated penitentiary, closure was finally announced in September 1969. By January the following year, the penitentiary was closed and sold to the City of Philadelphia. Almost immediately, the cells were back in use as overflow from the city's crowded carceral institutions.[70] However, in 1971, the site fell into a period of abandonment. The neglect during this period, paired with the lack of maintenance that began while the prison was still in operation, enabled vegetation to proliferate and water to enter the structure, further damaging already deteriorating roofs, walls, windows, and interior finishes.

Eastern State Penitentiary was designated a historic property in Philadelphia in 1958 and a National Historic Landmark in 1965, notably while still operating as a prison.[71] Despite the recognition of its significance in America's history, when the City of Philadelphia sought bids for development in the 1980s, many proposals called for substantial demolition, citing the prolific decay. City officials ultimately aligned with a group of concerned citizens, the Eastern State Penitentiary Task Force, thereby saving the site from demolition and giving the group permission to reopen the campus as a museum. Today, Eastern State Penitentiary Historic Site (ESPHS), the nonprofit that manages the site, advances public understanding of the criminal justice system and its impact on the lives of those affected by it to inspire a more just future.[72] More than 250,000 visitors from around the world visit the site annually, learning about its history through exhibits, art installations, audio and guide-led tours.

Today, the deteriorating building is a palimpsest—a massive physical archive of the innumerable ways the campus was repeatedly adapted while in use as a prison. ESPHS preserves the site as a stabilized ruin, treating the entire building as physical evidence of change over time for an institution with otherwise limited records of historic construction work. Since the 1990s, ESPHS has worked to restore the exterior envelope to prevent water entry while applying a strategy of minimal intervention to the interior. Exposed layers are stabilized and left available for study to better understand how people modified the campus over time, whether as a means of personal expression or to implement changing penal policies and practices.

Areas of particular value, however, are treated differently. Selective restoration is often preferred for spaces that embody a unique interpretive opportunity, when coupled with extensive documentation about the historic use and appearance. The Alfred W. Fleisher Memorial Synagogue is one such example. When studies began in the early 2000s, the space was treated as an archaeological site whereby fragments of the building were meticulously cataloged and analyzed to thoroughly document the appearance of the synagogue when it was last used by the congregation. The Star of

David, formed in plaster on the ceiling, was identically recreated and painted based on an archival photo and a corner of the star found in the rubble. Through detailed research, today's synagogue faithfully represents its appearance in 1970. The space is accessible to the public and available for mini tours with ESPHS staff.

Synagogue, after restoration, circa 2009. Photograph by Liz Trumbull, 2025.

Similar efforts were made in the chaplain's office with particular attention to the protection of Smith's twenty-three murals. After remaining covered by a temporary, protective treatment for nearly two decades, the murals were meticulously cleaned and readhered to the walls. While intact sections of the murals were retouched, large areas of loss were not repainted in keeping with ESPHS's stabilized ruin philosophy. Like the synagogue, climate control was reinstalled in the space to provide long-term protection for the delicate historic finishes. Today, visitors can access the chaplain's office through mini tours with ESPHS staff.

The historic chapel remains in a state of ruin, closed to staff and the public and protected by temporary roofing until funding is available to better preserve and activate the space. Like prison administrators in the 1920s, ESPHS has difficulty finding adequate space for

Chaplain's office, after stabilization, circa 2011. Mysteries of the rosary are visible along the skylight opening and the portrait of Martin de Porres is in view above the door. Photograph by Liz Trumbull, 2025.

large groups to congregate on a deteriorating campus that often lacks sufficient power and plumbing. ESPHS hopes to rehabilitate the former chapel into an education center, leveraging the historic fabric and its significance to create a space for community and dialogue—in keeping with the chapel's historic use.

Chapel interior located on the second floor of the Industrial Building, as found during the abandonment period. Historic American Building Survey, "Eastern State Penitentiary, 2125 Fairmount Avenue, Philadelphia, Philadelphia County, PA," 1998.

Religious practice remained a valued tool for rehabilitation throughout Eastern State's 141 years in operation, evolving in tandem with changing penal philosophies to stay relevant in an environment that was largely inhospitable to religion. After almost a century of imperfectly executed individual religious practice, three powerful spaces came to embody the role of religion as a congregate activity, creating moments of community and beauty in a place meant to deny those very experiences. The penitentiary's chapel represents the importance of communal gathering, the first space at Eastern State dedicated to this purpose. The Alfred W. Fleisher Memorial Synagogue embodies the importance and power of volunteerism, enabling a relatively small Jewish population to thrive with the support of committed incarcerated people and dedicated outside volunteers. The chaplain's office symbolizes the role of religion in reform and the impact that one individual can make on an institution through creative expression. Together, these spaces of worship represent the power of placemaking to create spaces of refuge in a carceral setting and continue to inspire moments of reflection in people who visit Eastern State Penitentiary Historic Site today.

1
"Eastern State Penitentiary Historic Structures Report," Philadelphia: Marianna Thomas Architects, 1994, 45–46.

2
Norman Johnston, Kenneth Finkel, and Jeffrey A. Cohen, *Eastern State Penitentiary: Crucible of Good Intentions* (Philadelphia Museum of Art, 1994), 32.

3
Norman Johnston, "Letter from Norman Johnston to Eastern State Penitentiary Historic Site Re: Foreign Radial-Plan Prisons," March 31, 2007. Eastern State Penitentiary Archives.

4
First and Second Annual Reports of the Inspectors of the Eastern State Penitentiary of Pennsylvania (Philadelphia Society for Alleviating the Miseries of Public Prisons, 1831), 9.

5
Eleventh Annual Report of the Inspectors of the Eastern State Penitentiary (Philadelphia, 1840), 38.

6
Johnston, Finkel, and Cohen, 49.

7
Johnston, Finkel, and Cohen, 53.

8
Tenth Annual Report of the Inspectors of the Eastern State Penitentiary (Philadelphia, 1839), 23. Negley K. Teeters and John D. Shearer, *The Prison at Philadelphia, Cherry Hill; The Separate System of Penal Discipline: 1829–1913* (Columbia University Press, 1957), 152.

9
"Eastern State Penitentiary Historic Structures Report," 85; Johnston, Finkel, and Cohen, 53.

10
"Warden's Daily Journal" [various dates between 1838 and 1900]. Pennsylvania State Archives, Department of Justice, Eastern State Penitentiary, RG-015-GG-B-50, ms.

11
"Warden's Daily Journal, December 1, 1895." Pennsylvania State Archives, Department of Justice, Eastern State Penitentiary, RG-015-GG-B-50, ms.

12
Sixteenth Annual Report of the Inspectors of the Eastern State Penitentiary (Philadelphia, 1845), 23.

13
"Warden's Daily Journal" [various dates between 1838 and 1900]. Pennsylvania State Archives, Department of Justice, Eastern State Penitentiary, RG-015-GG-B-50, ms.

14
Twenty-Seventh Annual Report of the Inspectors of the Eastern State Penitentiary of Pennsylvania (Philadelphia, March 1856), 42. *Twenty-Eighth Annual Report of the Inspectors of the Eastern State Penitentiary of Pennsylvania* (Philadelphia, March 1857), 81.

15
"Warden's Daily Journal, May 22, 1885." *56th Annual Report of the Inspectors of the State Penitentiary for the Eastern District of Pennsylvania* (Philadelphia, 1886), 32.

16
"Warden's Daily Journal, April 21, 1889." *60th Annual Report of the Inspectors of the State Penitentiary for the Eastern District of Pennsylvania* (Philadelphia, 1890), 3; "Warden's Daily Journal, March 9, 1904." *75th Annual Report of the Inspectors of the State Penitentiary for the Eastern District of Pennsylvania* (Philadelphia, 1905), 75.

17
Commonwealth vs. Robert Payne (Oyer & Terminer, Philadelphia County 1960). *City of Philadelphia, Department of Records, City Archives, RG 21, Court Records.*

18
"Warden's Daily Journal, September 6, 1959." Pennsylvania State Archives, Eastern State Penitentiary, RG-015-GG-B-50, ms. Knuckles v. Prasse (U.S. District Court for the Eastern District of Pennsylvania, July 31, 1969).

19
Saul Kohler, "Five Negro Inmates Ask Court to Allow Muslim Rites in Jails," *The Philadelphia Inquirer*, October 16, 1967; Knuckles v. Prasse.

20
Knuckles v. Prasse.

21
"Eastern State Penitentiary Historic Structures Report," 197.

22
[Prisoner Number] B-6076, "Jewish New Year in Prison," *The Umpire*, October 8, 1913. *Eighty Fifth Annual Report of the Inspectors of the State Penitentiary for the Eastern District of Pennsylvania* (Philadelphia, 1915), 10.

23
Eighty Fifth Annual Report of the Inspectors of the State Penitentiary for the Eastern District of Pennsylvania, 10.

24
"Minute Books of the Board of Inspectors and Board of Trustees, May 4, 1914." Pennsylvania State Archives, Eastern State Penitentiary, RG-015-GG-B-44, ms. "Warden's Daily Journal, March 19, 1914." Pennsylvania State Archives, Eastern State Penitentiary, RG-015-GG-B-50, ms.

25
"Eastern State Penitentiary Historic Structures Report," 184.

26
Insurance Maps of Philadelphia, Pennsylvania, Volume 4. New York: Sanborn Map Company, 1917.

27
"Convicts Who Pray in Dingy Loft Want to Build a Chapel," *Evening Public Ledger*, December 28, 1914. "Minute Books of the Board of Inspectors and Board of Trustees, May 4, 1914."

28
Eighty-Seventh Annual Report of the Inspectors of the State Penitentiary for the Eastern District of Pennsylvania (Philadelphia, 1917), 6.

29
"Catholic Easter Service," *The Umpire* V, no. 17 (April 26, 1916).

30
"Beautiful Catholic Christmas at the E.S.P. Chapel," *The Umpire* V, no 52 (December 27, 1916).

31
Annual reports from the years 1926, 1930, 1940, and 1943.

32
"Eastern State Penitentiary Historic Structures Report," 130.

33
"New Year Resolutions," *The Umpire* II, no. 42 (December 31, 1913); "Home Runs," *The Umpire* V, no. 36 (September 11, 1918).

34
"Pennsylvania State College Professor Lectures at the E.S.P.," *The Umpire* V, no. 9 (March 1, 1916); *Eighty-Eighth Annual Report of the Inspectors of the State Penitentiary for the Eastern District of Pennsylvania* (Philadelphia, 1918), 9.

35
"Warden's Daily Journal, November 14, 1926." Pennsylvania State Archives, Eastern State Penitentiary, RG-015-GG-B-50, ms.

36
Irene Becci and Joshua Dubler, "Religion and Religions in Prisons: Observations from the United States and Europe," *Journal for the Scientific Study of Religion* 56, no. 2 (June 2017): 245–46.

37
"Minute Books of the Board of Inspectors and Board of Trustees, September 133, 1951." Pennsylvania State Archives, Eastern State Penitentiary, RG-015-GG-B-44, ms. "Eastern State Penitentiary Historic Structures Report," 243. "Obituary, Adolph Frei," *The Philadelphia Inquirer*, April 30, 1935.

38
L. J. Biancone, "Spotlight on the B and T Department," *Eastern Echo*, 1957.

39
L. J. Biancone, "Spotlight on the B and T Department."

40
Bernard Farley, "March 30, 1932" in "Diary of Father Bernard Farley for the Years 1929 to 1939," Eastern State Penitentiary Archives.

41
Farley. See entries on December 24, 1934 and December 24, 1935.

42
"Pardon Given to Slayer of Woman and Son," *The Times Leader*, November 28, 1944.

43
Various "Warden's Daily Journal" and "Diary of Father Bernard Farley" entries between 1935 and 1938.

44
[Prisoner Number] B-6076, "Jewish New Year in Prison."

45
"Eastern State Penitentiary Historic Structures Report," 319.

46
"Convicts Observe Yom Kippur with Solemn Services," *The Evening Ledger*, September 30, 1914.

47
Laura A. Mass, *The Synagogue at Eastern State Penitentiary: History and Interpretation,* Master of Science in Historic Preservation, University of Pennsylvania, 2004, 30–31.

48
Mass, 28–30.

49
"Eastern State Penitentiary Historic Structures Report," 303; Mass, 42.

50
Insurance Maps of Philadelphia, Pennsylvania, Volume 4; Mass, 12 and 31.

51
Annual Report of the Eastern State Penitentiary for the Year Ending May 31, 1924 (Philadelphia, 1924), 26. Mass, 42.

52
Eastern State Penitentiary Historic Site. *Synagogue Hands-On History*. Eastern State Penitentiary Historic Site, Philadelphia, 2014.

53
Annual Report of the Eastern State Penitentiary for the Year Ending May 31, 1928 (Philadelphia, 1928), 43.

54
"Hoffman-Henon, Co." in *Philadelphia Architects and Buildings*, https://www.philadelphiabuildings.org/pab/app/ar_display_projects.cfm/22982, accessed December 30, 2024. Sandra L. Tatman, "Henon, Paul J., Jr." in *Philadelphia Architects and Buildings*, https://www.philadelphiabuildings.org/pab/app/ar_display.cfm/21996, accessed December 30, 2024.

55
Emily T. Cooperman and Sandra L. Tatman, "Demchick, Israel," in *Philadelphia Architects and Buildings,* https://www.philadelphiabuildings.org/pab/app/ar_display.cfm/22676, accessed December 20, 2024.

56
Mass, 41–42.

57
Annual Report of the Eastern State Penitentiary for the Year Ending May 31, 1928, 43. "The Entire Stock of Kayser and Allman Half Price," *The Philadelphia Inquirer*, December 6, 1931.

58
"Warden's Daily Journal, April 21, 1929". Pennsylvania State Archives, Eastern State Penitentiary, RG-015-GG-B-50, ms.

59
Mass, 85. [Prisoner Number] B-8874, "Jewish Holidays," *The Umpire*, April 3, 1918, Vol. V, no. 14 edition.

60
Mass, 85.

61
"Warden's Daily Journal" [various dates between 1951 and 1961]. Pennsylvania State Archives, Eastern State Penitentiary, RG-015-GG-B-50, ms.

62
Joseph Roach, "Progress Report" (Eastern State Penitentiary, April 13, 1960), 2.

63
Joseph Roach, "Letter to Rabbi Rothstein," December 2, 1959. Joseph Roach, "Progress Report" (Eastern State Penitentiary, May 15, 1960), 1. Eastern State Penitentiary Archives.

64
Joseph Roach, "Progress Report" (Eastern State Penitentiary, November 14, 1960), 2. "Synagogue Rededication Memo," February 23, 1962. Eastern State Penitentiary Archives.

65
Works Progress Administration, *Block 6 Ground Floor Plan (B6-1A)*, 1/8"=1'-0", Eastern State Penitentiary (Philadelphia, October 1938); "Eastern State Penitentiary Historic Structures Report," 317.

66
"Annual Report June 1, 1954–May 31, 1955," 1955, 33, Pennsylvania State Archives, RG-015-GG-B-34, ms.

67
George Riggins, "Young Robber Finds New Career in Prison; Gift of Water Colors Turned Him to Art," *The Evening Bulletin*, May 17, 1955.

68
Chaplains' Office Murals Hands-On History. Eastern State Penitentiary Historic Site, Philadelphia, 2014.

69
Chaplains' Office Murals Hands-On History.

70
Johnston, Finkel, and Cohen, 98.

71
Johnston, Finkel, and Cohen.

72
"About Eastern State," 2024, https://www.easternstate.org/about-eastern-state, accessed December 30, 2024.

Grégoire Korganow,
Prisoner Setting Fire to their Cell in a Detention Center,
photograph from the series "Prisons," France, 2013.

Above: Corridor convertible into a refectory thanks to retractable tables, Montpellier central prison, 1930, photograph. Courtesy of Henri Manuel / Fonds Manuel / ENAP – CRHCP, M-07-042.

Below: "Chicken cages," Aniane reformatory for juvenile delinquents, 1930, photograph, ENAP – CRHCP, notice: I73862. Courtesy of Michel Basdevant.

ADDENDA

ADDENDA ADDENDA ADDENDA ADDENDA ADDENDA ADDENDA ADDENDA

⁂

Kennedy Mattes and Charlie McWeeny

NOT MUCH IS GOING TO CHANGE: REFLECTING ON "THE ARCHITECTURE OF CONFINEMENT"

"Until you can bring the humanity level in somewhere and not have this mentality of 'they're just criminals, who cares,' not much is going to change."

–Lydia Thornton, activist who was formerly incarcerated at Edna Mahan Correctional Facility

As students in "The Architecture of Confinement", taught by Professor Basile Baudez at Princeton University, we heard from formerly incarcerated activists about how prison architecture influenced their experience. Activists included women formerly incarcerated at Edna Mahan Correctional Facility (EMCF), located in Union Township, New Jersey. The course traced the parallel history of the architecture of prisons and mental asylums in Europe and the United States in collaboration with community partners and Princeton's Program for Community-Engaged Scholarship (ProCES). It culminated in a report on the history, architecture, and future of EMCF.[2]

Our contribution drew upon interviews with women formerly incarcerated at EMCF and public officials connected to the prison to evaluate the effectiveness of the facility's closure on shielding the incarcerated women from abuse. These interviews highlighted the importance of grounding conversations on architectural prison reform in the perspectives of people who have lived within the architecture.

Edna Mahan Correctional Facility, originally known as Clinton Farms when it opened in 1913, was New Jersey's first correctional facility solely for women.[3] In 1928, Edna Mahan, for whom the prison was later renamed, began forty years of service as the prison's superintendent.[4] She operated the prison on, in her words, "the belief in human dignity, in trust, and in the worth of all individuals."[5] Her approach emphasized rehabilitation instead of incapacitation and punishment, which people considered to be progressive at that time. The history of EMCF is simultaneously marred by abuse. A 2020 report by the U.S. Department of Justice's Civil Rights Division exposed a "pervasive culture" of sexual and physical abuse by prison officials.[6] The report found that the correctional facility "fails to keep [incarcerated residents] safe" and that EMCF lacks adequate systems for reporting abuse, enabling abuse to occur "undetected" and "undeterred."[7] Following this report, on June 7, 2021, New Jersey Governor Phil Murphy pledged to close the facility.[8] As of September 2024, a majority of the incarcerated people have been moved from the facility to an interim satellite unit 5 miles away. They will reside here until a new prison is built.[9] Corrections Commissioner Victoria Kuhn assured the public that the new prison "will provide normative conditions that are conducive to rehabilitation, reentry, and improved safety and security."[10] With EMCF as a case study, our class pondered how this architectural decision will affect the lives of the incarcerated people. A *Washington Post* article by Jessica Adler similarly questioned whether the relocation would solve "the rights violations, violence and sexual abuse that have long defined the experience of incarceration in the United States."[11] We sought clarity to this question through interviews, speaking to formerly incarcerated women, public officials, and architects.

We interviewed Stephen Carter of CGL Companies, a consulting firm hired to assist with planning the relocation of EMCF residents.[12] Carter argued that the collection of old cottages and outbuildings dotting the facility's campus contributed to abuse because "there were just too many places and spaces that were unobservable."[13] He noted that architectural changes, including electronic surveillance, casual supervision through the windows of a case manager's office, and *en suite* bathrooms could limit future opportunities for abuse. "Ultimately, the design of the facility is how to eliminate [abuse]," Carter argued, while recognizing that "[i]f you've got staff that are intent on abuse, it's very difficult to eliminate [abuse] 100%."[14] As a solution, Carter cited CGL's partnership with The Moss Group, a consulting firm that specializes in cultural changes to address prison officials' behavior.

Bonnie Kerness, a member of EMCF's Board of Trustees, expressed doubts about the ability of Moss training to shift a deeply ingrained culture of abuse: "I don't know how you train bias."[15] According to her, "it's very clear that the culture shift has not taken place ... the move itself is not a panacea."[16] In public-facing interviews as a board member, however, Kerness expressed more optimism about the move. Of the new prison she said that "we anticipate these modern, normative settings will enable the incarcerated women to grow personally and build dignity and diligence in themselves."[17]

In addition, we interviewed Nafeesah Goldsmith, Lydia Thornton, and Tia Ryans, all of whom were formerly incarcerated at EMCF and, at the time of our interview, were actively involved in prison reform efforts.[18] Goldsmith and Thornton co-chaired the New Jersey Prison Justice Watch, and Ryans founded F.O.R.T.E. House (Forcing Out Recidivism Through Education). We asked each activist about their thoughts on EMCF's closure and the move to a new building. They all expressed concerns about whether architectural changes alone can eliminate abuse. For them, prison culture among officials is the culprit.[19] Goldsmith analogized the architectural move to a woman moving into a new house with her same abuser. Thornton professed a similar stance on prison architecture, saying that even if the same people move to "the most high-class, new, shiny, beautiful, clean facility you want ... how does that change anything? [They] still [are] the same people." At present, prison officials generally have the "mentality that [people who are incarcerated] are just criminals, [so] who cares." Thornton concluded that until the culture within prisons emphasizes each person's humanity, "not much is going to change." The architectural move must be coupled with a cultural shift.

The perspectives of activists who were also formerly incarcerated at EMCF is essential in providing insight into which changes will work and which won't. Their lived experience of the facility's practices is valuable precisely because those experiences did not align with the prison's ostensibly progressive mission. As students, we have greatly appreciated the community-engaged component of "The Architecture of Confinement" and would encourage future conversations on architectural prison reform to center the voices of people with direct experience of incarceration.

1
Kennedy Mattes and Charlie McWeeny, "The Past or the Present? Reconstructing the Experiences Within Edna Mahan Through Interviews," April 27, 2022, https://confinement.princeton.edu/sites/g/files/toruqf1281/files/documents/ART329%20Mattes%20and%20McWeeny.pdf, accessed January 6, 2025.

2
"New Jersey Prison Justice Watch | American Friends Service Committee Prison Watch Collaboration with Princeton Students," The Architecture of Confinement, 2022, https://confinement.princeton.edu/new-jersey-prison-justice-watch-american-friends-service-committee.

3
Colleen O'Dea, "The History of Only NJ Women's Prison," *NJ Spotlight News*, October 30, 2023, https://www.njspotlightnews.org/special-report/edna-mahan-nj-only-womens-prison-history, accessed January 6, 2025.

4
Mary Q. Hawkes, *Excellent Effect: The Edna Mahan Story* (Laurel: American Correctional Association, 1994); New Jersey Department of Corrections, "Edna Mahan Correctional Facility: Phase 1 Full Minimum Compound Relocation," October 30, 2023, https://www.nj.gov/corrections/pdf/PressRelease_PS/231030_EMCF_Relocation.pdf, accessed January 6, 2025.

5
Michael Mitchell, "This Is Who Edna Mahan Was and How Her Dream of a Reformist Prison Died," *NJ.com*, June 13, 2021, https://www.nj.com/opinion/2021/06/edna-mahan-the-slow-erosion-of-a-prison-reformists-life-work-opinion.html, accessed January 6, 2025.

6
United States Department of Justice Civil Rights Division and U.S. Attorney's Office for the District of New Jersey, "Investigation of the Edna Mahan Correctional Facility for Women (Union Township, New Jersey), April 2020. https://www.justice.gov/opa/press-release/file/1268391/dl, accessed January 6, 2025.

7
United States Department of Justice Civil Rights Division, 1.

8
State of New Jersey, "Governor Murphy Announces Intention to Close the Edna Mahan Correctional Facility for Women," Press Release, *Official Site of the State of New Jersey*, June 7, 2021, https://nj.gov/governor/, accessed January 6, 2025.

9
Sophie Nieto-Muñoz, "N.J. Seeks Reduced Oversight of Women's Prison, Citing 'substantial Compliance' with Fed Monitor," *New Jersey Monitor* (blog), September 12, 2024, https://newjerseymonitor.com/2024/09/12/n-j-seeks-end-to-oversight-of-womens-prison-citing-substantial-compliance-with-fed-monitor/, accessed January 6, 2025.

10
S.P. Sullivan, "N.J. Is Closing Its Scandal-Plagued Women's Prison. Its Replacement Will Cost at Least $90M," *NJ.com*, June 14, 2024, https://www.nj.com/news/2024/06/nj-is-closing-its-scandal-plagued-womens-prison-its-replacement-will-cost-at-lea st-90m.html, accessed January 6, 2024.

11
Jessica L. Adler, "Inhumane System of Incarceration in U.S. Poses Special Danger to Women," *Washington Post*, June 16, 2021.

12
Mattes and McWeeny, "The Past or the Present? Reconstructing the Experiences Within Edna Mahan Through Interviews," 50.

13
Mattes and McWeeny, 13.

14
Mattes and McWeeny.

15
Mattes and McWeeny, 40.

16
Mattes and McWeeny.

17
S.P. Sullivan, "N.J. Is Closing Its Scandal-Plagued Women's Prison."

18
Unfortunately Lydia Thornton passed away on October 1, 2022, shortly after having given this interview.

19
Mattes and McWeeny, "The Past or the Present? Reconstructing the Experiences Within Edna Mahan Through Interviews," 5.

⁂

Basile Baudez

A MODERN ARCHITECTURAL HISTORY OF CARCERAL FACILITIES IN FIVE PROJECTS

In Europe, dedicated penal institutions were rare before the early eighteenth century. Instead, makeshift prisons, such as castle basements, gatehouse chambers, and monastic cells, housed only a small number of detainees. Notable exceptions include the New Prisons in Venice, designed by Antonio Rusconi and Antonio da Ponte between 1560 and 1614, and the Hospice of San Michele in Rome, built in 1705 by Carlo Fontana. The widespread construction of large-scale facilities specifically for incarcerating individuals only began around the turn of the nineteenth century, as imprisonment became a formalized component of European penal codes. This shift was driven by the view that incarceration offered a more humane alternative to previous punishments such as forced labor on galleys, branding, or execution.

Newgate, London, by George Dance the Younger (1769–1782)

This new building, designed by London's City Architect, replaced a fourteenth-century urban gate that had become overcrowded at a time when incarceration was formalized in British penal law. The facility housed prisoners in large rooms surrounding three courtyards, each designated for a specific group: debtors, "male felons," and "female felons." Five individual cells were reserved for punishing the "refractory." At the center of the complex stood a chapel, serving as the facility's symbolic and spiritual core. The imposing rusticated façade and lack of windows were intended to convey strength and evoke fear. After being destroyed by fire in 1782, Newgate was rebuilt and remained in use until 1902.

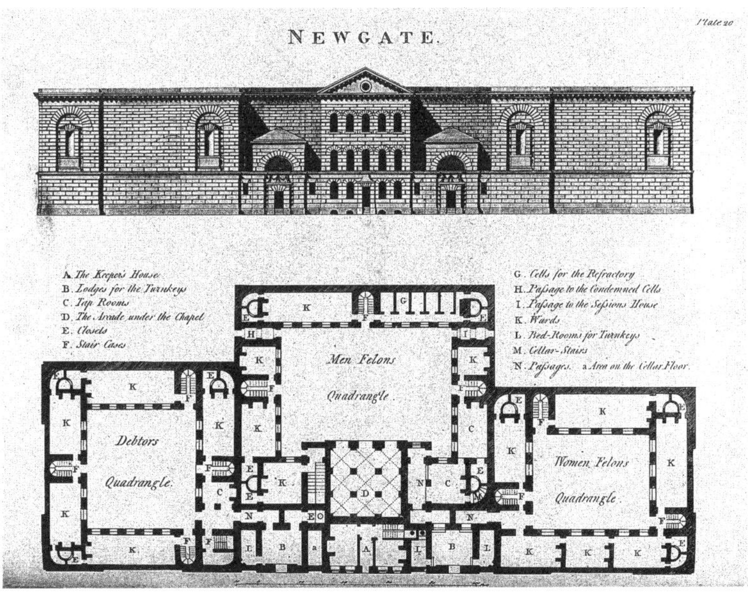

Newgate, engraving, in John Howard, *State of the Prisons*, third edition, 1783, plate 20. Public domain.

Eastern State Penitentiary, Philadelphia, by John Haviland (1829)

Built in a rural area of Philadelphia, Cherry Hill Prison—commonly known as Eastern State Penitentiary—adopted the popular radial plan but became renowned for implementing the Quakers' vision of reform through solitary confinement. The prison featured seven one-story cellblocks radiating from a central rotunda,

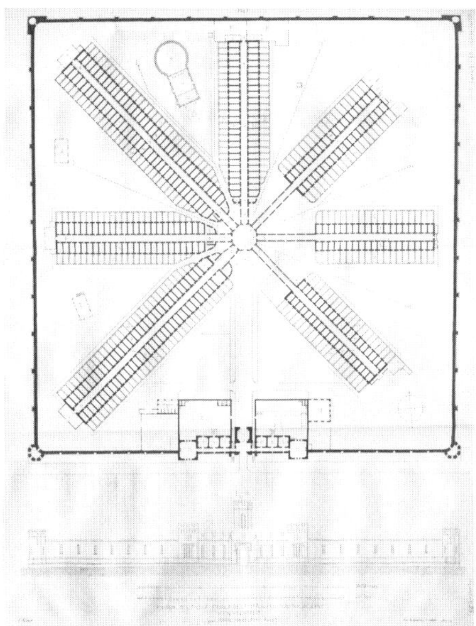

Plan of the ground floor and elevation of the exterior wall and main gate, in F.-A. Demetz and A. Blouet, *Rapport... sur les pénitentiers des Etats-Unis* (Paris: Imprimerie Royale, 1837), pl. 23. Public domain.

each containing thirty-six cells. These cells connected to a central corridor via small peepholes, through which food and work materials were passed. Each cell opened onto an individual exercise yard and was equipped with a flush toilet, a bed, and a tap for fresh water. Incarcerated individuals lived in complete isolation, eating, sleeping, working, and exercising without ever seeing another person. Even before its completion, the rising number of incarcerated individuals compelled architect John Haviland to design additional two-story wings.

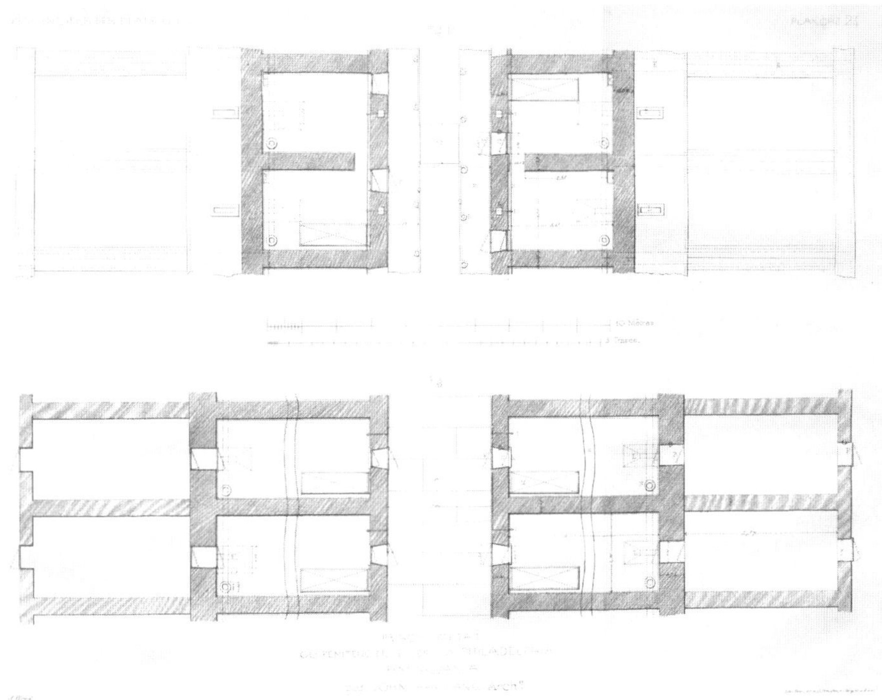

Guillaume-Abel Blouet, Eastern State Penitentiary, plan of ground-floor cells, exercise yards, and upper-floor cells, engraving, in F.-A. Demetz and A. Blouet, *Rapport... sur les pénitentiers des Etats-Unis* (Paris: Imprimerie Royale, 1837), pl. 24. Public domain.

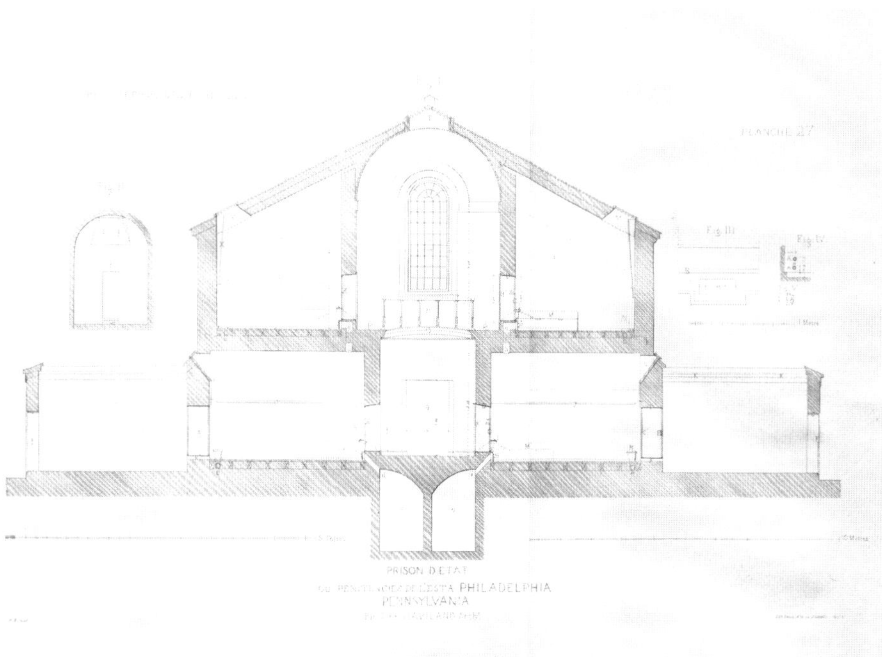

Guillaume-Abel Blouet, Eastern State Penitentiary, section of one of the cellblocks, engraving, in F.-A. Demetz and A. Blouet, *Rapport... sur les pénitentiers des Etats-Unis* (Paris: Imprimerie Royale, 1837), pl. 27. Public domain.

Mettray Penal Colony by Guillaume-Abel Blouet (1839)

The Mettray Penal Colony, established near Tours, France, was a pioneering institution aimed at rehabilitating young male delinquents between the ages of six and twenty-one. Founded by penal reformer and jurist Frédéric-Auguste Demetz and designed by Guillaume-Abel Blouet, the Inspector General of French Prisons, Mettray was conceived as a "reformatory without walls." Its innovative approach combined agricultural labor, spiritual guidance, and moral education. The central chapel was surrounded by ten pavilions, along with gardens, stables, and farmland, reflecting its guiding principle: "Improve man by the land and the land by man, under the watch of God." The colony's unique structure divided residents into "families," each overseen by a *chef de famille* who maintained military-style discipline. Initially celebrated as a model for reform, Mettray later faced criticism, particularly in the 1920s, for its increasingly severe disciplinary practices. Writer Jean Genet, who spent time at the colony, vividly depicted its oppressive environment in his works. The institution ultimately closed in 1937, leaving behind a complex legacy in the history of penal reform.

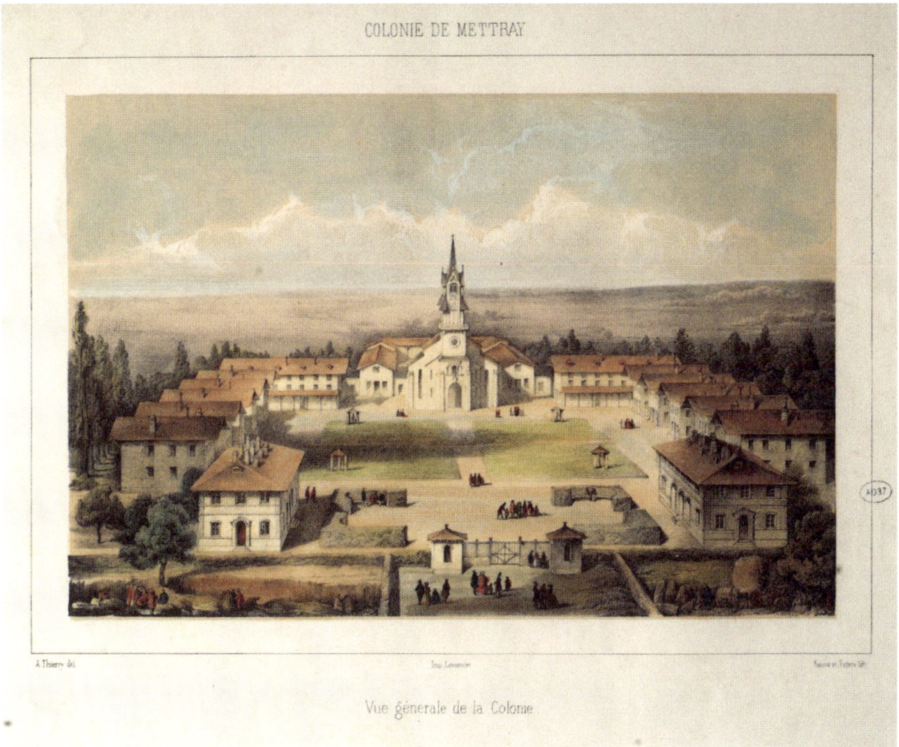

A. Thierry, *Colonie de Mettray*, 1844, chromolithograph by Sauvé & Faivre, 244 × 162 mm. Tours, Archives départementales d'Indre-et-Loire, inv. 114J33. Public domain.

Metropolitan Correctional Center, Chicago, by Harry Weese (1975)

The Metropolitan Correctional Center (MCC) is a distinctive federal prison facility located in the heart of downtown Chicago, Illinois. Designed by architect Harry Weese and completed in 1975, the MCC is re-

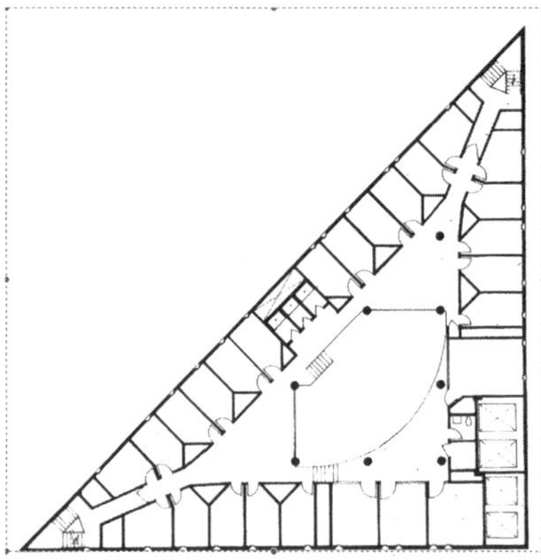

Plan of the MCC Chicago, in Leah Ray, "Opposing Mies: The Triangular Constructs of Harry Weese," in *Chicago architecture: histories, revisions, alternatives*, edited by Charles Waldheim and Katerina Rüedi Ray (University of Chicago Press, 2005), 285–291.

nowned for its bold triangular shape and impressive twenty-eight-story height, making it one of the tallest prison buildings in the world. It serves as an innovative experiment in urban vertical incarceration. The triangular design enhances security by providing guards with clearer sightlines while maximizing spatial efficiency. Its narrow, vertical slit windows allow natural light to enter while deterring escape attempts. Inside, the cells open onto a two-tiered multi-purpose dayroom, fostering a sense of openness. Additionally, the facility features a rooftop exercise yard, designed primarily for high-security inmates. While the MCC's architectural innovations aim to balance security with humane living conditions, the facility has drawn criticism over the years for issues such as overcrowding and inadequate living standards, highlighting the challenges of managing a high-rise correctional environment.

Harry Weese, Metropolitan Correction Center (1971–1975) viewed from the Sears Tower, Chicago. Photograph by Marcin Wichary, 2008, via Wikimedia Commons.

Anstalten complex, Greenland, by Schmidt Hammer Lassen and Friis & Moltke (2019)

Located near Nuuk, Greenland's seaside capital, this correctional facility, designed by Danish architectural firms Schmidt Hammer Lassen and Friis & Moltke, is the first high-security carceral facility on the island. Known as Anstalten, the facility spans 8,000 square meters and aims to resemble a small village, with multiple blocks connected by walkways. The architects' goal was to integrate the buildings into the surrounding landscape instead of closing the cluster behind high walls. It houses seventy-six individuals—forty in closed cells and the remainder in open cells, each featuring a window that frames the surrounding scenery. The complex also includes a variety of facilities, such as workspaces, educational and sports areas, a library, a health center, and a chapel.

Anstalten complex, Nuuk, Greenland, 2019, by Schmidt Hammer Lassen and Friis & Moltke. Courtesy of Schmidt Hammer Lassen Architects, Adam Mørk photographer.

Anstalten complex, Nuuk, Greenland, 2019, by Schmidt Hammer Lassen and Friis & Moltke, diagram. Courtesy of Schmidt Hammer Lassen Architects.

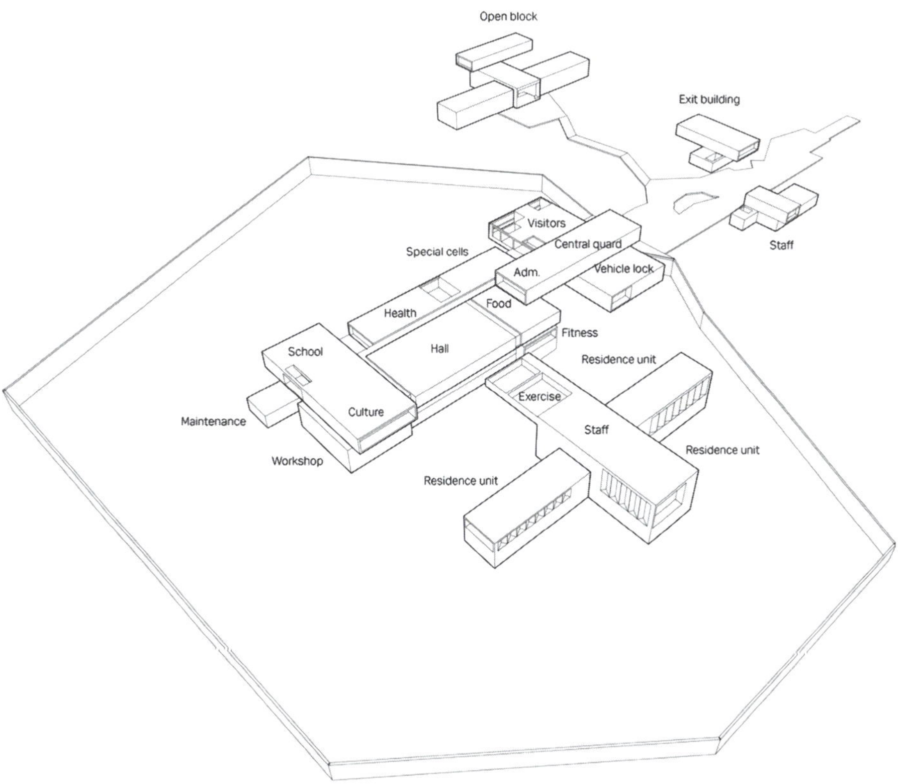

Anstalten complex, Nuuk, Greenland, 2019, by Schmidt Hammer Lassen and Friis & Moltke, plan.
Courtesy of Schmidt Hammer Lassen Architects.

BIBLIOGRAPHY

ESSENTIAL BIBLIOGRAPHY ON THE HISTORY OF THE ARCHITECTURE OF CARCERAL INSTITUTIONS

Bender, John. *Imagining the Penitentiary*. Chicago: University of Chicago Press, 1987.

Bienert, Andreas. *Gefängnis als Bedeutungsträger. Ikonologische Studie zur Geschichte der Strafarchitektur*. Frankfurt: Peter Lang, 1992.

Brodie, Allan, Jane Croom, and James O. Davies. *Behind Bars: The Hidden Architecture of England's Prisons*. London: English Heritage, 1999.

Brooke-Eisen, Lauren. *Inside Private Prisons*. New York: Columbia University Press, 2017.

Davis, Angela. *Are Prisons Obsolete?* New York: Seven Stories Press, 2003.

Day, Joe. *Corrections & Collections: Architectures for Art and Crime*. London: Routledge, 2013.

Dubbini, Renzo. *Architettura delle prigioni: i luoghi e il tempo della punizione, 1700–1880*. Milan: Franco Angeli, 1986.

Evans, Robert. *The Fabrication of Virtue: English Prison Architecture, 1750–1840*. Cambridge: Cambridge University Press, 1982.

Fairweather, Leslie and Seán McConville, eds. *Prison architecture: policy, design, and experience*. London: Routledge, 2000.

Finzch, Norbert and Robert Jutte, eds. *Institutions of Confinement: Hospitals, Asylums, and Prisons in Western Europe and North America, 1500–1950*. New York: Cambridge University Press, 1996.

Foucault, Michel. *Discipline and Punish: The Birth of the Prison*. Translated by Alan Sheridan. New York: Vintage, 1979.

Howard, John. *State of the Prisons in England and Wales. with preliminary observations, and an account of some foreign prisons*. Warrington: printed by William Eyres, and sold by T. Cadell and N. Conant, London, 1777.

Irwin, John. *The warehouse prison: disposal of the new dangerous class*. Los Angeles: Roxbury Publishing Company, 2005.

Jackson-Retondo, Elaine. "Manufacturing Moral Reform: Images and Realities of a Nineteenth-Century American prison." *Perspectives in Vernacular Architecture* 8 (2000): 117–137.

Jewkes, Yvonne, ed. *Handbook on Prisons*. London: Routledge, 2007.

Johnston, Norman. *Forms of Constraint: a History of Prison Architecture*. Urbana: University of Illinois Press, 2000.

Kann, Mark E. *Punishment, Prisons and Patriarchy: Liberty and Power in the Early American Republic*. New York: NYU Press, 2005.

Kirkham-Lewitt, Isabelle, ed. *Paths to Prison: On the Architectures of Carcerality*. New York: Columbia Books on Architecture and the City, 2020.

McKelvey, Blake. *American Prisons: A history of good intentions*. Montclair: Patterson Smith, 1977.

Morrison, Kathryn. *The Workhouse: A Study of Poor-law Buildings in England*. Swindon: Royal Commission on the Historical Monuments of England, 1999.

O'Brien, Patricia. *The Promise of Punishment: Prisons in Nineteenth-Century France*. Princeton: Princeton University Press, 1982.

Pugh, Ralph B. *Imprisonment in Medieval England*. Cambridge: Cambridge University Press, 1968.

Robinson, Willard B. *The People's Architecture: Texas Courthouses, Jails and Municipal Buildings*. Austin: Texas State Historical Association, 1983.

Semple, Janet. *Bentham's Prison: A Study of the Panopticon Penitentiary*. Oxford: Clarendon Press, 1993.

Simon, Jonathan, Nicholas Temple, and Renée Tobe, eds. *Architecture and justice: judicial meanings in the public realm*. Farnham: Ashgate, 2013.

Spens, Iona, ed. *Architecture of Incarceration*. London: Academy Editions, 1994.

Spierenburg, Pieter, ed. *The Emergence of Carceral Institutions: Prisons, Galleys and Lunatic Asylums, 1550–1900*. Rotterdam: Erasmus Universiteit, 1984.

Spirienburg, Pieter. *The Prison Experience: Disciplinary Institutions and their Inmates in Early Modern Europe*. New Brunswick: Rutgers University Press, 1991.

Urrutia-Moldes, Alberto. *Health and well-being in prison design: a theory of prison systems and a framework for evolution*. London: Routledge, 2022.

EDITORS/AUTHORS

EDITORS:

Basile Baudez is Associate Professor of Architectural History in the Department of Art and Archaeology at Princeton University. His latest single-authored book, *Inessential Colors: Architecture on Paper in Early Modern Europe* (Princeton University Press, 2021) was awarded the Alice Davis Hitchcock Medallion by the Society of Architectural Historians of Great Britain. He is co-editor of *Textile in Architecture: From the Middle Ages to Modernism* (Routledge, 2023), which explores the interconnections between soft and hard architecture in the *longue durée* from diverse geographic contexts. He regularly teaches community-engaged courses in partnership with New Jersey-based NGOs, such as the East Trenton Collaborative and the New Jersey Prison Justice Watch.

Victoria Bergbauer is a Mellon Postdoctoral Fellow at The Fox Center for Humanistic Inquiry. Her dissertation, entitled "Fragments of Freedom: Incarcerated Adolescents and their Afterlives in Nineteenth-Century Europe" (Princeton University, 2025) provides the first transnational history of formerly incarcerated individuals and shows how rehabilitation was embedded in legal, political, and economic frameworks. Her broader research on normalization in the nineteenth century has appeared in English, French, and Italian publications, and she has contributed to a collective project on "Sick Architecture." A former fellow at the Princeton University Center for Human Values, she served as a humanities tutor at East Jersey State Prison through the Prison Teaching Initiative.

AUTHORS:

Anna Arabindan-Kesson is an Associate Professor of Black Diaspora Art in the Department of African American Studies and the Department of Art and Archaeology at Princeton University. She practiced as a registered nurse before completing her PhD, and focuses on African American, Caribbean, and British art, with an emphasis on histories of race, empire, medicine, and transatlantic visual culture in the long nineteenth century. Her first book is called *Black Bodies, White Gold: Art, Cotton, and Commerce in the Atlantic World* (Duke University Press, 2021). Other projects include a co-written book on Black diaspora artists and a monograph, *An Empire State of Mind* (forthcoming), on the intersection of art and medicine in plantation imagery. She is the director of the digital humanities project Art Hx: Visual and Medical Legacies of British Colonialism.

Andrea Armstrong is a 2023 MacArthur Fellow, and the Dr. Norman C. Francis Distinguished Professor at the College of Law, Loyola University New Orleans, where she teaches incarceration law, constitutional law, criminal procedure, and race and the law. Armstrong founded incarcerationtransparency.org, a database and website that documents and memorializes deaths behind bars in Louisiana and supports similar efforts across the United States. Her interdisciplinary work focuses on carceral mortality, healthcare, and labor as well as on the intersection between race and conditions of incarceration, and public oversight of detention facilities. Her research has been profiled by the *New Yorker*, and has appeared in the *Atlantic*, *Harvard Civil Rights-Civil Liberties Law Review*, *The New York Times*, and *Stanford Law & Policy Review*, among others.

Elizabeth Austin is an architect, artist, and community educator dedicated to advocating for disability justice in the built environment. Her commitment to advancing anti-ableist, human-centered design is deeply rooted in her personal queer, neurodivergent, and psychiatric survivor identities. Elizabeth currently serves as an inclusive design consultant at Ennead Architects.

Tommaso Bardelli is the Principal for Justice Initiatives at Ithaka S+R, where he oversees a variety of projects aimed at expanding incarcerated people's access to higher education and technology, and preserving their artistic and intellectual production. His research on mass incarceration has been featured in newspapers and magazines, as well as academic and public interest journals.

Isabelle Bonzom is a painter, muralist, and a frescoist. The French Ministries of Justice and Culture commissioned her to paint murals at Saint-Malo Prison, France. With a doctoral degree in Art and Art History, she has authored a reference book on frescoes and was invited to talk about Goya's frescoes by the College Art Association thanks to a grant awarded by the Kress Foundation. Paintings by Isabelle Bonzom are held by public and private collections in France, Belgium, South Korea, and the United States.

Falk Bretschneider is a historian of the early modern period and *directeur d'études* (full professor) at the School for Advanced Studies in the Social Sciences, Paris. He works on the history of confinement in German-speaking countries, focusing in particular on the spatial aspects of early modern prisons. Among his many publications, he is the author of *Gefangene Gesellschaft. Eine Geschichte der Einsperrung in Sachsen vom 18. bis zum 19. Jahrhundert* (Uvk Verlag, 2011) and of the series *Enfermements* (Éditions de la Sorbonne), which he published with Julie Claustre, Isabelle Heullant-Donat, and Élisabeth Lusset.

Christopher Talib Charriez is a justice-impacted scholar, advocate with Higher Education in Prison (HEP), and community organizer with East Brooklyn Congregations (EBC). With over twenty-four years of lived experience, Charriez has spent the past decade deeply involved in prison education. As a teacher, mentor, and public speaker, he has empowered justice-impacted individuals while advocating for reform via re-entry and access to higher education. Through research and outreach, Charriez works to promote understanding and to create meaningful change for those affected by the justice system.

Regina Chen is Senior Principal in Process & Learning at MASS Design Group, where she views design as a catalyst for restoration. With a multidisciplinary background in architecture, engineering, planning, and research, she focuses on using the built environment to address legacies of inequity. Her work, spanning community engagement, research, narrative development, and process design, guides partners to ask questions that drive meaningful impact. She has led the Restorative Justice Design Lab since 2017, emphasizing community engagement, truth-telling, and collective action, and has launched MASS's Narrative (now Advocacy) team, overseeing publications such as *Justice is Beauty* (The Monacelli Press, 2019) and exhibitions including *Design and Healing: Creative Responses to Epidemics* at Cooper Hewitt, Smithsonian Design Museum.

Chris Etienne is Student Engagement Coordinator at the Prison Teaching Initiative, a journalist, and an Africana Studies scholar. With over a decade of experience working with justice-impacted communities, he seeks to spotlight injustice, raise awareness about social issues, and instruct justice-impacted individuals. In 2015, he joined the NJ-STEP program staff, where he tutored formerly incarcerated individuals looking to pursue post-secondary education. Since then, he has worked with various organizations such as Rutgers University, SOBA College Recovery, the Renaissance House, and Brooklyn CRAN.

rl Goldberg is Assistant Professor of Queer Studies at Hampshire College. Their first book, *I Changed My Sex! Pedagogy and Trans Narrative*, is under contract at Columbia University Press. They received their PhD jointly in English and Humanistic Studies from Princeton and are a long-time prison educator and abolitionist.

Nafeesah Goldsmith is the CEO of RISE (Real Intervention Supports Excellence), a mission-based sustainability effort that supports initiatives for at-risk communities and works toward a prison-free future. When she was twenty-one, she began serving a fifteen-year prison sentence at the Edna Mahan Correctional Facility for women in New Jersey. Since her release from prison in 2015, Nafeesah has dedicated her time to speaking on incarceration, re-entry, the school-to-prison pipeline, and the effects of incarceration on families and communities.

Isabelle Heullant-Donat is a medieval historian and professor at the University of Reims. She works on the cultural and religious history of medieval Italy between the twelfth and fifteenth centuries, in particular on religious mendicant orders and martyrdom in the late Middle Ages.

Een Jabriel has been an active speaker on university campuses and at national conferences, focusing on the potential for prison and re-entry education alongside combatting the stigma associated with currently and formerly incarcerated individuals. After having been incarcerated himself, Een studied Criminology at Rutgers. He now uses his lived experience and academic expertise to foster conversations and develop leadership skills among those who are impacted by the criminal justice system.

Sam Johnson is an architect and the Co-Director of Ennead Lab. With a robust background in historic preservation and sustainable design, Johnson brings a critical perspective on environmental justice and community engagement to Ennead Lab's latest projects. Outside of his work with Ennead Lab, he focuses on innovative educational spaces, in both the early education and post-secondary context. He has served as an editor for the architectural journal, *LUNCH*, and has exhibited work at the Smithsonian National Museum of American History.

Grégoire Korganow, a graduate of the Estienne School in Paris, began his career as a photojournalist in 1991. Since then, he has contributed to major newspapers (including *Libération*, *The New York Times*, *National Geographic*, *Marie Claire*, and *Le Monde*). He has frequently been invited to residencies and his works have been exhibited at international venues in Paris, Beijing, Milan, and Hamburg. He was awarded a Villa Albertine residency and regularly conducts workshops in France and abroad.

Sarah Lopez is an Associate Professor at the University of Pennsylvania in the Stuart Weitzman School of Design. Lopez is a built environment historian of twentieth-century Mexico and the United States whose research focuses on material histories of migration, remittance development and landscapes, and migrant incarceration. She is interested in experimental historical methods, ordinary landscapes, and the environmental humanities. Lopez's book, *The Remittance Landscape: Spaces of Migration in Rural Mexico and Urban USA* (University of Chicago Press, 2014), won the Spiro Kostof Book Award from the Society of Architectural Historians. She has been the recipient of Mellon Fellowships at Princeton, Dumbarton Oaks, and the Center for the Study of Visual Arts (CASVA) at the National Gallery.

Élisabeth Lusset is a historian of the Middle Ages and a Senior Research Fellow at the Centre National de la Recherche Scientifique (CNRS). She specializes in the history of monasteries and ecclesiastical justice in the West between the twelfth and fifteenth centuries.

Dolfinette Martin, Housing Specialist at Operation Restoration, oversees all housing programming and supervises staff, interns, and volunteers working within this program. A former panelist of the Criminal Background Review Board for the Housing Authority of New Orleans, she is a passionate advocate for safe and affordable housing for individuals impacted by the criminal justice system. In 2023, she was a keynote speaker at the Department of Justice's Zero Returns to Homelessness convening and serves on the advisory board of the Formerly Incarcerated Transitional Clinic. Martin co-authored the publication *Healthcare in Louisiana Prisons-Women*, serves on various advisory boards, and has contributed to art exhibitions such as *Per(Sister)* and *Unthinkable Imagination*. She was appointed to the Louisiana Women's Incarceration Task Force and the Survivor Informed Task Force. Martin is a Loyola School of Law graduate and Education Trust Fellow.

Kennedy Mattes graduated from Princeton University in May 2023 with a major in Politics and a minor in Statistics and Machine Learning. With her senior thesis on the causal effects of incarceration, she exposed uncertainties about the validity of assumptions for instrumental variable designs in the courtroom setting. She has worked as a criminal investigator in the Brooklyn office of the Legal Aid Society and is currently a student at Harvard Law School.

Charlie McWeeny is currently completing his undergraduate degree in Politics (with a minor in English) at Princeton University. His research focuses on the effects of judicial elections on the partisanship of state supreme court justices in electoral cases. He interned with the Magistrate Judge for the Eastern District of New York. McWeeny also serves as a Peer Representative, providing guidance to students under university investigation, and volunteers as a tutor for students incarcerated at Garden State Youth Correctional Facility through the Petey Greene program.

Amy Mielke is an Associate Principal at Ennead Architects and former Director of Ennead Lab. In her work, Amy has explored topics including urban resiliency and the spatial potential of water in infrastructure. One of her projects, *Poreform*, received the LafargeHolcim Gold Medal for North America, the world's most significant award for sustainable design. Mielke continues to pursue justice in the built environment through stressing the importance of ethical sourcing, transparency in environmental condition monitoring, and designing resilient supply chains.

Juan Moreno Haines is a journalist and an influential figure in prison reform. His understanding of the criminal legal system is shaped by being confined in California's prison system for over thirty-five years. Haines's commitment to revealing the often-overlooked realities of incarceration has received numerous awards, including the Society of Professional Journalists' Silver Heart, accolades from the California Newspaper Publishers Association for COVID-19 reporting, as well as an Evident Change Award by Media for a Just Society. As Editor-in-Chief of *Solitary Watch*, he has exposed unnecessarily harsh prison conditions. Haines is the co-founder of Humans of San Quentin, a website geared toward empowering incarcerated voices. He advises several nonprofits, each led by a justice-impacted person.

Sowande' M. Mustakeem is an Associate Professor of History and African and African American Studies at Washington University in St. Louis. She specializes in slavery at sea, Black women's history, medicine, memory, policing, gender, and executions. Mustakeem is renowned for her book *Slavery at Sea: Terror, Sex, and Sickness in the Middle Passage* (University of Illinois Press, 2016), which won the Wesley-Logan Prize and the Dred Scott Freedom Award. Her research has been published in *The Journal of African American History* and *Atlantic Studies*, among others. The audio version of her book was released in 2021, and Mustakeem has been featured on Vox, BBC radio and in Henry Louis Gates's PBS documentary series *Many Rivers to Cross*.

Joel Negron is a Research Assistant for the Department of Urban Education at Rutgers University-Newark. He holds a BA in Criminal Justice with a focus on Justice Studies and is currently pursuing his MA in Public Affairs and Administration with a focus on nonprofit management. Negron intends to create his own nonprofit organization specializing in addressing trauma for formerly incarcerated citizens.

Tammy Ortiz is a sociologist, accomplice, formerly incarcerated individual, and grandmother. As an analyst at Ithaka S+R, she pursues research that involves students and patrons who are or were formerly incarcerated, helping to increase their access to education. In addition, Ortiz is the editor of *The Warbler*, a newsletter that was created by the Alabama Prison Arts + Education Project during the COVID-19 pandemic as a way to reach incarcerated individuals. *The Warbler* is distributed weekly to prisons and to individuals in Alabama and across the nation.

Ess Pokornowski is a researcher, writer, and educator. They are a Senior Analyst at Ithaka S+R, where they research educational access and equity, and issues of censorship and academic freedom.

Katie Chizuko Solien is an architectural designer based in New York City. She holds a BFA and BArch from the Rhode Island School of Design and an MArch and graduate certificate in Media and Modernity Studies from Princeton University. She has practiced at design offices including Ultramoderne, SO – IL and AD–WO, and has also been a Teaching Fellow at RISD and an Associate Research Scholar for the Buell Center at Columbia University. Her work focuses on the spatial dynamics of carceral landscapes and the practices that emerge in spite of them. Since 2011, Chizuko Solien has been involved with the Heart Mountain Wyoming Foundation, a nonprofit museum preserving a site where 14,000 Japanese Americans were incarcerated during WWII. She volunteers, leads tours, and hosts workshops alongside former incarcerees and their descendants.

Syrita Steib is the founder, president, and CEO of Operation Restoration, a nonprofit organization, which has helped girls and women to restore their lives and overcome economic inequities. Steib's advocacy began after her own conviction at nineteen, when she was sentenced to 120 months in federal prison, twenty years in state prison, and $1.9 million in restitution for her involvement in a crime of theft and transportation of automobiles across state lines. In 2021, she was granted a full pardon. In Louisiana, Steib is known for her "Ban the Box" initiative, leading to the passage of Louisiana Act 276, which prevents public post-secondary institutions from inquiring about criminal history during student admission. She helped draft the First Step Act, which reformed federal criminal law to reduce recidivism.

Jill Stockwell directs the Prison Teaching Initiative at Princeton, a higher-education-in-prison program serving incarcerated students across the state of New Jersey and supporting summer internships at Princeton for formerly incarcerated students.

Ibrahim Suleimani is the Executive Director of Transformative Justice LLC, a consultancy led by individuals with carceral experience. In 2018, he was released from prison after serving a thirty-year sentence for a crime he committed at fifteen. During his time in prison, Ibrahim focused on education and advocated for people in prison, on probation, and on parole to gain democratic rights. He has been featured on NJTV news, Spotlight, and in local newspapers, and has spoken at Swarthmore, Princeton, and Rutgers. Ibrahim co-founded Meet him at the Gate, which supports individuals transitioning out of prison, and is involved in several re-entry and advocacy groups, including the New Jersey Prison Justice Watch and the Prison Survivors Union.

Miriam Taylor Fair is a PhD candidate in Urban Studies through Tulane University's City, Culture, and Community program. Her forthcoming dissertation explores the memorial landscape of Jackson, Mississippi and the role of place-consciousness in promoting a place-based ethics of care. She is a former Mellon Fellow in Community-Engaged Research and Mellon Sawyer Seminar Fellow. Miriam previously served as the Interim Director of the Newcomb Art Museum, overseeing the museum's closure, restructuring, and reopening in response to the COVID-19 pandemic. She also served that museum in the roles of Deputy Director, Curator of Special Projects, and External Affairs Manager.

Liz Trumbull is the Senior Director of Preservation and Operations at Eastern State Penitentiary Historic Site, a museum interpreting the legacy of American criminal justice reform from the site of the world's first penitentiary. Since 2018, Trumbull has been involved in the preservation and planning of the 11-acre National Historic Landmark in Philadelphia, as well as ongoing stabilization and restoration campaigns. She also manages the Preservation Trades Center at Eastern State, a workforce development program that engages communities underrepresented in the building trades through paid, on-the-job preservation training while fostering connections to long-term careers in the construction sector. Trumbull earned her MSc in Historic Preservation from the University of Pennsylvania and a BSc in Civil Engineering from Northwestern University.

Spencer J. Weinreich is a Lecturer on the History of Science at Harvard University and a Junior Fellow at the Harvard Society of Fellows. He is currently writing *An Experimental Box: A History of Solitary Confinement*. He received his PhD in the History of Science from Princeton University in 2022, and his work has appeared in *Journal of the History of Ideas*, *Punishment and Society*, *History Workshop Journal*, *Journal of Social History*, and the *Los Angeles Review of Books*.

Jessica Womack earned her PhD in Art and Archaeology from Princeton in May 2024, with graduate certificates in Latin American and African American Studies. Her dissertation, "Nation in the Making: Art, Politics, and Statecraft in Jamaica after 1962," examines post-independence Jamaican art by tracing the relationships between artists, arts institutions, and government agencies. In probing the politics and practices of exhibition in Jamaica, her research explores how these relationships were informed and shaped by broader concerns as Jamaica transitioned to statehood. Womack holds an AB from Dartmouth and an MA from Princeton, where she was a Graduate Fellow in the Scholars Institute Fellows Program and project manager for Art Hx: Visual and Medical Legacies of British Colonialism.

Cover:
Grégoire Korganow,
200 meters from the
prison of Marseille,
photograph from the
series "Périphéries," 2018.

Acquisitions editor:
Felix Torkar

Project management:
Franziska Schüffler

Copy editing:
Cecilia Tricker

Design and setting:
Floyd E. Schulze

Production:
Susanne Rösler

Lithography:
Bild1Druck

Printed in the
European Union.

For questions about the
General Product Safety
Regulation please contact:
productsafety@degruyterbrill.com.

Bibliographic information published by the Deutsche Nationalbibliothek
The Deutsche Nationalbibliothek lists this publication in the
Deutsche Nationalbibliografie; detailed bibliographic data are available on the
internet at http://dnb.d-nb.de

jovis Verlag
Genthiner Straße 13
10785 Berlin

www.jovis.de

jovis books are available worldwide in select bookstores. Please contact your nearest
bookseller or visit www.jovis.de for information concerning your local distribution.

ISBN 978-3-98612-205-8 (softcover)
ISBN 978-3-98612-206-5 (e-book)